SALES MANAGEMENT AND PERSONAL SELLING

Prof. Anil Keskar
B.E., M.B.A., Ph.D.

and

Prof. Suresh Abhyankar
B.Sc., P.G.D.M. (FAM), M.P.M., Ph.D.

First Edition : 2013

Himalaya Publishing House

MUMBAI • NEW DELHI • NAGPUR • BENGALURU • HYDERABAD • CHENNAI • PUNE • LUCKNOW • AHMEDABAD • ERNAKULAM • BHUBANESWAR • INDORE • KOLKATA • GUWAHATI

First Edition : 2013

Published by : Mrs. Meena Pandey for **Himalaya Publishing House Pvt. Ltd.**, "Ramdoot", Dr. Bhalerao Marg, Girgaon, **Mumbai - 400 004.** Phone: 022-23860170/23863863, Fax: 022-23877178 **E-mail: himpub@vsnl.com; Website: www.himpub.com**

Branch Offices :

New Delhi : "Pooja Apartments", 4-B, Murari Lal Street, Ansari Road, Darya Ganj, New Delhi - 110 002. Phone: 011-23270392, 23278631; Fax: 011-23256286

Nagpur : Kundanlal Chandak Industrial Estate, Ghat Road, Nagpur - 440 018. Phone: 0712-2738731, 3296733; Telefax: 0712-2721215

Bengaluru : No. 16/1 (Old 12/1), 1st Floor, Next to Hotel Highlands, Madhava Nagar, Race Course Road, Bengaluru - 560 001. Phone: 080-32919385; Telefax: 080-22286611

Hyderabad : No. 3-4-184, Lingampally, Besides Raghavendra Swamy Matham, Kachiguda, Hyderabad - 500 027. Phone: 040-27560041, 27550139; Mobile: 09390905282

Chennai : No. 8/2, 2nd Madley Street, Ground Floor, T. Nagar, Chennai - 600 017. Mobile: 09345345055

Pune : First Floor, "Laksha" Apartment, No. 527, Mehunpura, Shaniwarpeth (Near Prabhat Theatre), Pune - 411 030. Phone: 020-24496323/24496333; Mobile: 09370579333

Lucknow : House No 731, Shekhupura Colony, Near B.D. Convent School, Aliganj, Lucknow - 226 022. Mobile: 09307501549

Ahmedabad : 114, "SHAIL", 1st Floor, Opp. Madhu Sudan House, C.G. Road, Navrang Pura, Ahmedabad - 380 009. Phone: 079-26560126; Mobile: 09377088847

Ernakulam : 39/176 (New No: 60/251) 1st Floor, Karikkamuri Road, Ernakulam, Kochi - 682011, Phone: 0484-2378012, 2378016; Mobile: 09344199799

Bhubaneswar : 5 Station Square, Bhubaneswar - 751 001 (Odisha). Phone: 0674-2532129, Mobile: 09338746007

Indore : Kesardeep Avenue Extension, 73, Narayan Bagh, Flat No. 302, IIIrd Floor, Near Humpty Dumpty School, Indore - 452 007 (M.P.). Mobile: 09301386468

Kolkata : 108/4, Beliaghata Main Road, Near ID Hospital, Opp. SBI Bank, Kolkata - 700 010, Phone: 033-32449649, Mobile: 09883055590, 07439040301

Guwahati : House No. 15, Behind Pragjyotish College, Near Sharma Printing Press, P.O. Bharalumukh, Guwahati - 781009, (Assam). Mobile: 09883055590, 09883055536

DTP by : HPH, Editorial Office, Bhandup (Harshali)

Printed at : M/s. Aditya Offset Process (I) Pvt. Ltd., Hyderabad. On behalf of HPH.

पुणे विद्यापीठ

University of Pune

डॉ अशोक जोशी

अधिष्ठाता: व्यवस्थापन विद्याशाखा
सदस्य: विद्यापरिषद

गणेशखिंड, पुणे-४११००७
Ganeshkhind, Pune-411007

Dr. Ashok Joshi

Dean: Management
Member: Academic Council

FOREWORD

It gives me a great pleasure to write a few lines about the book on SALES MANAGEMENT AND PERSONAL SELLING written by Professor Anil Keskar and Dr. Suresh Abhyankar.

Selling has been the most important activity in any business. As mentioned by none other than Peter Drucker that the purpose of any business is to create a customer, I will go a step further and state that the purpose of any business is to sell its produce. Thus, the authors have written this book on the most appropriate subject.

I know both Professor Anil Keskar and Dr. Suresh Abhyankar have started the professional careers in corporate sector before deciding to shift to Academics. Both of them have spent a substantial period of their corporate careers in selling. In this book, they have used their corporate experience in writing of this book. They have given live cases to substantiate the various theoretical concepts. There are very few authors who have this unique combination to their credit.

In today's competitive business environment, selling has attained a great importance. Gone are the days when markets were dominated by producers. Today, in all the industries, be it automobiles, consumer durables, non-durables, electronic goods, the competition has reached its peak. Further, the phenomenon of Globalization has made it more complicated and competitive. Thus, the process of Selling has become more important.

In this book, all the aspects of this subject are appropriately covered with lot of live Indian cases.

I am confident this book will be helpful not only for the students, but also for the selling professionals.

Date: *15th August, 2012*

Dr. Ashok Joshi
Director, IndSearch &
Dean, Faculty of Management,
University of Pune,
Pune.

कार्यालय: इंडियन इन्स्टिटयूट ऑफ कॉस्ट ॲण्ड मॅनेजमेंट स्टडिज ॲण्ड रीसर्च (इडसर्च), ८५/१, लॉ कॉलेज रोड पुणे - ४११००४.
दूरध्वनी: ०२० - २५४३१९७२, २५४४१५२४

College: Indian Institute of Cost & Management Studies & Research (IndSearch), 85/1, Law College Road, Pune-411004.
Phone: 020-25431972, 25441524
e-mail: joshiashok@hotmail.com ashokjoshi@indsearch.org

Preface

We are happy to present this book to all MBA/MMS students who are preparing themselves for joining the industry in sales and marketing departments. We are both teaching in various reputed institutes for last two decades and have always felt that there are no books which explain the secrets of success in sales management as most of the books available are written by foreign authors having no or limited knowledge of Indian market conditions or have been written by academicians who have second-hand knowledge of working in sales departments. The gap was big and having successfully worked and climbed the ladder of positions in sales department, we felt that we should put forward our experiences and knowledge in book format for the interested students and working executives/officers.

Both of us show a good combination of knowledge with Dr. Anil Keskar having vast experience in industrial sales and Dr. Suresh Abhyankar having vast experience in FMCG leading to perfection of all-round information in sales management.

We look forward to suggestions and queries from both academicians and corporate about the information in the book and will be very happy to add newer areas of sales in this book to enrich this book further.

Dr. Anil Keskar
drkeskar@yahoo.com

Dr. Suresh Abhyankar
drsureshabhyankar@gmail.com

Contents

Part I: Sales Management

Part II: Personal Selling

Detailed Contents

Part I : Sales Management

Part II : Personal Selling

List of Tables

Part I: Sales Management

Part II: Personal Selling

List of Boxes

Part I: Sales Management

Part II: Personal Selling

Part – I

Sales Management

CHAPTER 1 INTRODUCTION

Sales Management is most important part of any business enterprise. Manufacturing is one time process, if you manufacture and do not sell the process of manufacturing stops. The process of manufacturing can become continuous only if you are able to sell what you are producing. The process of manufacturing may stop even after you are able to sell what you produce, if you do not recover - the cost of production plus the cost of selling and get reasonable profit – to sustain manufacturing process which will keep requiring additional investments to take care of increase in raw material cost, increase in labor cost and increase in sales volumes. Customers are not willing to pay high overheads of process costs, and selling and promotional costs so the selling should take place without spending high amount cost and at a price that is affordable to the customers and recovers the costs and expenses and get reasonable profit. To understand this in detail we will look at selling process in detail and understand what is required to ensure successful selling and its management.

1.1 Evolution of Sales Department

Historically manufacturing and selling of various products required by villagers was part of duty of village craftsmen called Balutedars in most parts of India. These are the craftsmen (12 in total) like - 1. The Potter (Kumbhar), 2. The Glass Manufacturers (Kasar), 3. The Iron Smith (Lohar), 4. The Carpenter (Sutar), 5. The Cobbler (Chambhar), 6. The Oil Seed Crusher to get oil (Teli), 7. The Utensil-maker (Tamboli), 8. The Goldsmith (Sonar), 9. The Washerman (Dhobi, Parit, Rajak), 10. The Tailor (Shimpi), 11. The Cloth-weaver (Sali), 12. The Barber (Nhavi, Hajjam). These craftsmen will do their work without asking for immediate payment and will be paid every year by way of grains and cereals that the people produce on their farms. You will see that there is no sale involved it is only "Live and let live" principle. So even if a person does not need services of one of the craftsman, the craftsman will be paid his share (Hissa) in agro produce. The craftsmen will do work for other poor people free of charge.

The actual process of sale started when the craftsmen started becoming artisan. When I use the word ARTISAN, I mean a craftsman with creativity and difference in making the things artistically (Aesthetically) beautiful and making them stand out in comparison with all other craftsmen. People started giving preference to artisan over the craftsmen and when artisan started getting overburdened by the work load due to high demand he started refusing more work. People (consumers) with wealth started offering him more returns for preferential treatment by way of cash and valuables. The artisan came to know the VALUE of their PRODUCT and some ambitious artisan went to the large towns and cities or to meet the King of the land to get more and more returns for their ART. Some of them started large scale manufacture (more than the consumption of their town or city) by using assistants (similar to the concepts of ghetto which was present in European countries) and started selling their PRODUCTS to customers from other places (Either buyers/customers coming to purchase or artisans going for sale). This started growing and the process of selling started at different locations like weekly bazaars etc.

During this phase the trader community/banias (till that time dealing in grains and cereals only) stepped into this trade also. They started buying products from artisans and selling them to distant countries. These traders used to move in groups along with soldiers for protection in bullock carts or carts driven by horses and even the camel (this entire group was called popularly as CARAVAN). This is the evolution of sale and you will understand that the possibility of higher sale of product led to production in larger quantity, i.e., manufacturing units, i.e., industry.

Discovery of America (Columbus) is due to interest in selling process of condiments which were available in India and Columbus was trying to find out safer route to India for this trade. Voyages of SINDBAD was due to selling. (He sailed to different countries in search of good buyers for his carpets etc. and buying valuable products that could be sold in his country of residence). Voyages of MARCO POLO was also for selling (Silk trading route to China). All the buying and selling in this ERA was done on BARTER system.

Modern day selling was started after industrialization. The industry could produce articles on a large-scale and high quantity selling was required to sustain the production process. As the competition grew the manufacturers increased the number of sales people and sent them to distant areas to reach to customers which were not being serviced by competition. Some sales people worked honestly and efficiently getting good sales volumes but there were many sales people who cheated on work and were not efficient enough to get good sales volumes, this compelled the manufacturers to appoint supervisory staff to monitor the work done by the sales people. As the organization became larger and larger the supervisory staff needed to be monitored by managers and senior managers leading to formation of sales organization and requirement of sales management.

So, a salesman who is taking care of all the above deterrents and tries to sell a product at high rate can be left with profit even if he loses on all of above accounts during transit. The main idea is to "buy low and sell high". This was possible to persons who have the art of salesmanship. All those people who were able to convince the buyer to purchase the product, sometimes even unwanted ones (sometimes even by cheating) were called GOOD SALESMEN or people with SALESMANSHIP. Over a period of time this art was analyzed and found to be a craft, which can be learned and mastered. Let us look at different selling situations in today's life.

1.2 Selling Organization

Selling Organizational structure depends on types of product the manufacturer is selling and the type of selling situation they adopt. Each type of selling situation will require different types of selling organization structure. Let us first look at the different types of selling organizations structures.

1.3 Geographical Area Wise Organizational Structure

Sales staff is appointed to cover the available number of customers on the basis of geographical area. All the Sales Personnel will be then grouped under respective Area Managers. The area manager reports to Regional Managers who in turn report to National Sales Managers. Fig. 1.2 illustrates the structure in detail.

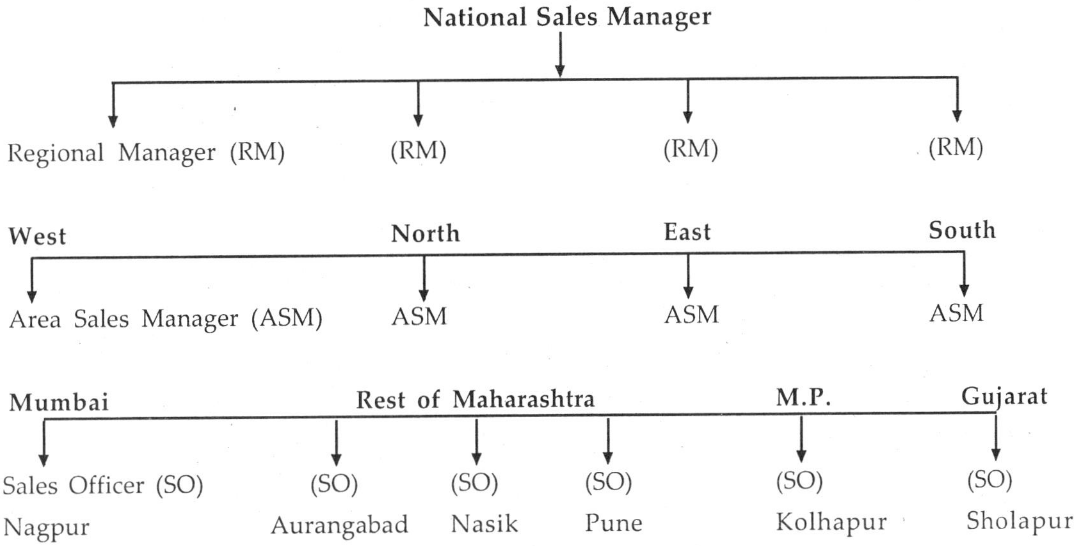

Fig. 1.2: Geographical Sales Organizational Structure

1.4 Product Wise Organizational Structure

Sales Staff is appointed for selling particular product or product group. The individual sales people will only sale that product or product group. Fig. 1.3 will illustrates the point clearly.

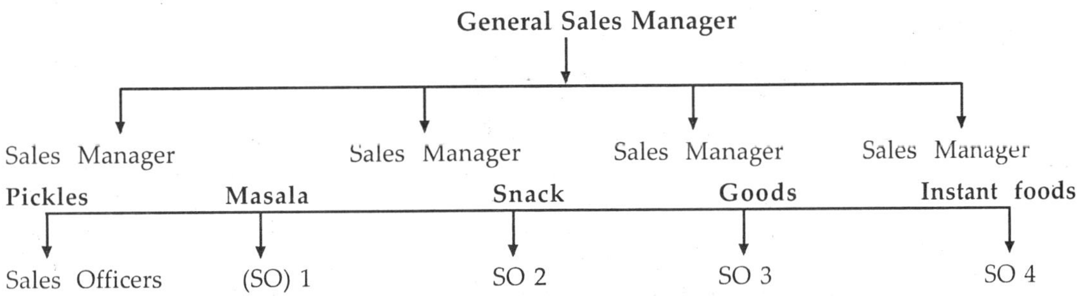

Fig. 1.3: Product Wise Organizational Structure

If the sales are high or customers are more in this type of organization, geographical structure or customer structure is used also.

1.5 Customer Wise Organizational Structure

If the company is manufacturing different product/product groups being sold to different types of customers. The sales organization can be made up of sales personnels' visiting different customers. Fig. 1.4 illustrates the point clearly.

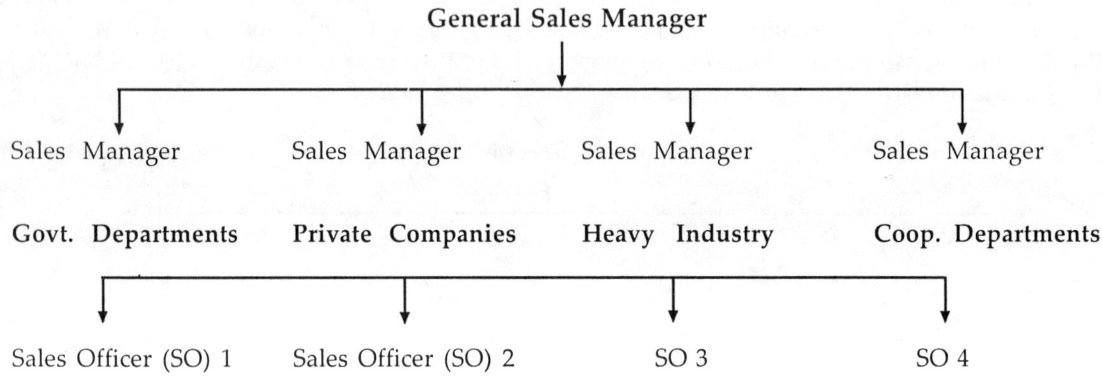

Fig. 1.4: Customer Wise Organizational Structure

If the manufacturer is selling in larger area, this type is combined with area wise organizational structure to get better results.

1.6 Selling Process Wise Organizational Structure

A manufacture may use different processes for selling his products. For each process he will have separate staff giving organizational structure as shown in Fig. 1.5

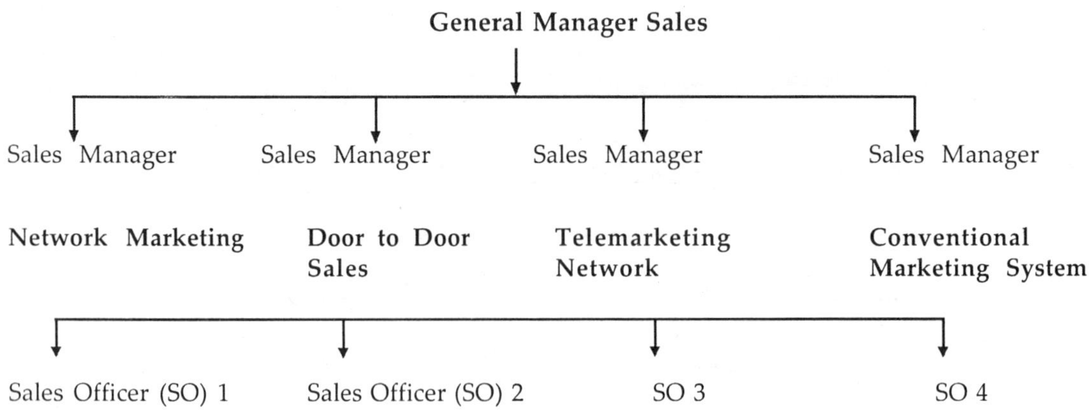

Fig. 1.5: Selling Process Wise Organizational Structure

The size and type of organizational structure will always depend on the number of customers, type of products, number of products to be sold, area of operations and the volume of sales. We will look into decision of type and size of organizational structure when we will look into field sales management in detail.

1.7 Selling and Marketing

The words Selling and Marketing are generally used interchangeably. In many Indian industries Sales and Marketing departments are one and same; with no separate staff for marketing functions and sales functions. In fact many people working in such organizations do not even know that selling and marketing are two words with different meanings. Let us look at them separately.

Selling

Selling is the term used for exchange of products for money (in case of monetary sale) or other product (in case of barter). It does not include what the buyer expected and what he has received. It does not also include buyer's satisfaction level or does not even consider whether buyer is satisfied with the purchase or is unsatisfied with it. Seller has sold what he had with him; buyer has bought what was available. Seller has made profit; buyer may be or may not be satisfied. If buyer is satisfied, he will purchase again or if other products are not available he will keep purchasing the products out of necessity and helplessness. Seller will keep selling to whoever is ready to purchase what he has for sale.

This is what was happening in India through most of Indian industries. Indian consumers went on purchasing what was available out of necessity and helplessness.

Marketing

Marketing is a term used where CONSUMER has more say. The product is made according to consumer's requirement and aggressively promoted to make him aware of it, attract him and persuade him to buy it once, try it and keep buying regularly. The emphasis is on the consumer satisfaction. The Marketing Companies know that if the consumer is satisfied he is willing to buy the product over and over again and will suggest and recommend the products used to his family and friends and acquaintances. The large number of consumers will give the manufacturer ECONOMY OF SCALE and he will start making high profits through high volumes without fear of competitors.

1.8 Comparison of Selling and Marketing

Comparison of Selling and Marketing is obvious. In today's liberalized and globalized economy, Selling-oriented Companies will not be able to sustain market forces and will collapse and close. Only the Marketing-oriented Companies can survive and grow.

Table. 1.1: Comparison of Selling and Marketing

Selling	*Marketing*
1. Sell what you produce.	1. Produce what consumer wants.
2. Sell to consumers who demand your product.	2. Persuade consumers to buy your product.
3. Search for consumer who is likely to buy your product and approach them.	3. Inform all the consumers that a product what they were looking for is available.
4. Rigidity about features of product no modification allowed.	4. Flexibility of features. Modification done according to the needs of buyer.

5. Rigidity of pricing.	5. Willing to loose money to capture market and then recover the losses.
6. Short-term views and strategies.	6. Long-term plans and strategies.
7. If customers are not available for a product, it is phased out and another product is developed to take its place.	7. If customers are not available for a period of time the manufacturing unit gets closed with LAY OFF to workers.
8. Small product range.	8. Ever increasing product range.
9. Backward and forward integration not done.	9. Backward and forward integration done to save costs and remain competitive.
10. Price competition handled by reduction in cost through reduction in quality (sub-standard materials used to cut costs).	10. Price competition is aggressively met by increasing features and improving quality to justify price through aggressive promotions.

1.9 Importance of Sales Management to Business Enterprise

In today's world, Marketing has become a KEYWORD for any Business Enterprise. A modern Business Enterprise will have Marketing department established first and the production department will produce what Marketing department decides to sell, through their Market Research, Product development and Test Sales department in the Business enterprise. Marketing department cannot survive without strong support of selling organization. Let us know look at the importance of Sales department to and old or Modern Business Enterprise.

Importance of Sales Department

1. Sales department gives personal interface with consumers.
2. Sales department ensures placement of stock as close to consumers as possible increasing availability of product, thereby increasing the effectiveness of marketing strategies.
3. Sales department services the consumer regularly there by creating RELATIONS which many a times help combat competition and sustain sales volumes (creation of loyalty).
4. Sales department services the chain of distributors; retailers etc., and keeps it well oiled for smooth working without any problems.
5. Effective Sales Managers can reduce cost of selling with innovative thinking.
6. Effective Sales Managers come out with cost effective localized sales promotions which give higher returns and also motivate the channel members in distribution set-up.
7. Sales Department works as EYES and EARS to Marketing Department and feed them with AUTHENTIC (first hand) information about competitor's activities, market response to these activities and possible counter measures to be taken.
8. Sales forecasting methods are many but the best and dependable method amongst them is the OPINION OF SALES TEAM.

9. Marketing Promotions if not properly executed are not effective. The execution of all marketing promotions depends on the Sales department and their market relations.

10. Sale department works as a link between consumers and business enterprise and also distribution chain and business enterprise. Both these elements are very important for growth of any business enterprise.

1.10 Scenario in India before Liberalization

Before liberalization scenario in India was very distinct, all the multinationals were aggressively marketing their products and succeeding in speeding their popularity and distribution all over India. Most of the Indian companies barring few were happy earning profits by selling sub-standard products to Indian masses under government protection. Many Indian companies enjoyed MONOPOLY through protectionism so there was no need for marketing and in some cases even selling. Consumers were after them for supply of stock (At whatever quality) and were even willing to pay premium for this sub-standard, outdated (according to world market) products. In consumers consumables the situation was little better with some companies like AMUL, TOMCO, (Tata Oil Mills Company manufacturing-Hamam, hair oils etc.), Swastik (Sway, Det), Wipro (Sunflower vanaspati, Santoor Soap), MSIL (Mysore Sandal Soap), Godrej (Cinthol, Key detergent), VICCO (Vajradanti, Tumeric cream), Parle(Gluco, Monaco), Parle(Thumsup, Limca, Frooti), Dukes (Lemonade, Mangola), Quality (Ice-cream), Uncle Chips (Potato wafers) maintaining quality and so maintaining market share and sale. In most of the other products Indian Companies could not gain market share and kept losing to Multi nationals as consumers started feeling 'Anything Indian is of sub standard materials and quality' and they were not wrong. At this time most of the Indian Companies sponsored SWADESHI movements and slogans like BE INDIAN, BUY INDIAN to gain market share by appealing to Indian consumers patriotic emotions instead of improving quality and marketing efforts. If only they could have improved and established quality standards as done by companies like HMT (wrist watches) who never required SWADESHI movement and BE INDIAN, BUY INDIAN slogans, their quality increased their sale and market share.

In pharmaceutical sector Indian Companies had very good time. With no PATENT LAWS (International) stopping them, they were selling all IMPORTED formulations under their own names on par with Multinational products' prices. With negligible expenses on manufacturing (many times in Garages) and zero R&D expenses and royalty, they made huge profits and also offered very high margins and credits to Chemist shops, distributors and incentives to Medical practitioners (Car, T.V., fridge, foreign tour etc.). They monopolized government supplies and cases of drug deaths (J.J. Hospital's case in Mumbai) due to poor quality standards were hushed up/prolonged through political support.

In consumer durables Indian Companies like Godrej; government companies like ECTV and Indian companies with foreign technology like Videocon were doing fine and giving tough competition to foreign companies. But automobile sectors had problems with exceptions like TELCO and Mahindra the products manufactured by Indian companies were all World War II designs with reduced quality. The situations changed after public sector MARUTI brought Japanese models.

Quality maintenance was not the only problem with Indian Companies; the other problem was the sales management and absence of marketing totally. Many Indian Companies do not understand the difference between selling and marketing still. Sales department were generally handled by relatives of the company's owners. Since there was no tension of the job retention, the sales managers enjoyed their life and did nothing to improve the distribution level and selling quality. The main job of sales manager was COLLECTION OF PAYMENT and everything resolved around it. The sales staff coming to office with collection was treated well and was declared as efficient. The selection process of sales staff was faulty. Since evasion of tax was one of the MAIN methods of earning profit or competing with competition, the staff was selected more for trust worthiness (known people) and less for salesmanship. Salaries were very low so the good people tried to get jobs only in multinationals. The experience in Indian Companies was also not treated as experience in Multinationals as there was very little to learn in those companies. In this situation MNCs paid higher salary (in comparison to Indian companies) and exploited the sales force (nobody wanted to lose their job). MNCs trained their sales staff to get better efficiency and quality work. MNCs trained even the distribution channel members to get better results.

So one can summarize that only MNCs (Multinational Corporations) had marketing departments and sales departments and by and large other companies managed their operations (barring exceptions mentioned above) with the help of protected environmental conditions and illegal transactions.

1.11 Scenario after Liberalization and Globalization

The scene is changing but still not in Sales and Marketing. The Indian Companies are busy reducing staff to become cost effective. They have also started improving quality. They have also started creating marketing departments but the sales departments are not still changing. Sales training is still not accepted as investment but expense. But market forces are operating and survival of sales personnel is becoming difficult. Since companies are not providing training opportunities, individuals should seek training from outside sources, and through books giving practical tips.

1.12 Exercise

1. Discuss with village elders and find out how they procured their daily requirements and compare with current situation.
2. Read voyages of Sindbad again to understand his methods of sale. What was the currency he used? Was it sale against money or barter system?
3. Read Marco Polo's travels through silk route, list all the problems he must have faced during the voyages and compare them with current situations.
4. Discuss with some elderly shopkeeper and ask him how he started his shop and where did he get his requirements initially; ask him what changes he has seen in trading atmosphere.

1.13 Questions for Practise

1. Explain difference between sales and marketing
2. Explain the importance of sales department to any organization.

CHAPTER 2 SALES MANAGEMENT – PLANNING OF SALES EFFORTS

Learning Objectives:

- Definition of Sale
- Definition of Management
- Definition of Sales Management
- Duties of Sales Manager
- Planning of Sales Efforts
- Goal Setting

Every individual is involved in buying function and is buying something or the other from another person who is selling. Every individual has an understanding of what is sales and many people give many different definitions of sale. Some of them are as follows:

1. Sale is exchange of goods with money
2. Sale is transfer of ownership of something for consideration

The most accepted definition is as follows:

"Sale is exchange of goods with money where the seller gets profit."

This definition was widely accepted and was useful till recently, but as the business scenario started changing with increased competition in every category of products and wide range of products including services came in the market and the consumers buying power and frequency of purchase increased the definition of sale needed a change. Because of the competition and the increased frequency of buying another element and that of customer's long term satisfaction needed to be added in the definition of sale. While adding customer's satisfaction, one cannot neglect the satisfaction of the seller also, so the redefined definition of sale is as follows:

Modern definition of sale: "sale is exchange of goods, services or knowledge for money where the seller gets profit and both buyer and seller get long-term satisfaction"

With this definition of sale following factors got focused and are important to sale

1. There should be exchange
2. Money has to be paid. If money is not paid sale remains incomplete
3. Seller should get satisfied with the profit he earns.
4. Buyer should be satisfied with the purchase and there should be no feeling of being cheated.
5. The satisfaction of buyer and seller should be long-term so that they are willing to do business again and again.

2.1 Definition of Management

Management is defined in various ways by various people. Some of the definitions are as follows

Management means "Organization and coordination of the activities of an enterprise in accordance with certain policies and in achievement of clearly defined objectives".[1] Definition with productivity as focus

Fredrick Winslow Taylor: "Management is the art of knowing what you want to do in the best and cheapest way"

John F. Mee: "Management is the art of securing maximum prosperity with minimum efforts so as to secure maximum prosperity and happiness to both the employer and employee and give the public the best possible service"

Definition with personnel administration as focus

Lawren A. Appley: "Management is development of people and not the direction of things – Management is personnel administration"

Harold Koontz: "Management is art of getting things done through and with people in formally organized groups. It is art of creating environment in which people can perform and individuals could cooperate towards attaining of group goals. It is art of removing blocks to such performance, a way of optimizing efficiency in reaching the goals."

Definition with decision making and leadership as focus

Stanley Vance: "Management is simply the process of decision making and control over the action of human beings for the express purpose of attaining pre determined goals."

Ralph C. Davis: "Management is function of leadership anywhere."

Donald J. Clough: "Management is the art of and science of decision making and leadership."

1. Businessdictionary.com

Other definitions

Dalton E. McFarland: "that process which managers create, divert, maintain and operate purposive organization through systematic, coordinated, cooperative human effort."

Joseph Massie: "Management is defined as the process by which a co operative group directs action towards common goals."

Theo Haimann and William G. Scot: "Management is social technical process which utilizes resources, influences human action and facilitates changes in order to accomplish organizational goals."

George R. Terry: "Management is a distinct process consisting of planning organizing, actuating and controlling performance to determine and accomplish stated objectives by the use of human beings and other resources."

According to this writers the definition of management with focus to business is "handling business activities in such ways so as to maximize profits (if profitable business enterprise), avoiding losses (if not a profit making enterprise) or reducing losses (if loss making enterprise) successfully."

As a discipline, management comprises of the interlocking functions of formulating corporate-policy and organizing, planning, controlling, and directing the firm's resources to achieve the policy's objectives."[2]

"Definition of sales management: Various people define sales management in different manner following are some of the definitions "Sales management" means management of all marketing activities, including advertising, sales promotion, marketing research, physical distribution, pricing and product merchandising.

"Sales management is attainment of an organization's sales goals in an effective and efficient manner through planning, staffing, training, leading and controlling organizational resources."[3]

2.2 Duties of Sales Manager

Many people define duties of sales manager differently with the limited perspective they gain in various organization. What they define is the organizational focus on the sales manager's duties. In an organization where selling of product is easy but getting the money from the buyers is difficult the definition given is "Ensuring that the collection of money is done in time"

In an organization where the sales staff is sending false reports of working the definition of duties will be given as "Ensuring that all the sales staff works as directed and no one cheats"

In an organization where getting leads is a difficult task the duties will be defined as "Ensuring that the sales staff creates " × " number of leads every month" In an organization where achievement of sales is difficult the duties are defined as "Ensuring that sales targets are achieved regularly"

One must have an all encompassing definition of sales manager's duties. We can list them as primary duties/responsibilities and secondary duties/responsibilities

2. Businessdictionary.com
3. Wikipedia

Primary duties/responsibilities: There is one and only primary responsibility and that is to achive targeted sales as per the company policy at lowest cost of selling. With the modern definition of sale, collection of money is not separated from the selling function so it need not be separately mentioned.

Secondary duties/responsibilities: Secondary duties/responsibilities are all the activities that are needed to accomplish the primary duties/responsibilities. The secondary duties/responsibilities can be listed as follows

1. Planning the sales by forecasting it and discussing it with the management
2. Planning the sales staff, their areas, travel plans, costs of coverage to the available customer base,
3. Increasing the number of customers
4. Planning the distribution channel, recruiting the channel members and keep them motivated.
5. Monitoring and controlling the efficiency of the sales staff and training them whenever required, controlling the channel members and keep them motivated.
6. Planning various sales promotions

If we look at all the responsibilities we can match them to the basic management activities of

1. Planning – sales, selling activities, promotions
2. Organizing – sales staff, distribution channel
3. Directing – sales staff, channel members
4. Control – sales staff, channel members

We will look and understand the sales manager's duties and activities as core management activities.

2.3 Objectives

Like any manager the sales manager has the basic objectives. These objectives can be divided or classified as primary and secondary objectives.

Primary Objectives

The sales manager is an integral part of an organization. Basic objective of an organization is always earning MONEY. Similarly, the basic objective of sales manager is to earn MONEY for organization. Sales Manager is the REVENUE EARNER of the organizations without the sales and sales revenue, the organization will become dead. So, the primary objectives of a sales manager are to SELL the company products and to sell them in increasing quantity to maximum possible level.

As the modern definition of the sale is — Exchange of Goods/SERVICES/KNOWLEDGE FOR MONEY in which seller gets PROFIT and both buyer and seller get long-term satisfaction. Exchange of goods with money (reaching/delivering the product to customer and collecting money) the primary objective becomes:

1. Reaching the product at customer doorstep by-
   (a) Spreading the availability to maximum possible level
   (b) Contacting maximum number of customers
2. Collecting money for the product sold.
3. Controlling the cost of sale the lowest possible level to gain PROFIT.
4. Maintain good customer relationship to get long-term satisfaction.

Secondary Objectives

Secondary objectives are directed towards achievement of primary objectives. The secondary objectives are as follows:

1. Appoint more and more distributors/dealers.
2. Set up coverage pattern, which takes care of maximum number of retailers.
3. Maintain good relationship based on healthy commerce with distributors (Company should reduce cost of selling and distributor earns good ROI)
4. Maintain and increase sales volumes.
5. Maintain high level of visibility/availability of products.
6. Train and motivate sales force for efficient and cost effective selling.
7. Build up company reputation in the market.
8. Handle consumer complaints if any effectively

2.4 Planning Sales Efforts (Sales Forecasting)

Planning of sales efforts starts with planning of sales or sales targets. Planning of sales targets is always based on the market which is going to accept the product the sales manager or the marketer is trying to sell. This will depend on the marketing activity STP, i.e., segmentation, targeting and positioning. The sales target will always depend on the size of the segment chosen for selling activity. The sales target will also depend on competition present in the market. Normally the demand for the market is deciding on following analysis of the market which divides the market in four distinct categories.

1. **Potential market:** it will be the set of customers who keep have potential to use it or may have interest in using the product. E.g., for entry level automobiles (Maruti 800, Alto, A Star, Santro I10, Santro I20 etc.) all the customers with steady income and are working as executives or lower level managers or owners of small scale business enterprise (self-employed persons)
2. **Available market:** it will be the set of customers who have interest and ability to buy the product. E.g., all those potential customers who have stability in life and are seeking esteem needs in Maslow's need hierarchy will form the available market for entry level automobile.
3. **Target market:** it is the part of available market that is being earmarked for attacking marketing activity in immediate future. E.g., the marketer may target a

specific geographic area say Maharashtra and also decide a particular expenditure level on automobile purchase as ₹ 3 lakh. The customers in this category will be called target market.

4. **Penetrated market:** It is part of available market which has been targeted earlier successfully and the customers are already using the product. E.g., all those customers who have already purchased the product are called as penetrated market. The marketer may try to influence these customers to go in for exchange of their current automobile and declare loyalty promotions.

Decision on sales target is based on the sales demand forecasting. Various methods of demand forecasting are used by various people. We can list these methods as follows

(a) **Census survey:** This is done by physically counting all the potential customers and deciding on availability of the customers and the quantity they are likely to purchase. This will give the marketer the size of the potential market. On the basis of the market potential thus ascertained the market may find the available market and take decision on targeting its part.

(b) **Expert opinion method:** Marketer may get in touch with experts who know the market very well and take their opinion on the size of potential, available market and decide on the market to be targeted.

Estimating the current demand (sales forecasting) will depend on various factors as said earlier on the size of available market, the competition present, the current market share of the product the marketer is selling, the promotions planned etc., various methods of current demand/ expected sales forecasting are used by various marketers. We can list some of them as follows

(i) **Composite of sales force opinion:** This method is widely used method and if used properly can give best results. In this method entire sales force is asked to forecast the expected sales for their respective area of operation. Since the sales force is aware of all the environmental conditions that may affect their respective sales areas they are in a better position to forecast the sales closure to the actual sales. Totalling the individual forecasted sales the marketer can estimate the total sales forecast.

Using this method a good sales manager can get good results but a sales manager who does not know the sales staff working under him/her properly will not be able to get good results. The reason is very simple every sales person will have three distinctive attitudes

(a) Over ambitious behavior which will lead to his forecast being over ambitious

(b) Pessimistic behavior will lead to forecast being overly cautious

(c) Realistic/meticulous behavior will lead to realistic forecast

A sales manager is required to accept the forecast given by each individual after applying a correcting factor according to the attitude shown earlier by each individual that can lead to correct forecast.

(ii) **Expert opinion:** Companies can obtain the sales forecast from the experts like the dealers, distributors, suppliers, marketing consultants etc., and decide the expected sales.

Marketer must ensure that the experts are not already working for the competitive products and are not giving misleading or biased opinions.

(iii) **Past sales analysis:** Marketers can analyze the past sales records and decide the sales forecast on it. Past sales analysis has various methods of using the past sales records which are as follows

Table 2.1: Showing the Sales in Units

Month	*Sales units*
April	100
October	120
May	120
November	100
June	100
December	110
July	110
January	100
August	130
February	100
September	90
March	100

(a) **Time series method:** In this method the past sales are put on a graph to get the trend and based on the trend the future sales are forecasted e.g., if following sales figures are observed for the months April to December one can forecast the sale for January to March shown in red as follows

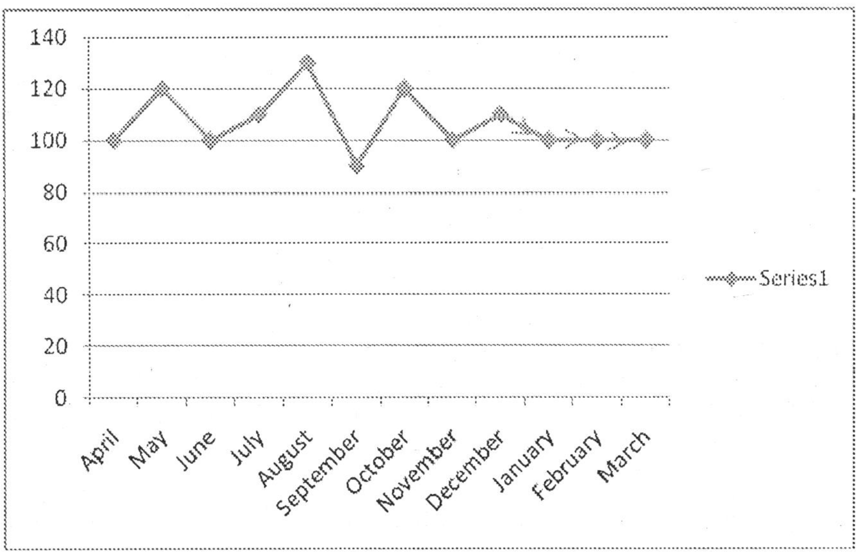

Fig. 2.1: Showing Sales Trends

The forecast here is based on the average sale and the downward trend shown from October.

(b) **Moving average totals:** Instead of taking sales for a period sales average are taken in this method to streamline the effects of external environmental impacts caused by various environmental aspects time to time. E.g., in the above example if we take quarterly averages it will show the forecast for January–March quarter as follows

Table. 2.2: Showing Average Totals

Period	*Average Sales for the quarter*
April-May-June	320
July-August- September	340
October- November- December	330
January-February-March	330

Moving average totals can be taken for various periods, in the above example, we have shown it for a quarter but it can be taken for six months or a year (12 months). The choice of period will change from product category to product category. For fast moving consumer goods (FMCG) it is normally taken for 12 month period average to streamline

Sales forecasting in sales department is basically done on historic data along with other aspects like:

(a) Retail audit

(b) Sales promotional aspects

(c) Competitive activities

(d) Other environmental aspects

Let us look at these methods in detail

(a) Retail audit:

The retail audit indicates the consumer off-take for the previous month. The consumer off-take indicates similar off-take for the next month (if the off-take is showing a trend over a period of time it can also be incorporated in the forecasting).

Field sales planning is very important job the for entire organization. Entire planning of an enterprise depends upon the sales estimates given by the field force. The sales manager does not have any support system to depend on the market information available is of no good quality. Market research organizations are not dependable. The retail audit data provided by research organization is not dependable. The Sales Manager is required to depend on his judgments only. Some good professional sales managers set up Retail Audit Panels for their own territories to get help in sales planning. But monitoring retail audit panel is a very difficult task, if done properly is the best tool. This writer had developed his own retail audit panel in Mumbai and was able to forecast the sale for immediate next month with variation of + 2% only.

How to set up Retail Audit Panel?

Following steps need to be taken in setting up of retail audit panel.

1. **Finalize retail universe**

   To set up retail audit panel one must know the exact population of retailers keeping the products. The population of retailers is called as retail universe for a product.

2. **Prepare sales data**

   To set up retail audit panel one must have the historic and current sales data for the area. This sales data will help in determining sales averages per call basis.

3. **Classify retailers**

   The retailer should be classified in ABC categories depending on their purchase/sales to customer pattern. Generally, following parameter is used which is decided by the sales manager himself.

   A Class 170% of average sale per outlet and above

   B Class 71 to 169% of average sale

   C Class 70% of average sale and below

4. **Categories retailers**

   Categories retailers as follows, which will help to find category wise sale per outlet.

   Ch – Chemist

   Gr – Grocers

   Gm – General merchants

   Co-op – Co-operatives

   Super stores – etc.

5. **Find category wise sales**

   Find the contribution of sale per category to total sale.

6. **Find class wise sales**

   Find contribution of each class of retailer to total sale.

7. **Find representative sample**

   Find retailers who can constitute representative sample as retail audit panel with:

   (a) Categories represented as per actual constitution, e.g., if 200 chemists are in retail universe of 2000, e.g., 10% in the representative sample 10% outlets should be chemists.

   (b) Class represented as actual constitution, e.g., if A class declares are 400 in retail universe of 2000, e.g., 20 % and B class 40% and C class 40 % the representatives sample should have 20% A class 40% B class and 40% C class retailers.

   (c) Representation from all routes should be taken.

   (d) The retail audit panel should be at least 10% size of total universe *vis-a-vis* number of retailers and sales generation.

Monitoring Retail Audit Panel

Following steps are taken to monitor retail audit panel.

(a) Opening stock of beginning date is taken physically.

(b) Subsequent purchases are recorded correctly.

(c) Closing stock for current month, e.g., opening stock of next month is always taken by physical check.

(d) The stock check is done for entire panel of retailers on the same date + 1 day every month.

(e) Do not give special treatment to panel outlets.

(f) Check the off-take sale co-relation. Change panel outlets to bring stability/uniformity in the relation of panel to universe.

(g) Once you are sure of panel to universe relation start forecasting sale for next month based on retail audit off-take information safely. Previous months off-take < sale next month. (By extrapolation panel to universe).

Sales planning based on retail audit is very safe and without risk.

Sales promotional aspects

The planned sales promotions have effect on the sales and consumer off-take. The previous experience about the planned promotions or advertisement campaigns effect on sale can be taken as indicator while forecasting sales based on promotions planned.

Some promotions lose their attractiveness after using them over and over again, but some promotions remain attractive even after using them many numbers of times.

Competitive activity

As the promotions help sell more quantity of your product. Promotions planned by competition affect your sale adversely. A sales manager should consider the effect of competitive activity while forecasting the sale.

Other environmental aspects

Environmental aspects like:

(i) Elections

(ii) Finance budget presentations

(iii) Agricultural yield condition

(iv) Condition of main industry

(v) Festivals

(vi) Seasons, etc.,

Their favorable or adverse effects on the sale, a Sales Manager should consider these effects. All these aspects have diverse effects on sale and are different in different areas.

A Sales Manager is required to give sale estimates for the coming periods continuously. He must do so considering all these aspects and not monotonously without considering them.

Example 1.1

Sunil Balgu was preparing sales forecast for next four months. He has the following facts at hand

1. Sales for Jan 99 200 units

   Sales for Feb 99 200 units

   Sales for Mar 99 150 units

   Sales for Apr 99 100 units

   Sales for May 99 100 units

2. The sales trend improves in 2nd week of June every year due to school opening (end of vacation).
3. Company has planned consumer promotion in the month of July 99. Consumer promotion gives nearly 2½ times normal sales.
4. Sale in the next month of sale is 80% of average sale.

Sunil Balgu prepares his forecast for June, July and August 99 as follows:

June 99 200 units (normal level of sale Jan., Feb.)

July 99 500 units (2½ times normal level)

Aug 99 160 units (80% of normal level).

Example 1.2

Pravin Gandhi was making his sales forecast for Jan. to March 2000. He had already achieved his previous sale (April 1998 to March 99) till December 1999. The sale achieved in January–March 2000, will be over and above his previous year sale. The company expected him to do 10% more than previous year but he planned to end at 20% more to get best Sales Officer prize and ensure sales next year. (April 2000 to March 2001) also, from the following facts he had –

1. Sale of previous year (April 98 to March 99) – 2500 units
2. Sale till this month (April 99 to December 99) – 2500 units
3. Additional sale required to show 20% growth – 500 units
4. Monthly average for previous 3 months – 300 units

Pravin Gandhi made forecast as follows:

January 2000 – 250 units

February 2000 – 150 units

March 2000 – 100 units

Example 1.3

Arondekar was analyzing his budgets at the end of 3rd quarter. He found the following:

1. Expenditure budget was on par with planned expenditure.
2. Major expenditure 60% of total was coming from touring small towns.

3. Monthly expenditure budget was ₹ 1,00,000/-.
4. If small towns are not visited in a particular month there is a saving of ₹ 45,000/– in that month.
5. Volume sales were on par with previous year but below the budgeted sales of 5% above previous year.
6. Competition with strong in major towns and weak in smaller towns.
7. New super stores with 5 branches had opened. They were demanding rental for display but were willing to purchase more than the required quantity to achieve the budgeted volumes. The rental worked out to be ₹ 15,000 × 5 = ₹ 75,000/ (₹ 5000/- per month per store).
8. Effect of superstores was going to be felt by surrounding retailers.

Arondekar decided the following plan for the last quarter, e.g., January, February and March.

(a) **January** – (i) The smaller towns will not be visited. Instead the bigger towns will get concentration. (ii) Superstores will be given okay for rental and orders collected and supplied.

(b) **February** – Smaller towns to be visited as normal.

(c) **March** – Smaller towns will not be visited.

Result:

(a) Saving of ₹ 45,000 × 2 = ₹ 90,000/-

(b) Additional expenditure of ₹ 75,000/- super store rental.

(c) Achievement of sales volume quota/budget.

(d) Saving of ₹ 15,000/- in expenditure budget.

2.5 Sales Target/Budget Planning

A sales manager is required to prepare sales targets based on the sales forecast. The professional sales managers will plan sales targets for the entire year in advance and then break them in to area wise and month wise targets. In many FMCG (fast moving consumer goods) companies, the sales force opinion combined method is used. Sales force will base their opinions on past sales records and the effects of competition and economic development in their area of operation. Preparing targets this way is called as "Bottom up method" of preparing the targets.

In some organizations planning of targets is done by the senior management based on the past trends and company's growth objectives. These targets are then broken down area wise and given to respective sales personnel. This method is called as "Top down method".

Bottom up method is liked by the sales force and the chances of achieving these targets is high as the sales force have a feeling of ownership towards its and they try to prove that they are able to forecast accurately. Bottom up method does not incorporate the company objective and can reduce the pace of growth of the company.

The top down method takes in to consideration the company objectives and the promotional plans but many times does not consider the area wise deviations into considerations. The promotional plans are also not divulged to the sales staff for fear of leakage of information to competition and competition planning counter promotions nullifying the effect of promotions. Because of this there is always a fear of sales force not accepting these targets wholeheartedly and work towards it. To avoid this many organizations go in for a third type of method which is a compromise of both the methods. In this method the regional manager prepares targets with bottom up method and the senior managers prepare target by top down method, the difference in the quantities is negotiated to arrive at acceptable target to both. The regional manager will accept higher figure and negotiates promotional efforts to help achieve that figure. Since the promotions or promotional budgets are discussed with regional managers the leakage of information is avoided. Many times the regional manager is authorized to propose various promotions for various areas at various times with the budgeted limits.

Breaking the annual targets area wise and month wise is the next thing the sales manager is required to do. Breaking of the sales targets area-wise requires following considerations

1. **Area potential:** A particular area may be achieving low sales due to the inefficient or unskilled efforts of a particular sales person manning that area. The sales manager must analyze the true potential by investigating the competitions activity, the number of customers available and under coverage and the market share enjoyed. Unless he plans for increase of market share and complete coverage equal to more than that of competition the area will never develop.
2. **Economic environment of the area:** The target must be planned in consideration with the economic development of the area. If the area is growing rapidly the targets must be planned higher accordingly and if the area is showing negative growth the targets must be planned lower accordingly (see box).

Box 2.1: Changes in sales patterns with movement of population

(a) In the city of Mumbai, south Mumbai is to be thickly populated once upon a time. As the business started growing and more and more commercial space was required in the vicinity of the backbay reclamation. So the population started shifting to suburbs after taking hefty sums they offered to handover their residences. This population shift started reducing the demand for most of the consumer products. Many sales managers not accepting this theory kept on pressurizing their sales staff with high targets for the south Mumbai area and loosing good sales people to other companies.

(b) The wholesale market in Bhat-bazaar in Mumbai used to be a feeder to entire Maharashtra towns and villages which were not under proper coverage up to the early eighties. When the maximum retail price inclusive of all taxes (MRP) was enforced by the Government the shopkeepers in these remote towns and villages were unable to charge higher rates than the printed MRP for recovering the extra cost they have incurred in getting the products from Mumbai; the shopkeepers started demanding the products locally. At the same time most of the manufacturers appointed distributors at all these places as the demand was increasing with advent of television advertisements. The sales in the wholesale market started dropping and the share of Mumbai area to total Maharashtra started dropping from 80% earlier to 50% later. All the manufacturers were required to reduce the targets for Mumbai area and increase the targets for rest of Maharashtra area substantially.

3. **Previous sales records:** Sales targets must be based on the sales trends shown by a particular area. A sales manager can never break the sales targets equitably as all the sales areas do not have same potential, same economic environment and sales trends.

4. **Seasonal variation in sales:** The sales manager must consider the seasonal variation in sales while breaking the annual targets to month wise figures and that to by understanding the trends of high primary (company to distributors) and high secondary (distributors to retailers) variations properly, e.g., though the consumer off-takes (purchase of goods from retailer by consumers) of school stationery and notebooks etc., is highest in June when the schools open the order booking starts in January and the actual primary and secondary sales takes place in May. If a sales person tries to book orders in June he will not get them because the retailers and distributors have already stocked themselves to take care of coming demand.

Some sales managers increase or decrease the sales targets based on the efficiency level of a sales person. This practice is unhealthy and does not do justice to the more efficient sales personnel.

Breaking of sales targets from territory total to distributor/town wise and further in day wise should be best left to be done by the territory sales in-charges, but should be ensured that they do it meticulously.

Planning of sales targets can be done in two ways

1. **Volume targets:** Which are based on the quantity to be sold in the given period of time

2. **Value targets:** These are based on the value of the products to be sold in given period of time

In the author's opinion setting value targets is a wrong method in most of the cases as it only guarantees the turnover of the organization but not the growth. For long-term benefit of any organization the sales manager must insist on the volume (quantity) targets which guarantee the growth of the organization. One should always remember that the prices of the products rarely fall but they normally rise and value targets can easily be achieved by increasing the prices of products even when the volumes (quantity sold) are dropping as a last resort.

Budget planning: When the word budget is used it talks about the expenses incurred in achieving the sales volume targets. Various organizations have various ways to plan budgets. Budgets can include the following

(a) Salaries of the staff

(b) Travelling expenses of the staff

(c) Office expenses of the branch (Electricity, rents, stationery, telephones, postage, entertainment, etc.)

(d) Promotional expenses

(e) Transportation costs

The budgets are generally planned on the basis of volume targets and are in proportion to the previous period actual expenditures incurred for achieving previous period sales volumes.

2.6 Planning of Sales Efforts (Sales Force)

Second most important part of planning of sales efforts is the planning of sales force. Planning of sales force depends on various factors as follows

(a) **Area under coverage:** When area under coverage is very large the number of sales personnel required also becomes more and if the area under coverage is small the number of sales personnel required is small. Sometimes the area under coverage is not very large but the terrain is difficult making it physically difficult for the sales people to cover the entire area, then it is important that additional sales person are appointed.

(b) **Number of customers to be serviced:** The number of sales persons required is directly proportionate to the number of customers required to be serviced. Normally, a sales manager fixes the number of customers a sales person can visit efficiently in one working day and the calculates the number of working days required to cover the customers to be serviced. As every month has approximately 25 working days and for every 25 working days required one sales person is appointed. E.g., if a sales person is able to visit 10 customers in a day and there are 1000 customers to be serviced every month then the number of sales persons required is calculated as follows

1000 customers/25 working days per month × 10 customers per day = 4 sales persons are required to be appointed.

(c) **Product range:** If the product range is cohesive one sales person can sell all the products together, but if the product range is not cohesive the organization requires different sales person to sell different products, e.g., Mohan Meakins sells food product range consisting of corn flakes, fruit juices, etc., and also the liquor range of whisky, beer, etc. Since the customers to be serviced differs completely they are required to have two sets of sales force to service both type of customers increasing the number of sales persons in the sales force.

(d) **Frequency of service required:** Depending upon the products and the quantity being purchased at a time by the customers, the frequency of service required changes. This leads to increase or decrease in number of sales persons required to cover the customers. E.g.,

(i) in above example in "b" if the frequency required is weekly instead of monthly as shown the number of sales person will increase fourfold to 16 as shown below

1000 customers × 4 visits per month/25 working days a month × 10 customers per day = 16 sales persons to be appointed

(ii) if the product is say bread in above example then the frequency of coverage required will be daily and that too twice daily the required number will change as follows:

1000 customers x 60 visits per month (30 days × 2 visits per day)/30 working days a month x 50 customers per day (one can cover more customers for selling bread) = 40 sales persons

(e) **Budgeted expenditure on sales force:** The budgeted expenditure also decides the number of sales persons to be appointed as follows

1. If the budgeted expenditure on sales force is ₹ One lakh and the sales person is required to be paid ₹ 10,000/- per month one can appoint only ten sales persons even if the requirement is of sales persons is more than ten.
2. If the budgeted expenditure on sales force is 2% of the monthly targeted values of sale say ₹ One crore the available amount for expenditure is ₹ Two lakhs and if the sales persons is to be paid ₹ 10,000/- per month then one can appoint 20 sales persons.

   1,00,00,000 × 2/100 = ₹ 2,00,00

   2,00,000/10,000 = 20 sales person
3. Organizations can also decide to have one sales person per say ₹ 20 lakh per month sale. In such case if the average sale per month is ₹ 2 crore the number of sales persons will be 10.

(f) **Competitive activity:** In competitive product sales one has to follow the competition and have sales persons equal to the competition and the coverage pattern and frequency is needed to be matched with the competition. E.g., if Pepsi has 10 sales person covering the area once daily the frequency coke has to match, and have equal to or more than that number.

(g) **Selling strategy:** An organization can decide to cover the customers by their own sales force or through the distributor's sales force. If the coverage is to be done through the distributor's sales force then the organization can have lesser number of sales persons in their sales force, e.g., Hindustan Unilever Ltd., operates through distributor's sales force so their total sales force is very limited as compared to the area under coverage and the volume of sales they generate. Their territory in-charge may control a large area having say 4000–5000 customers being covered once every week.

Examples Manpower Planning

Example 1

An electronic company has following number of customers:

'A' class – 33

'B' class – 64

'C' class – 40

'D' class – 103

If the coverage frequency is decided to be

'A' class – 33 daily

'B' class – 64 twice a week

'C' class – 40 once a week

'D' class – 103 once a month

If a sales officer visits 8 customers every day.

How many sales officers are required to be appointed? A sales officer works 25 days a month.

Solution

(a) We must work out the work load per month as follows:

'A' class 33 daily	= 33 × 25	= 825
'B' class 64 twice week	= 64 × 8	= 512
'C' class 40 once a week	= 40 × 4	= 160
'D' class 103 once a month	= 103 × 1	= 103
		1600

(b) One sales officer visits 8 customer calls daily, i.e.,

25 × 8 = 200 calls every month

(c) If we require 1 sales officer for every 200 calls for 1600 calls we will require

1600/200 = 8 Sales Officers

Example 2

An FMCG company has 1200 retailers to be visited every week. If the sales officer visit 25 retailers every day, how many sales officers are required for them? Tip = 24 working days per month.

Solution

Let us find work load.

25 retailers = 1 man day

So, 1200 retailers = 48 man days

Since, every retailer will be visited once every week, i.e., 4 times a month.

Monthly work load is = 48 × 4 = 192 man days

Since, one month is = 24 working days we have (6 days × 4 weeks)

192/24 = 8 man months.

The sales officers are appointed on monthly basis. So we require 8 sales officers.

Example 3

A cigarette company has a retail universe of 2000 retailers. If a salesman visits 50 retailers every day and all retailers need daily visit, how many salesmen does the company require?

Solution

One salesman visits 50 retailers.

All retailers require daily visit.

So for every 50 retailer one salesman

For 2000 retailers 2000/50 = 40 Salesman required.

Use of ISR/DSRs

Many a time companies need to give daily/weekly coverage for a large retail universe. Giving such coverage through company sales officers is very costly. Not giving coverage affects the company business in such case use of ISRs (Interim Sales Representatives) or DSRs (Distributors Sales Representatives) or Pilot Sales Representatives is prevalent. These ISRs/DSRs/Pilots are paid their salaries through distributors and is reimbursed by the company in various ways. The difference between the salary structure of the company sales officers and ISRs is very large. A company can avail of 4 to 5 ISRs in place of one company sales officer.

Compensation of ISRs/DSRs/Pilots

The reimbursement of ISR/DSR salary can be on absolute value terms or can be additional margins on sales. Giving additional margins ensures business as the money is available only when sale occurs.

2.7. Planning of Sales Territories

Formation of territories is very important job. Before getting into the formation of territories let us understand what territory is.

Definition

Territory is grouping of customers and prospects (potential customers) assigned to an individual sales person.

Sales territories are made in different ways like –

1. **Based on product:** Each salesman is assigned one product and all customers purchasing it is the sales person territory.
2. **Based on consumer type:** Consumers are classified – (a) A Class, B Class or C Class (based on the size of their business) .
   (b) They are classified as bulk buyers, small lot buyers.
   (a) They are classified on their nature of business like chemical industry, sugar industry, pharmaceutical industry etc.
   (b) On their qualification: Gynecologist, orthopedic, ophthalmologists, urologist, general practitioners etc.
3. **Based on skills of the sales person:** Companies may use different sales person to contact same customer, based on their (sales persons) skills in handling the situation. This is similar to the one explained above (based on the product) but has small difference like, e.g., Sales person specializing in say "electronic eye" may visit all the customers using products having "electronic eye" as its part .
4. **Based on geographical divisions:** This is the most common method in most FMCG products. The salesman will be assigned part of town, cities, etc. He will look after all the customers in that area.

Precautions while taking territory decisions

There are many precautions a sales manager must take while taking the territory decisions.

1. **Equitable work load:** The work load in each territory should be equitable. Nobody should be overburdened and nobody should be made under loaded. The growth prospects also should be able to show growth by reasonable amount of effort.
2. **Equitable business opportunity:** In case of salary + commission or commission only businesses, the sales person should be able to generate equal expenses. If the opportunities are not equitable sales person can get demotivated and frustrated.
3. **Equitable treatment for each territory:** A sales person based in large city may get large turnover due to concentration of large number of customers. At the same time a sales person based in remote area may be getting substantially lesser business with very high level of efforts (troublesome travel without proper facilities). If the sales person from remote area is not treated properly and his efforts are not recognized it will lead to demotivation and frustration.
4. **Minimum number of days with his family:** A sales person should be given territories in such a way that he spends at least 8 to 10 days (inclusive of holidays and weekends) with his family. That means the base town should be a bigger town where he can keep his family safely in his absence and spend at least 8 to 10 days with them. This will keep them motivated.
5. **Avoid long journeys:** If a sales person is required to travel longer durations at a time:
   (a) He will get tired due to journey and his efficiency will go down.
   (b) He will lose valuable working time for unproductive work, e.g., travel.
   (c) Company will be playing higher allowances for unproductive time spent in travel.

As long as possible the journey time from one customer to another customer, or one town to another should not be more than 3 to 4 hours and may be occasionally one overnight journey where the travel arrangements are comfortable (sleeper coach in train).

6. **Night stay should be in better place:** If the sales person is travelling continuously (Van Salesman) his territory plan should be in such a way that he can have food and rest in reasonably good locations. This will avoid sickness among sales staff and demotivation and frustration of the sales staff.
7. **Territory should avoid backtracking:** If the sales person is required to travel the same distance repeatedly it will lead to unnecessary travel expenditure and payment of excessive allowances. Fig. 2.1 and 2.2 illustrates the same.

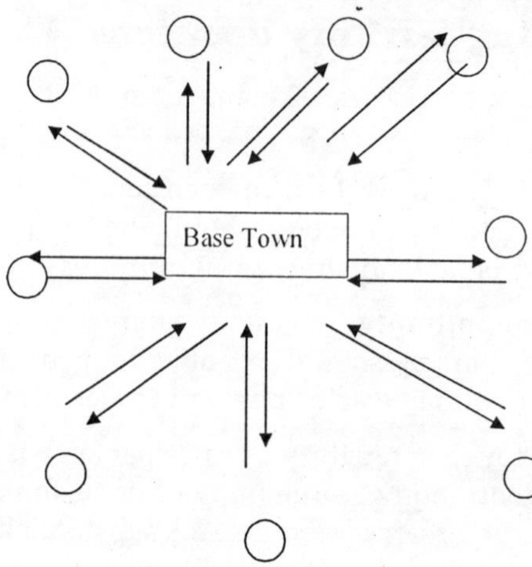

Fig. 2.1: Backtracking

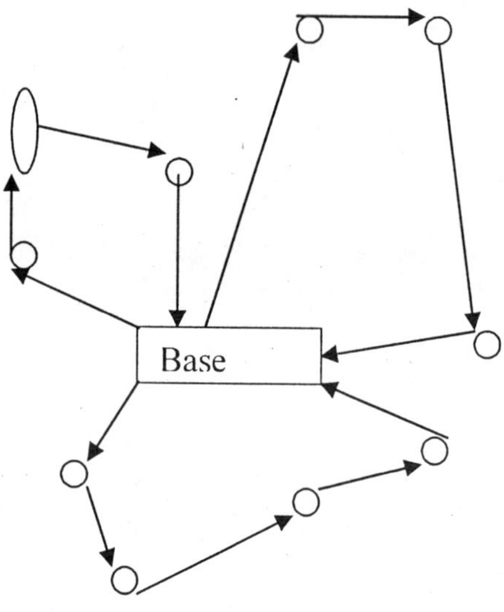

Fig. 2.2: No Backtracking

The expenses saved on travelling are more than the night away allowances paid. Popular shapes of territories are as shown in Fig. 2.3.

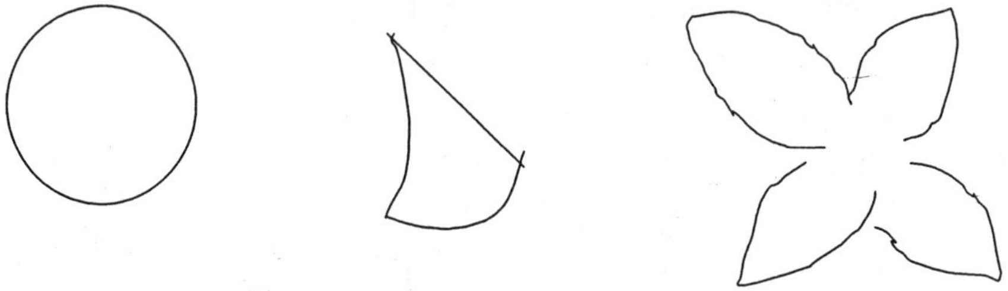

Fig. 2.3: Popular Shapes of Territories

8. **Avoid sharing of customer:** Two sales persons should not be allowed to call on the same customer for same product range. (For different product ranges it can be done). The customer may create misunderstanding between the two sales persons and take benefit of the situation.
9. **Clear demarcation of territory:** The adjoining territories should have clear-cut demarcations to avoid area crossing by sales persons. The demarcation can be a railway-line, river, main road etc.
10. **Manageable size:** The sales territory should not have large geographical area as possible. Large territory even with low volume sale becomes unmanageable.

Concept of PJP (Permanent Journey Plan) in deciding territories

PJP is a good method of deciding territories as it helps in deciding the work load effectively. To understand PJP one must understand the following terms:

JC – Journey Cycle: For monitoring the progress of sales the financial year (April – March or January, December as may be the case in each company) is divided into different periods. At the end of the each period the sales person reports to sales manager on his sales plan and actual achievement. In each of this period sales person is required to undertake journey from one customer to another or one route to a another or one town/city to another etc. The sales person will have cyclic journey during this period before he comes back to sales office for reporting. This journey from sales office to customers to sales office is called as Journey Cycle (JC).

A Sales person may visit same customers every time or different customers every time but the period of JC are fixed.

A JC can be of one week duration or of fortnight duration or of 4 week duration or a month's duration. Generally, the monitoring period is not greater than a month. In many companies JC was 4 weeks period with 1/12 of yearly sales budget giving the Sales Manager 13 JCs to achieve years sales budget with at least 1/12 additional sales as growth. This system is discontinued by most companies now as planning becomes difficult for other facilities.

JCM – Journey Cycle Meeting

The Sales Manager conducts a review meeting of the sales personnel at the end of each JC which is called JCM – Journey Cycle Meeting.

EJC – Every Journey Cycle: Depending upon the business potential of the customer the frequency of visit by sales personnel is planned. If the sales person visits a customer in every journey cycle the customer/route/town is called as EJC customer/route/town.

AJC – Alternate Journey Cycle: If the customer/route/town is visited in every alternate journey cycle it is called AJC customer/route/town.

QJC – quarterly Journey Cycle: As the normal period of Journey Cycle is a month, visit frequency to any particular customer/route/town once in every three cycles is called Quarterly Journey Cycle (Three months is quarter of year). QJC customer/route/town. In actual fact it can be:

(a) Every third day if JC is of single day (for white goods)

(b) Every third week if JC is of a week duration (most FMCG companies)

(c) Every third month if JC is of a month duration

Deciding Work Load in PJP system

In PJP system the work load has to be decided for each working day. Following methods are used.

1. Time required per customer: Time required to call on a customer varies from company to company and product to product. We will consider standard times for product groups.

(a) White Goods (fridge, TV, music systems, automobiles etc.):

There are many aspects involved in a sales call for white goods like:

(i) Stock available with customer in all products, product categories, product variation etc., e.g., Fridges: 90 lt, 165 lt, 200lt, 220lt, 300lt, 330lt, 600lt.

Conventional, frost free

With CFC, without CFC

One door, two doors, three doors etc.

White, pink, red, blue, yellow, gray, silver colors

(ii) Stock available with customer for competition.

(iii) Stock on display for the company and competition.

(iv) Shop demonstrators' activities, his training level, and his efficiency.

(v) POP in the shop for the company and competition.

(vi) Promotional schemes for the company and for competition

(vii) Emphasis of customer on your company and competition, reasons for it.

(viii) MOP – Market Operating Price (The price at which the product is being sold generally lower than suggested price) for the company and for competition.

(ix) Payment position – Details of outstanding payments.

(x) Actual sales closing (Taking order based on above considerations).

To do all these things in a busy outlet the sales personnel may require from 45 minutes to 2½ hours also. As the white goods customers (retailers) are scattered in many cases, a white goods sales person can do no more than 5 to 8 calls in a day of 8 hours. (See Box 2.2)

Box 2.2 Effects of Defective Call Procedure

When Kelvinator and TVS were acquired by Whirlpool the two teams were having two cultures and two working styles; this lead to a situation where Whirlpool's market outstanding amounts reached to around 300 days putting pressure on working capital. At this time Whirlpool was setting up a Global No-frost (GNF) refrigerator plant at Ranjangaon Pune. The company looked for the reasons for the market outstanding and found following reasons

1. Call procedure of sales staff was faulty
2. Only major retailers were being visited and smaller one were being neglected
3. Sales staff complained that they were overburdened and needed to reduce work load.
4. There was no proper MIS (market information system) available

Whirlpool launched a all India sales force training program under a Hindustan Unilever veteran Mr. Talwar with three others (one of them was this author) to do field training of the sales staff (all staff being experienced they were not open to any training) showing practically their weak points.

The author found that the selling call procedure was faulty leading to the dealers cheating the sales staff on the stock holding and refusing payment on the basis of high stock holding. This author developed a daily calls report for them and helped prepare PJP for individual sales officers. This improved the coverage and payment collection and at the end of field training the market outstanding amount came down to 90 days from initial 300 days.

(b) Pharma Sale: A Medical Representative (also called as officer or executive) visit general practitioners (GPs), and specialists along with some calls to chemists. A sales call generally requires only 2 minutes completing but the travelling between the customers and waiting period is large. The working hours are also limited like 1000 to 1300 hrs in the morning session and 1800 to 2130 hours in the evening session. The Chemists can be visited in the afternoon hours only. So the work load plan is generally 10 to 12 GPs and 2 specialists a day with one or two chemists per day.

(c) Industrial Institutional Sale: In Industrial sale the time taken for travels, waiting is very large. Even if one is visiting an industry with prior appointment number of calls cannot exceed more than 2-3 calls per day. If the salesman is visiting smaller industrial units the numbers can go up to 6 calls a day.

(d) Consumer Products (FMCG): In consumer product category the sales call takes about 2 to 15 minutes to complete depending on:

(a) Product popularity

(b) Retail outlet size

(c) Promotional offers present not present.

(d) Arrangement of display done not done

(e) POP fixing done not done

The time required for travel between the calls is negligible in most cases as the routes are planned accordingly. In smaller towns and in larger routes the time between the calls can be arranged to 2-3 minutes per call. If we consider 5 hours, e.g., 300 minutes of actual working and 18 minutes per call (at maximum) a minimum of 17 calls can be made. If we consider 4 minutes per call (at minimum) we can do 75 calls. So we find that the call norms are set in the range of 20 to 50 calls by different companies.

2. Total number of customers available: Once the maximum work load per sales person is decided; number of workdays (mandays) required can be decided on the basis of:

(a) Number of customers available: In a town/city there can be many customers (in case of FMCG number of retailers stocking the company products) available. A Sales Manager can arithmetically find the number of mandays required to cover the available customers e.g.:

(i) For 100 customers with a call norm per day as 20, number of days required is 5.

(ii) For 100 customers with a call norm per day as 50, number of days required will be 2.

These outlets will constitute that day's route. A route list can then be prepared showing the names of the retailers/doctors/customers to be visited in a particular day.

(b) Proximity of towns/villages: If a town village has lesser number of customers than the calls norms, the sales person can be asked to go to another town/village to complete the quota of calls (call norms) for that day provided:

(i) The towns are in close proximity and can be reached by available conveyance easily.

(ii) The sales person has been given a vehicle/vehicle allowance to complete the quota by reasonable distances of travel.

(iii) The customers are available for a sales call when the sales person reaches the destination. (Most of the retailers/doctors/customers in Indian subcontinent are closed for afternoon lunch and Siesta for long duration of time say 12 Noon to 4.30 pm) and do not object sales persons visit. (Many retailers do not entertain sales person in the evening rush hours). If these things are not available the sales person may be permitted to do lesser number of calls on that particular day.

(d) Ease of coverage: Many a times a sales person may start working from one town/village and travels on a route to cover entire lot of customers (more than the prescribed quota of customers even) because he is required to take that route to reach another important destination, where he can rest, have dinner before proceedings to other towns. In such cases, the sales person visits the customer's irrespective of their wish for visiting time (explaining them this way or else he may not visit them at all). Table 2.3 explains the situation properly. The Pachwad customers whether they like it or not will have to accept the visit of sales person in the evening.

Table. 2.3: Ideal Coverage Pattern

Sr. No.	*From*	*To*	*Distance Kms*	*No. of Customers*	*Approx time to cover the market Hrs*	*ETA*	*ETD*
1	Pune	Starting point				0800	
2	Pune	Shindewadi	15	10	1	0820	0920
3	Shindewadi	Shiwapur	5	3	0.20	0930	0950
4	Shiwapur	Nasarapur	15	20	2	1030	1330
5	Nasarapur	Shirwal	15	20	2	1400	1600
6	Shirwal	Pachwad	30	6	1	1645	1745
7	Pachwad	Satara	30	Night halt		1830	

On the basis of these norms and the total number of customers the total number of working days can be decided for giving at least one visit per customer per month .

3. Frequency of visit to each customer: The frequency of visit may differ from customer to customer. On the following basis:

(a) Size of the business: Visit to every customer is cost to the company as it requires the sales personnel time, energy and traveling cost. If the cost cannot be recovered through the business generated, the visit is futile, e.g., the company spends more money than it earns.

The expenditure is always worked out as average cost of visit and not as individual cost of visit. If the business generated is more the frequency of visit can be planned at higher level and if the business generated is less than frequency can be reduced.

(b) Market Trend:

(i) The retail associations in many towns/cities force the companies to give weekly coverage instead of fortnight/monthly coverage to reduce their own investment and increase profitability.

(ii) A company is forced to give higher coverage to match the coverage of competitor.

(c) Company Policy: A company may decide to give particular frequency of visit as a policy decision.

(i) We will spend only so much on sales expenses.

(ii) We will give higher frequency which we belief will increase the turnover.

(d) Variable Frequency: A company may decide to give higher frequency of visit to not so important customers. In such cases the customer even in one route may have variable frequency of visit leading to large number of customer per route Fig. 2.4 illustrates the same.

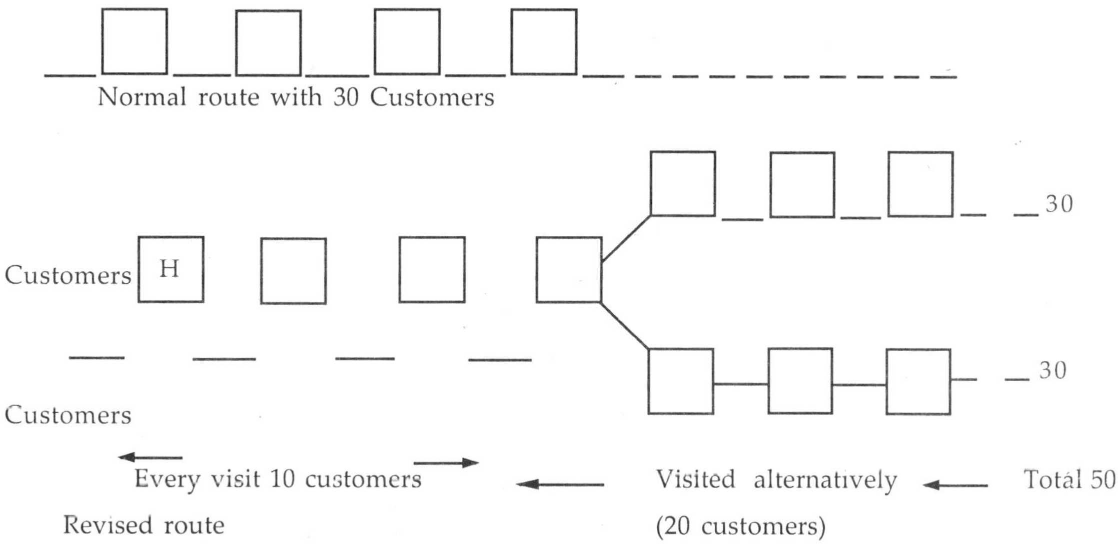

Fig. 2.4: Variable Frequency in One Route

Once we have decided the number of days required and the frequency the work load in PJP system can be prepared by entering it in PJP format. Table 2.4 shows the illustration.

Table 2.4: PJP with work load

Permanent Journey Plan

Name: Mr. Subbarayan HQ : Raipur

Period: Jan 2000 to Dec. 2000

Sr. No.	*Town/ Route*	*Freq.*	*No.Of Days*	*Jan.*	*Feb.*	*Mar.*	*Apr.*	*May.*	*Jun*	*July*	*Aug.*	*Sept.*	*Oct.*	*Nov.*	*Dec.*	*Total*
1	Raipur	Ejc	5													
2	Bhilai	Ejc	9													
3	Rajnan-dgam	Ajc	1													
4	Dalli-Rajhara	Qjc	1													
5	Dhamtari	Ajc	1													
6	Bilaspur	Ejc	4													
7	Chind-wara	Qjc	1													
8	Seoni	Qjc	1													
9	Jagdal-pur	Ejc	4													
10	Total		24													

Dec. 2000

2.8 Planning for Promotions

A sales manager should also plan for the promotions required in his territory. In some organizations the sales manager has a promotional budget at his discretion which is in proportion to the number of customers in the area under coverage and the sales volumes generated in the area. In such cases the sales manager can plan his promotions well in advance as per the area specific requirements and execute them effectively to get the planned results.

In case the sales manager is not having any budget at his disposal he should plan his budget well in advance and send the proposals to the highe sanctioning authority in the form of a proposal. Normally he should send the proposals at least 5-6 months in advance so that they can be executed properly to get the planned results.

He can plan following types of promotions.

1. Awareness creation

A sales manager can increase the awareness of the product by following means:

(a) Distribution of leaflets, brochures to customers.

(b) Giving advertisement in local newspapers.

(c) Wall paintings.

(d) Hoardings at important locations

(e) Giving signage to shopkeepers (Boards)

(f) City bus panels paintings.

(g) Auto-rickshaw/Taxi panels paintings.

(h) Displays at various locations.

(i) Demonstration and sampling activities

(j) Postering and use of POP (point of purchase) materials like stickers, streamers, danglers etc.

(k) Participation in seminar and exhibitions.

2. Push Promotions (Stock loading)

A sales manager can promote sales by giving quantity discounts to various channel members who in turn PUSH/recommend the product to end user to get benefits of the promotion. E.g., a sales manager may tell an electronics showroom owner to buy 200 refrigerators or television sets in a period and give Singapore trip free to him. The showroom will buy and push the 200 refrigerators or televisions to customers to avail the free trip to SINGAPORE.

Push promotions can also be used to increase the retail universe by inducing new retailers to start selling products while higher margins (because of extra discount) are being offered. This leads to use of the selling mantra for higher sale,

More customers
More number of times
More quantity everytime

PULL Promotions

A sales manager can promote sales by creating pull for the product by giving 'free on' promotion e.g.,

(i) Buy 3 get 1 free on soap.

(ii) Buy 1 get 1 free on shirts

(iii) Buy 150 gm get 50 gm free on tooth paste etc.

All these promotions is planned to be self-financing, i.e., the extra profit earned by extra sales covers the expense on promotion are sanctioned easily by the top management.

Planning for expense budget

All the sales staff is required to travel and communicate requiring expense budget. A sales manager should prepare optimum movement plan requiring minimum expenditure to achieve required sales volumes.

Planning for Promotions

Example 1

UTRAN KITE PROMOTION: AHAMADABAD

Background

Every year during UTRAN (Period of Uttarayan – Maker Sankranti) all over the state of Gujarat people fly kites. In Ahmadabad this is more pronounced. People of Ahmadabad are so engrossed in this sport that most of the communal riots in Ahmadabad started with kite flying. This kite flying sport touches their heart dearly. During UTRAN schools are given holidays even many business establishments are closed for four days. All the people are found to be on terraces of their houses with all the members of their family (inclusive of women, children and old family members) taking part in kite flying. They even have their food on the terrace.

Intensity: It is estimated that on an average each family buys at least 3 to 4 dozen kites of different sizes, shapes and varieties. An average family spends about ₹ 400 to 600 on kites and the treads etc.

The Promotion: To give a POLYSTER KITE worth ₹ Ten only FREE along with our product ABCD 500 gms. for a period of 14 days starting 1st of January this year.

The working: Ahmadabad city has 2000 outlets stocking our product ABCD in 500 gms. varieties. The average stock holding is about 4 units per outlet. The sale in first half of the month is about 2000 units every month. The plan is as follows. Our sales representative Mr. Amar Desai along with the able team of our distributor Mr. Sunil and Mr. Deepakbhai will distribute kites and sticker the existing stock of all the retailers (8000 units approx.) from 1st January. Along with the kites distribution they will also supply fresh stock which will be pre-stickered. This operation will take them 10 full working days and will ensure that all the outlets have promotional stocks, before the actual UTRAN period.

Announcement of Promotion

Since, the promotion is restricted to only Ahmadabad city the promotion will be announced by use of POP (Point of Purchase) material.

Objective of Promotion

To increase usership of the product.

To achieve higher sales.

To increase STR (Stock Turnover Ratio) in the market before the coming peak period of the year.

Costing

Cost of 16,000 kites @ ₹ 3/- = ₹. 48,000.

Cost of stickers (inclusive of stickering charges) @ ₹ 0.08/- per sticker of 16,000 stickers: ₹ 1280/-

Cost of promotional POP @ ₹ 4/- per unit x 2000 units = ₹ 8000/-

Cost of transportation = NIL (distribution through normal ready stock operation)

Total Cost of Promotion:

₹ 57,280/- for promotional sale of 16,000 units.

Cost per sale of promotional unit = ₹ 3.58/-

Cost per sale of additional unit (8,000 - 2,000, i.e., normal sale = 6,000 units) is ₹ 9,547/-. The sale is not expected to drop after the promotional period.

Planning of Promotions

Example 2

PARTICIPATION IN CONSUMER EXHIBITION AT PRAGATI MAIDAN

Objective:

1. To create awareness about our new products.
2. To give opportunity to try our new product at discounted rate.

Background

CONSUMER Exhibitions are held every year at Pragati Maidan. It is found that lot of companies display their new and existing products and achieve high sales and awareness during the exhibition period of 8 days.

Almost about 1,00,000 people visit Consumer Exhibition everyday.

Working

The exhibition is open from morning 10 AM to evening 8 PM, i.e., almost 10 hours. So, we need two teams of 2 demonstrators and a helper along with the staff of our distributor Mr. Subhash Agarwal.

A stall will be booked in strategic high traffic location, and will be decorated with the help of existing POP and some special POP like cut-outs; banners etc. All the people manning the stall will be given special T-SHIRTS and CAPS printed with our products name and company logo.

All the visitors to the stall will be explained the features and benefits of our new products and will be allowed to purchase with a discount of ₹ 5/- per pack.

Expected Sales

Considering four peoples to a family of visitors almost 25,000 families would be made aware of our product of this if only 5% are expected to purchase our product (MRP. ₹ 20/-) so we expect to sale about 1250 x 8 days = 10,000 units.

Costing

Rent of stall	:	₹ 15,000/-
Demonstrators	:	₹ 4,800/- (₹ 150/- per day per
person x 32 man days) Helpers	:	₹ 1,600/- (₹ 100/- per day x 16 man days)
Incidental Charges	:	₹ 500/- (tips to watchmen, sweepers etc.
T-SHIRTS and CAPS	:	₹ 3,000/-
Special POP	:	₹ 3,000/-
Discount offered	:	₹ 50,000/-
Total Cost	:	₹ 77,000/-
Cost per person sampled	:	10,000 x 4 users in a family = 40,000/50,000 = ₹ 0.08 paisa
Cost per person made aware of the product	:	27,000/ 1, 00,000 = ₹ 0.27 paisa (₹ 77,000-50,000)

Example 3: Healthy baby contest (Baby product company)

Mr. Amar Chitnis ASM for SKACO Company dealing in baby products like baby oil, baby soap, baby talk etc. wanted to increase awareness about his company products amongst the consumers. Since the parents of small children are concerned about the health of their children he thought of having a healthy baby contest which can work to his benefit.

Working: the working of the promotion was as follows

1. All the consumers purchasing any of the SKACO company products during the period of promotion (45 days) were given entry form for the contest.
2. A panel of Doctors was appointed that was required to check the baby's' health individually at their clinics spread across the city and select top three contenders for the final round from their area.
3. The panel then selected the top three healthy babies in the final round.
4. All the selected healthy babies will be given gift hamper containing SKACO company products that will last them for a period of three months.
5. Top three healthy babies from the final round will be given gift vouchers for the SKACO company products that can be used for one year.
6. Photographs of parents and the healthy babies would be published in the daily and a popular weekly.

Cost: the cost of the promotion was as follows

- Cost of printing 10,000 entry forms @ 40P per form= ₹ 4,000/-
- Cost of distribution of entry forms ---NIL (retailers did the same willingly)
- Cost of POP for announcing the scheme 1000 posters @ ₹ 10/- 10,000/-
- Cost of advertising the scheme in local news papers fours advertisements@ ₹ 1,000 = ₹ 4,000/-
- Fee for doctors ---- NIL (they were getting free publicity and probable patients)
- Hall booking for the area wise contest six areas @ ₹ 500/- per area = ₹ 3,000/-
- Hall booking for the final round ₹ 2,000/-
- Chief Guest cost--- ₹ 2,000/-
- Cost of gift hampers ₹ 500 x 3 x 6 = ₹ 9,000/-
- Cost of prizes 500 x 3 x 3 = ₹ 4,500/-
- Cost of publicity in the daily and weekly through the reporter ₹ 3,000/-
- Photographs, tea coffee snacks at the final round ₹ 3,000/-
- Miscellaneous ₹ 500/-
- Total ₹ 45,000/-
- Average sale ₹ 10, 00,000 /-PM
- Expected sale ₹ 15, 00,000/-PM
- Increase in product awareness 100%

Success of the scheme: if all the six centers get at least 100 entries total 600 entries the scheme should be treated as success as the similar scheme by the brand leader had 1200 entries one year ago.

2.9 Planning for Major Customers

Advent of organized retail chains has made the sales manager to do separate planning for the organized retailers as they buy goods in bulk and give major business to the sales manager. These customers if not treated specially with difference may divert their business to your competition reducing your overall market share.

(a) Major customers in retail: Treating major customers differently started when Sahakari Bhandars were established in 1976, in Delhi and Mumbai. Sahakari Bhandars were treated on par with the distributors and were supplied the products at distributors invoicing price directly from the manufacturers instead of being supplied through distributors at retailer's invoice price. This way the distributor's margin was passed on to the Sahakari Bhandars as additional margin and bulk discount. Today most of the manufacturers negotiate the pricing and supply terms for various organized chain retailers separately. The decision has to be taken based on the size of retail shops and the number of retail outlets the chain has in a particular town. Every self service counter should not be treated as a major customer unless they prove to be stock pullers and volume generators. (see Box 2.3)

Box 2.3 Major Customer Dealing

1. Khetan and Deewan started their first super stores (KD's super store) in Char Bunglow area Andheri Mumbai west in 1982. These promoters were displaced from east Africa and had come to India with the ideas from east Africa. Mr. Deewan who was operating the store wrote to all the FMCG company corporate office about the starting of this stores and requested them to give them special treatment and special pricing. The senior management at the corporate offices forwarded these letters to their regional offices in Mumbai and asked them to do the needful. Some of the sales managers immediately started treating KD's specially and offered them special discounts. Mr. Suresh Abhyankar who was then area sales manager for Mumbai for Smithkline Beecham (then HMM ltd.) refused to treat KD as special retail outlet unless they prove themselves different and start buying stocks in bulk. Mr. Deewan was furious and informed the matter directly to the sales Director Mr. Amit Sarker in Delhi. Mr. Amit Sarker replied to him saying such matters are decided by the regional office on case to case basis and company does not have any special policy for super stores.

Mr. Suresh Abhyankar was not willing to give special treatment to them as he was not giving any special rates even to Apana Bazzars in Mumbai who used to purchase in bulk at 13 branches throughout Mumbai. If he gives special treatment to KD he will be required to give special treatment even to Apana Bazzars reducing his profitability.

(b) Major customers in industrial products: when we say major customers in industrial products we talk about the distributors of the industrial products and not the end customers as the end customers always negotiate the prices based on competitive bidding.

A sales manager should plan the quantity discounts for major customers (distributors) in advance and should relate them to targeted achievements. It should not become an item in the price list for them and they should not take quantity discounts for granted. The targeted achievements can be of various types, e.g.,

1. Growth over previous year's achievements in sales volumes
2. Growth over previous year's achievements in number of customers
3. Growth over previous year's achievement in area under coverage etc.

2.10 Setting Goals

A sales manager should set goals for himself and his staff. The goals are not always related to company target achievements. There are many other aspects which need to be looked after for individual's growth prospects and getting job satisfaction. Following goals can be set by the sales manager and his subordinates.

2.10.1 Achievement of sales "x" per cent more than the given target by the company

Achieving targets as per company requirement is done by many managers but if you are trying and achieving higher sales than given targets you stand out amongst the crowd.

2.10.2 Training subordinates to become capable of getting promoted

A sales manager must plan to develop subordinates who can take his position. Many times a sales manager may not get promoted just because there is no one who can replace him and ensure the sales volumes. If your subordinates develop they may get promoted in the same organization or they may get higher position in other organization. In both the cases you are benefited as your subordinates will always remain highly motivated and work for you better and help you achieve your targets easily.

2.10.3 Increasing width of coverage in the area of operation

Width of coverage is the number of customers being serviced by the sales team. It is not possible to achieve 100% coverage for any sales team as

(a) It may not be economically viable to reach to each and every customer (the cost will be higher than the earnings achieved by covering all customers)

A sales manager can run a campaign to find out such customers who are not under coverage and try to bring them under coverage either by company representatives or by distributor's sales staff which has lesser cost of coverage due to lower salary and wages.

(b) One may not know the existence of some of the customers as they are buying products of competition only or are buying their requirement from wholesale markets.

2.10.4 Increasing the depth of coverage in the area of operation

While the width shows the number of customers the depth talks in term of the average stock holding by the existing customers. Increasing the depth means make the existing customers hold higher stock per customer increasing the STR (stock turnover ratio). This reduces the chances of any retailers going out of stock due to temporary stock shortages at distributor level. STR is always denoted in number of days and a marketer would like to have the STR levels ideally above 20 days, i.e., even if you do not supply stock to retailers for 20 days consumers will keep getting the product in the market.

2.10.5 Improve the coverage by the distributor

Ideally the distributors should give good coverage making the company sales staffs free to plan various promotions and give focus on increasing the width and depth of distribution. The company staff can spend time on training the distributor's sales force in call procedures and improving their efficiency in getting higher and higher sales. Company staff can also keep watch on competitive activity and plan for countering their promotional efforts.

2.10.6 Motivating distributors and their staff

A sales manager can plan for keeping the distributor's and their staff's motivation level high so that they work to their fullest capacity and keep achieving better sales returns. This can be done by training the distributor's staff in selling skills. (See box 2.4)

Box 2.4 Distributor Sales Representative Training

This author developed sales training program to train the distributor's sales staff first in Marathi (the regional language of Maharashtra) and then in Hindi. The program was successfully run for sales staff of Mumbai distributors at a conference hall of Bandra Hill Road hotel for two consecutive days. The staff had no previous experience of spending time in a three star hotel's A/c conference hall and having sumptuous buffet lunch. The training program improved their selling skills and the experience had great motivational effect on their working. This helped the Mumbai team to great achievements. The author was asked to run the program for benefit of the distributor's sales teams at Ahmadabad, Vadodara, Surat, Rajkot, and Pune by the then Regional Sales Manager Ranjan ray Choudhury. The program in its Hindi version was sent to other regions also.

2.10.7 Motivating subordinates

Sales manager can decide to increase motivation level of his subordinates by planning good motivational activities. A sales manager can plan various activities of motivating sales staff without requiring budgetary support from the organization (see box)

2.10.8 Motivating sales staff and team building

Motivation is the noun from the verb motivate. The verb motivate comes from the noun motive which means reasons for action, what induces person to act. Motivating sales person is providing reason for action (better, good) to sales personnel. Why should anyone be required to motivate sales person when the salary (or keeping job secure) itself is a good reason in itself? That is the question that comes to mind. The answer is salary and fear of losing the job makes a person works to acceptable (average output) level only. If you expect to

1. increase the output
2. increase/push the average level upward
3. find out the potential of the staff
4. find out potential of the market

You should motivate the sales staff but more important than motivation is to avoid demotivation. In most companies I have noticed that the cause of low results or below average performances is the demotivation factors. What are these demotivation factors that a Sales Manager should avoid?

Demotivation Factors for Sales Staff:

1. Treatment not proper by office staff and seniors (No due importance given).
2. Salary not paid on time.
3. Expenses not reimbursed on time.
4. Action not taken on reports sent to office.
5. Claims of customers not settled on time which leads to loss of prestige in front of customers.
6. Orders not supplied in time.
7. Checks banked before due time (reduction of credit to customers).

8. Supply of stocks not according to order placed.
9. Quality complaints of products not settled properly.
10. Transit delays and damages are not looked at and acted upon by company office staff.

If only the Sales Manager avoids these demotivators the performance of the staff will improve by at least 30-35 %. If there are no demotivators and the staff is working normally, motivation is required for the reasons discussed above.

It is very important for the sales manager to motivate his subordinates and build a strong team. Team building happens when the staff spends quality time together in activities other than the company work. Staff picnics if possible with the family members always help in building the team.

Always remember that all the subordinates cannot keep achieving high sales returns all the time and if the sales manager wants to keep achieving at highest levels all the time the shortfalls of one staff member should be covered by another staff member without creating any problem. To achieve this, building team spirit is immensely important, as it can be done as team target easily by the strong team.

Box 2.5 Motivating Sales Staff

1. This author as a sales manager of rest of Maharashtra, used to have quarterly JCMs at various locations. He had a sales staff of four sales officers covering rest of Maharashtra. Two of his sales officers were headquartered at Pune and third was at Thane and the fourth was at Nagpur.

At the beginning of the quarter he is to declare the next quarter end JCM to be held at " X" location only if the quarter targets are achieved. The arrangements at the location were the responsibility of the sales officer in-charge. The JCM will be planned with two days rest leave attached to it after the JCM. This way he had JCM cum picnic at Nashik, Matheran, Kolhapur and Aurangabad etc., instead of Pune which was normal location with two sales officers on HQ allowance and two on up-country allowance. The cost overrun was negligible and the regional managers never objected as targets were always achieved by the team. This had a big impact on the team's motivational level and had great achievements as, team.

2. This author had a practice of having the July end JCM for Mumbai team away from Mumbai and that too as a family picnic cum JCM. July used to be the peak sales month of the year after the lows of April-May-June. If the team achieves July peak then the achievements for rest of the year used to be very easy. The family picnics were held at Alibaug, Matheran, Lonavala, etc.

This had great motivational and team building effect. The Mumbai team achieved "best team" awards consecutively during the period and the entire team was promoted to senior sales officer level initially and then half the team was further promoted to Sales Development Officer (SDO) level subsequently. Team members achieved best sales officer awards at national sales conferences.

Sales officers/salesmen can also be motivated through different types of sales contests some examples are given below:

Conducting Sales Contests

Sales Contests are organized by various companies at various times. The principle of ACMEE which is used by all managers in planning all the activities (Sales, distribution, sales training etc.) is applicable here also. The meaning of ACMEE is as follows:

A-AIM: Aim is the objective of the activity. In this case the objectives are as follows:

Objectives of Sales Contest

1. To obtain new customers.
2. To increase the size of order.
3. To sell entire range of products.
4. To push slow moving products.
5. To sell profitable sale mix.
6. To improve performance of distributors and their staff.
7. To promote seasonal products
8. To improve visibility of products by better displays.
9. To launch new product with high productivity.
10. To increase width and depth of distribution.

C-Contests: This explains the details of activity and its format, the prizes to be won etc.

Contest Format: An innovative Sales Manager will devise different types of formats for sales contest to awaken interest of participants and hold them on and keep them motivated towards achieving the results.

Contest Awards (Prizes): As a rule all participants should have chance to win at least one award or else they will not get motivated towards participating in the contest. Normally the prizes are as follows:

1. One bumper first prize
2. Two second prizes
3. Four third prizes
4. Consolation prize to all participants achieving minimum level.

M-Method: The method explains details of contest.

E-Execution: Execution is crucial thing where monitoring the activity is done. It Is ensured that contest elements are available in plenty and there is no scope for any contestants to lose due to administrative problem.

E-Evaluation: Each contest should be evaluated for its results and usefulness. Useful contests can be repeated at a later date.

Product XYZ Launch Contest

Objectives: To achieve high degree of productive call average and high achievement of individual sales targets.

Place: Mumbai

Period: 20th Jan. '99 to 20th Feb. '99

Number of Salesmen: Ten, all the salesmen in Mumbai team.

Eligibility: For winning consolation prize a salesman should achieve at least 60% productivity of targeted calls (not calls made) and achieve at least 80% of targeted sales.

Method: For every per cent of sales above 80%, salesman gets one point to his credit up to 100% achievement level afterwards he gets two points for every additional % e.g., for achievement of 90%, he gets 10 point.

For achievement of 95% he gets 15 points.

For achievement of 100% he gets 20 points.

Foe achievement of 105% he gets 20+10=30 points.

(a) For every % of productivity achieved above 60% he gets half point till 100% achievement, afterwards he gets one point for every additional% achieved (obviously new calls).

(b) So a salesman with 70% productivity and 90% sales acheivement has

$$\left(10 \times \frac{1}{2} = 5\right) + (10 \times 1 = 10)\ 15 \text{ points.}$$

Prizes

First Prize : One = Philips Audio Recorder-cum-Radio

Second Prize : Two Philips Walkmans

Consolation Prize : All eligible salesmen will get Philips pocket radio

Cost

Prizes ₹ 7,000 /-

Function ₹ 3,000/-

Total ₹ 10,000/- ₹ ten thousands only.

Mumbai Salesman's Contest

Objective

(i) To achieve distribution objective of at least 80% outlets stocking product XYZ.

(ii) To achieve sales objective of 25% sales growth over the current average during the contest period.

Scheme

During the contest period the product XYZ will be offered to consumer with an offer of "₹ 2/- OFF" on each pack on sale.

Background

The product XYZ is unique product well supported by the company. But, is not achieving its sales objectives because of lesser support by the sales team. The sales team concentrates more on the company's major brand which contributes to 85% of company sales and profits. The brand manager of product XYZ thinks that product XYZ has potential to become big brand given the right support which can be obtained once the product starts achieving reasonable level of sales. The sales are not coming as the product is not widely distributed, not even in the company's normal outlets.

Working

(i) Opening stocks at all the distribution points will be checked at the beginning of the scheme period.

(ii) Entire opening stocks at the distributor's points will be stickered with promotional offer.

(iii) Targets will be decided strictly on the basis of previous three months sales average.

(iv) Sales achievement will be found from the actual closing stock verified at the end of scheme period.

Eligibility

All those salesmen who achieve the minimum standard of 80% distribution and 25% growth are eligible for consolation prize. The first and second prizes would be decided on the basis of sales growth achieved (Assuming that the growth is not possible without distribution extension)

Prizes

First Prize : One Godrej 165 litre Refrigerator

Second Prize : Two sumeet Mixer/Blender

Period

1st August to 31st October

Area	A	B	C	D	E	F	G	H	I	J	K	TOTAL
Average	65	76	59	84	74	72	76	45	130	9	665	842
Target	81	95	74	105	93	90	95	56	163	120	81	1053

2.11 Planning for Self Career Growth

A sales manager should always keep track of the career growth opportunities available to himself. If need be, he should keep improving his knowledge base by doing some correspondence courses and also seek opportunities to give his knowledge by doing guest lectures at various management institutes many of which do not have any faculty with hands down sales experience. While preparing to give a guest lecture on any one of the topic the sales managers gets opportunity to clarify his own thoughts and while answering questions raised by students çomes to know the areas in which he lacks knowledge.

2.12 Planning for Improved Distribution Network

The sales manager must keep planning for new distributors in the network either by bifurcating/rearranging territories, or finding new distributors willing to cover areas currently not under coverage. While doing this care should be taken that the current distributor is not unnecessarily being disturbed reducing his interest in your business. As long as possible the current distributor should be encouraged to increase his infrastructure and also being asked to start a branch office in far-flung areas which are not getting proper coverage by the existing infrastructure. (See box) are as following:

Box 2.6 Distributors Area – Bifurcation for Better Coverage

1. M/s Vithaldas Sakalchand & co. was covering Pune Pimpri and Chinchwad area efficiently for Hindustan Milkfoods which was having only two SKUs (stock keeping units) of product Horlicks, viz., plain Horlicks and Elaichi Horlicks in 450gms packs. When Boost was launched in 1976, the product had larger consumer base and it was found by this author who was area sales manager, rest of Maharashtra that due to improper coverage sales were not growing at required rate. The area sales manager Mr. Suresh Abhyankar had discussions with the owners of M/s Vithaldas Sakalchand but they were unable to increase the infrastructure. So Mr. Suresh Abhyankar trifurcated the Pune distribution area as ,

   (i) Pune old city plus cantonment

   (ii) Rest of Pune city

   (iii) Pimpri/Chinchwad with Pradhikaran

   The sales grew three times with Vithaldas Sakalchand not losing their sales volumes
2. M/s Khushal Biscuit Mart was handling area from Ambernath to Dombivli in Maharshtra including the towns (now cities) of Kalyan and Ulhasnagar. After cutting this area by Mr. Suresh Abhyankar with three additional separate distributors for Dombivli, Kalyan and Ulhasnagar the sales went up fourfold in the span of three months.
3. M/s Bombay Sales Agency at Santacruz was handling area from Bandra to Borivili in Mumbai city. After taking charge of Mumbai city as area sales manager, Mr. Suresh Abhyankar bifurcated this area in two part (i) Bandra to Andheri, (ii) Jogeshwari to Borivli the sales went up threefold.

If the sales manager spends enough time on the planning activity, executing the plan is not a very difficult task.

Case Study - 2.1

Sales Manager Dhurandhar goofs up

Mr. Dhurandhar the sales manager in SKACO company was earlier working in a popular company manufacturing toffees as a sales supervisor, when Mr. Ambekar who was also working in the same toffee manufacturing company joined SKACO as director, brought Dhurandhar along with him to SKACO and made him sales manager.

At the sales review meeting Dhurandhar said that the sales officers were not working to their full capacity and should be motivated by offering them some incentives. Mr. Ambekar accepted the suggestions and asked Dhurandhar to make incentive plan. Mr. Ambekar was Works manager in earlier company and he had no knowledge of how the incentive plans were made, so relying totally on Dhurandhar's knowledge he okayed incentive plan that was made by Dhurandhar as follows

Sales Officer's incentive plan August-October, 1992

Objective: Sales officer will be given targets which are 15% more than average sales for the planned quarter. Each sales officer gets ₹ 5000/- for achievement of basic target and then ₹ 2000/ for every additional per cent till he achieves 5% more on target and then he starts getting ₹ 5000/ - every additional percentage above target, e.g.,

If the target is 100% on achievement of 100% sales, the officer gets ₹ 5,000

If the sales officer achieves 105%, he gets 5 × 2,000=10,000 + 5,000 = ₹ 15,000

If the sales officer achieves 106% he gets 1 × 5,000 + 15,000 = ₹ 20,000/-

Total sales currently for the plan period is 9,000 cartons and target is 9900, but because of the incentives the expected sales are 12,000 cartons.

Expected expenses: if all the eight sales officers achieve their target at 105% the maximum expense will be ₹ 1,00,000/-

At the end of plan period the sales were found to be only 9500 cartons but the money spent was more than ₹ 2,00,000/-

What went wrong? To understand one must look at the sales and the targets set for each sales officer

	Dubey	*Gupta*	*Mishra*	*Panchal*	*Uke*	*Salvi*	*Desai*	*Mhatre*	*Total*
Average August-Oct.1991	210	180	210	4000	3000	180	600	620	9000
Target Aug-Oct. 1992	1250	1250	1250	1250	1250	1250	1250	1250	9900

After looking at the targets all the sales officers were demoralized and decided not to put any efforts in fact they collaborated with Panchal and Uke that the sales achieved by them should be added to the tally of Panchal and Uke and both Panchal and Uke should give some consideration for getting additional benefit. So both Panchal and Uke who covered the wholesale markets and so high sales volumes; were getting following benefit for achieving their normal sales

Panchal – Target 1250 achievement 4000= 325% incentive 5000+ 10000 +1,60,000= 1,75,000/-

Uke – Target 1250 achievement 3000 = 245% incentive 5000 + 10,000 + 70,000= 85,000/-

Targets were achieved only by Panchal and Uke and all others reported less than normal sales.

Dhurandhar should have planned targets on individual basis and his shortcut of preparing targets (target/8= individual target) lead to the fiasco.

Case Study 2.2 Sales Staff Planning in JTI

JTI India Pvt. Ltd. a wholly owned subsidiary of Japan Tobacco International, world's third largest cigarette manufacturer manufacturing world's first cigarette brand CAMEL and many other fast moving brands like MORE decided to start their operations in India. The market combing operations (find out the size of retail universe and its process –number of retailers and wholesalers), channel member appointment, deciding the size of sales force, their selection, recruitment and training and supervision of actual launch of their brand "MORE" was assigned to M/s Abhyankar and Associates as marketing consultants. Mr. Suresh Abhyankar, the Director after doing initial market research found following details:

Current market condition Pune

There were three major players in the cigarette market

1. Indian Tobacco Company (ITC – a division of British American Tobacco Company world's second largest cigarette manufacturer)
2. Godfrey Philips (division of Philip Morrison world's number one cigarette manufacturer)
3. Vazir Sultan Tobacco company (makers of Charminar brand cigarettes from Hyderabad)

    - The size of retail universe was over 47,000 outlets spread over Pune city with 115 wholesalers.
    - ITC operated through single distributor with three branch offices.
    - Godfrey Philips operated through single distributor and two branch offices.
    - Vazir Sultan sold their products through WIMCO distributor.
    - ITC had one sales officer and 125 cycle salesmen
    - Godfrey Philips had one sales officer six supervisors and 85 cycle salesmen
    - Vazir Sultan had no dedicated sales staff as they were going through bad patch.

Distributor margin and sales staff salary:

- ITC gave 1.5% margin to their distributor and supplies were against advance demand draft.

- The ITC distributor gave 0.8% margin on commission only basis to cycle salesmen and they must clear the accounts on daily basis.
- ITC gave 0.8% margin to wholesalers who supplied to all the dealers that were not covered/supplied by cycle salesmen.
- Godfrey Philips paid 2.5% margin to their distributor and supplies were against advance demand draft.

  Godfrey Philips paid 1% margin to the wholesaler
- Godfrey Philips paid ₹ 6000/- to supervisors and ₹ 3,500/- to cycle salesmen with target incentives over and above the salary.
- All salesmen of ITC, Godfrey Philips worked only one route on daily coverage basis

Distribution Policy Guidelines by the JTI

JTI wanted to have coverage on the ITC pattern and wanted to sell directly to the retailers avoiding wholesalers.

Mr. Suresh Abhyankar's suggestions to JTI

Mr. Suresh Abhyankar suggested following set up to JTI

- Appointment of three distributors to cover entire PUNE city
- Appointment of three supervisors and 40 two wheeler riding salesmen
- Supervisor's salary to be ₹10,000 (inclusive of daily allowance) to be paid by the distributor
- Salesmen's salary of ₹6000/- (inclusive of daily allowance) to be paid by the distributor
- Two wheelers (M80) to be purchased by distributor and the installments to be deducted from salesmen's salary every month
- Salesmen will cover all the retailers on weekly basis with special coverage on daily basis to "Super A class" retailers (Advertising ban on tobacco product was started, making it difficult to promote and create awareness)
- Distributor to be given 6% margin with ROI guarantee of 24% to be calculated on monthly basis.

All the suggestions of Mr. Abhyankar were accepted and implemented by the company.

What must be the reasons behind change in coverage pattern and reduction in sales staff when normal practice is follow the leader in deciding sales force size?

Case Study 2.3 Sales Staff Planning PICKWICK

Primlaks Waffles Pvt. Ltd. manufacturers of PICKWICK brand wafer biscuits was a loss making company when Mr. Suresh Abhyankar joined them as head of marketing; the factory worked for one shift ten a days a month and still the market had problems of old stocks which needed to be replaced. The company marketed their products through their own subsidiary Target Marketing Pvt. Ltd. (TMPL) in Maharashtra and Gujarat and rest of India they had super distributors at Kolkata, Delhi, Chennai and Jaipur.

Target Marketing had one sales manager, three sales executives and 20 sales representatives, after joining Mr. Abhyankar had a meeting with the sales manager and he discussed the plans for increase in sales volumes and reduction of cost of sale per box sold. The sales manager had no plans; he said he is trying to push the sales representatives but had no concrete plans. Mr. Abhyankar called meeting of entire sales staff in Mumbai and told them that the expenses on sales staff was upward of 10% and he wanted to reduce it to 2%, the only way to do so was by increasing sales volumes or reducing the sales staff; he is willing to give three months to have the change and he will take the action. Mr. Abhyankar had similar meetings in Pune and Ahmadabad for respective sales staff also.

At the end of second month, the sales manager resigned and went to some other company and Mr. Abhyankar conducted a two day sales training program for entire field force. At the end of three months the cost of sales dropped to 5% and then to 3%. As the direct sales through the super distributors also increased through 15 super distributors (11 more super distributors on advance demand draft basis were appointed) the company started working two shifts and all thirty days a month to become profitable.

If the cost of sale is high the profitability drops may lead to losses.

2.13 Exercise

1. Visit various shops and find out different types of pack promotions being offered by various companies. Discuss with the shopkeeper to find out the effect of these promotions. Have these promotions helped increase the sales? If yes which other product's sales were affected because of this? If no, what is the reason according to the shopkeeper for it?
2. Contact any company sales officer/area sales manager and ask him/her how they project/forecast their sales.
3. Contact any sales officer and find out how he covers distributors in his/her territory? Is he/she having any PJP for him/her? If no is he/she missing out on smaller distributors often?
4. Contact any medical sales officer find out how he/she plans the coverage of the medical practitioners/specialists in his/her area of operation. Do they have daily contact point to start their route?

2.14 Questions for Practise

1. In a market with 2000 retailers selling a particular product the salesman is required to visit 30 retailers per day. If the salesman works 25 days a month, how many salesmen are required to be appointed to cover the market on a monthly frequency basis?
2. Nanded has 240 outlets, if the company norm is to cover 40 outlets per day.If the company sales officer should plan to work is how many days in Nanded needed to cover all the retail outlets?
3. A company has a turnover of ₹ 2,00,00,000/- per month and plans to spend 1% of its turnover on sales staff. If the cost of sales officer is ₹ 20,000/- per month how many sales officers can the company appoint.

4. In Bengaluru market a company has 4500 outlets, out of them 400 are "A" class, 1000 are "B" class and remaining are "C" class. Company norm is 30 calls per day and a sales officer works 24 working days a month. If "A" class outlets need weekly visit, "B" class outlets need fortnightly visit and "C" class outlets need monthly visit how many sales officers are required to be appointed.

5. In Pune market a sales officer of an electronic goods company visit eight retailers per day. If there are 232 retailers in Pune out of which 20 are "A" class, 50 are "B" class and remaining "C" class. If "A" class outlets are visited every day, "B" class outlets are visited twice a week and "C" class outlets are visited every week and a sales officer works 24 days a month how many sales officers need to appointed to ensure proper coverage.

6. In Nagpur market there are 1160 medical practitioners out of which 200 are specialists and 960 are general practitioners (GPs), if a medical sales officer visits 12 GPs and two specialists every day, how many medical sales officers are needed to be appointed at Nagpur.

7. Mr. Pandit the area sales manager wants to plan territories for Karnataka with following information

S. No.	*Name of town/city*	*Frequency*	*No. of days per month*
1	Bengaluru	EJC	541
2	Chick Ballapur	QJC	1
3	KGF	AJC	2
4	Mysore	EJC	12
5	Mandya	AJC	2
6	KR Puram	QJC	1
7	Kollegal	QJC	1
8	Mangalore	EJC	10
9	Udupi	EJC	3
10	Manipal	AJC	2
11	Suratkal	QJC	2
12	Karwar	AJC	2
13	Ankola	QJC	1
14	Harihar	QJC	1

15	Haveri	AJC	11
16	Belgaon	EJC	6
17	Bijapur	AJC	2
18	Gadag	QJC	2
19	Raichur	EJC	4
20	Hubali	EJC	10
21	Dharwad	EJC	4
22	Gulburga	EJC	4
23	Tumkur	AJC	3
24	Tiptur	QJC	1
25	Hassan	AJC	2
26	Chitradurga	AJC	2
27	Davangere	AJC	2
28	Arcecare	QJC	1

If a sales officer works 24 days in a month how many sales officers should he appoint and where should they be headquartered? Give reasons for your answers.

8. Mr. Salgaonkar wants to forecast sales for 2012-13 and prepare targets for territories under him with following information

Territory	*A*	*B*	*C*	*D*	*E*	*F*	*Total*	*Target*
Expected sales 2011-12	500	400	550	600	900	250	3200	3000
Actual sales 2010-11	400	370	500	450	750	260	2660	2500
Actual sales 2009-10	340	320	420	400	600	260	2340	2200
Average previous three years	300	300	380	380	500	280	2140	

The area needs to grow at the rate 20% over 2011-12 but since territory F which is dropping due to commercialization of the area and consumers moving out, need to sustain at current level (no increase in sales) and area E which is growing faster due to new townships coming in should grow at 30%. Help Mr. Salgaonkar preparing the targets.

9. Explain the duties and objectives of sales manager.
10. Write short notes on (a) Backtracking, (b) ROI, (c) Precautions while doing territory planning, (d) Frequency of visit to customers.
11. Explain various methods of planning the strength of sales staff.

CHAPTER 3 SALES MANAGEMENT – ORGANIZING EFFORTS

Learning Objectives:

- In this chapter we will cover selection process of sales staff, training process of sales staff – induction training, on job training, skills improvement training for FMCG, skills improvement training for industrial sales person,
- Selection process of channel members—selection and appointment of distributor, selection and appointment of CFAs, selection and appointment of super distributors and selection process of transport operators.
- Sales manager should look in to organizing activity also very seriously. A sales manager is required to organize in two major areas
  1. Sales staff
  2. Distribution channel

3.1 Organizing Sales Staff

In the previous chapter, we have already seen the planning process of the number of sales personnel one should be appointing; now we will understand the process of recruitment of sales staff.

Recruitment process: Following steps are required to be done in recruitment process:

1. Preparing job description
2. Decision on the number of people to be recruited
3. Searching for good candidates
4. Selection process
5. Training of sales staff
6. Confirmation in the position

Let us look at this process one by one

3.1.1 Preparing job description

Job description of the sales person will change from company to company depending on the company focus and priorities, but it will include amongst other things,

- Name of the position
- Location
- Salary structure
- Allowances and other benefits
- Reporting to whom
- qualifications
- Experience
- Brief job requirements
- Age and sex specifications if any
- Physical requirements

3.1.2 Decision of number of people to be recruited

We have already discussed this aspect in earlier chapter number two

3.1.3 Search for candidates

Search of candidates can be done from internal or external source.

3.1.3.1. From Internal Source

Recruitment through internal source is very popular method.

Following Internal Sources are used:

- **From Other Departments:** Because of the job scarcity, people accept any job initially. After sometime they find that their liking is different and so look around for job which they like. A company may have such people in some other departments. Giving opportunity to shift to the department of their liking increases MORAL AND MOTIVATION LEVEL of the employee and is beneficial to the company. So the jobs are advertised internally to get responses for such employees.
- **Relatives of the Current Employees:** Relatives of current employees are interested in joining the company, if found SUITABLE can be employed. This increases the GOODWILL of the company and the MORAL AND MOTIVATION LEVEL of the employee whose relative is employed. Care should be taken that relatives of same employee are not given jobs over and over again.
- **Recommendation of Distribution Channel Members:** Distribution channel members (Distributors, transporters, C&F agents) etc., may recommend candidates, if found SUITABLE they should be recruited.
- **Upgradation of ISRs:** Distributors/Interim Sales Representatives if qualified and SUITABLE (working hard and enthusiastically) can be upgraded to join the company sales force. This motivates other such people to work better.

3.1.3.2 From External source

If candidates are not available internally then the organization is required to recruit people from external sources which are as follows

(a) **From Competitor's Organization:** Many a times a product is best sold due to personal relations and skills than the product superiority and distinction. In such cases sales personnel from competitor's organization with good selling skills, personnel contacts are selected for employment and offered job. This is best suited in pharmaceutical, industrial and institutional sales.

(b) **From Educational Institutes:** Many companies prefer to recruit people directly from educational institutes by CAMPUS INTERVIEW process. The idea is to find Bright, Enthusiastic, Unbiased, and raw talent which can be molded into company requirement while they have impressionable minds.

(c) **Through Employment Agencies (head Hunters):** There are many good employment agencies which provide recruitment help. Choice for using employment agency is done for following reasons:

- When number of people to be recruited is less and does not justify expenditure on advertisements, (Advertisements are very expensive) use of employment agency works out cost effective.
- When the job in question is not **likable** (Hardships and low wages are involved). There is high rote of attrition in employees, going through employment agencies who guarantee that the person will work for at least 6 months or provide a replacement candidate free of charge (up to two replacements) which works out to be cost effective for the company.
- When a company is thinking of replacing an existing employee they want to be secretive about it till such time that they select replacement. Employment agencies can be used in such situation to avoid advertising the job and making your intention public knowledge.

(d) **Through Advertisements**: Advertisement is a very good method of recruitment. A company can call upon eligible candidates to apply and get selected for the post. To cut short the process nowadays more and more people are using **WALK-IN** types of recruitment advertisements. By giving WALK-IN advertisements following objectives are achieved.

I. Process time in receiving the applications, calling of them for interview etc. is eliminated.

II. Can be arranged at short notice depending on availability of interview panel.

III. Walk-in gives flexibility to candidates appearing for interview as they can come according to their free time available during the day and increasing possibility of getting better candidates due to higher footfall.

IV. Removes uncertainty of called candidate's appearance for interview. Whoever comes is interviewed.

WALK-IN thought very popular has lot of disadvantages like-

- If the name of the company is not popular (known), no one comes for walk-in, leading to wastage of time, energy of interview panel and money for company.
- Walk-in arranged on a holiday is not found effective.
- Candidates may not get time for making them free to attend the interview.
- Walk-ins are required to be arranged at different locations to get local candidates for local vacancies. This increases cost.
- Unsuitable candidates also appear for interview, wasting the time.

Advertisement can give lot of scope for a company to attract better candidates by innovative advertisements. Many a times, a person not interested in change in a job may also get tempted to apply due to good quality advertisement. Following precautions are required to be taken while releasing the advertisement.

Choice of Newspaper/Periodical: All the newspapers and periodicals are not read by all types of people. So the company should choose à newspaper or periodical depending on:

(i) Its reach to required geographical area.

(ii) Its reach to required segment of people to which the candidate belongs.

(iii) The circulation of the newspaper or periodicals which will give high OTS (Opportunity to see) to the candidate. Circulation figures are available through research agencies like ABC (Audit Bureau of Circulation) etc.

Choice of issue of newspaper/periodical: The circulation figures keep fluctuating during the week for newspaper and during the month for a periodical. Newspapers have very high (peak) circulation a day of weekly holiday, and the chances of candidates noticing your advertisement is high. So your advertisement should be released on such day .The advertisement rates are comparatively higher on such dates but it is worth spending for it.

Choice of page in newspaper: All advertisements for employment are clubbed together and printed. If you have a choice, choose the right hand page for it.

Use of innovation: The advertisement layout and copy is very important. Your advertisement can stand out (even if it is very small) if it is done innovatively. Use of good copywriter and layout maker may require little extra money but will give good results.

Job portals on internet: Nowadays use of job portals is becoming very popular, but one must choose a proper job portal or else the advertisement in a wrong job portal will not get required response. It is better to advertise the job on a portal rather than downloading the CVs from the job portals as many of the CVs on job portals are not updated and the candidates seeking employment do not remove their CV after getting a job and do not respond to your call.

3.1.4 Selecting sales personnel

Selection procedure will involve the following steps:

(a) Shortlisting

(b) Interview

(c) Verification of information

(d) Finalization of wage structure

(e) Appointment order

Shortlisting: All candidates are many times asked to give information on standardized format, which makes it easy to check the suitability of the candidates on the basis of the job description you have prepared. Only the candidates who are suitable are called for interview. In walk-in type of recruitment this step is eliminated.

Interview: Actual interview can take place in various stages. Generally, it is done in 2-3 stages. If the number of candidates appearing for the job is more, the numbers of stages can increase and if the numbers of candidates are less, only a single stage interview is used.

Following stages may be used:

I. Written test

II. Group discussion

III. Initial interview for shortlisting

IV. Final interview for selection.

Criteria for selection in each stage: Following types of criteria are used for selection in each stage:

1. **Written test:** Questions involving job/aptitude/communication skill/analyzing skills and comprehension are used with different weightages. Candidates securing a minimum level (set above 60 out of 100) are allowed to pass.
2. **Group discussion:** Skills of communication (listening, understanding, speaking), and manner in which the candidate is trying to put forward his viewpoints, originally of views (thinking power) are judged. This is SUBJECTIVE in nature and can be biased if the observer is not skillful and good.
3. **Personal Interview:** Selection of candidates in personal interview depends upon the panel. Many companies use a standardized format and the panel members are asked to give weightages for different selection criteria.

Use of Psychological Tests: In place of group discussions or personal interview use of psychological tests is becoming popular. Psychological tests can be administered in written form or through computer program. Psychological test will give ratings for persons:

(a) Intelligence level

(b) Analytical skills

(c) Aptitude

(d) Leadership quality etc.

Many specialized software programs are available in market. Generally, these soft-wares are used at the time of promoting a person to higher level.

Table: 3.1: Interview Guide for Panel Members.

PART-1

Job——————————————

All conditions satisfied Yes/No

Scores on written test——————

Group discussion—————-

Current employment —————————— Employed Yes/No

Why are you seeking career change

(i) Better prospects

(ii) Job contents not of liking

(iii) Job environment not conducive

(IV) Problems with employer/supervisor

Past Employment

(v) Reasons for leaving

(vi) Are they similar to that of current employment

Rating

Good

Above average

Average

Below Average

Unsatisfactory

PART-2

Sales Experience: What kind of work have you done and for how long

- Retail ——————————————
- Door to door ——————————————
- Delivery or route ——————————————
- Missionary (Ethical) ——————————————
- Technical ——————————————
- Specialty ——————————————

Do you have experience in:

- Starting new accounts ——————————————
- Display/Merchandising ——————————————
- Product demonstrations ——————————————

- Price negotiations ————————————————
- Telephone sales ————————————————
- Sales to Govt. agencies ————————————————

Are you willing to get posted anywhere? ———————— Yes/No.

Can you take up extensive traveling ———————— Yes/No.

Have you traveled in rural areas ——————————— Yes/No.

Have you traveled in semi urban areas ——————— Yes/No.

Have you traveled in urban areas —————————— Yes/No.

Have you traveled in cities ——————————————— Yes/No.

Explain: How will you face a situation (Give a situation) and the reasons for it ———————————————

Rating:

Good

Above Average

Average

Below Average

Unsatisfactory

PART-3

Family Background:

What is/was your father doing?

Govt.

Private

Business

How long has he worked in same company ————————————

How long has he worked in same position ————————————

How are your brothers/sisters placed ————————————

Is he having family history of job hopping. Yes/No.

Does he have unstable mind about jobs. Yes/No.

Rating:

Good

Above Average

Average

Below Average

Unsatisfactory

PART – 4

Personal

What are your strong points ------------------

What are your weak points ------------------

Neatness/Cleanliness ------------------

Health ------------------

Dress ------------------

Poise and Manner ------------------

Speech Rating: ------------------

Good
Above Average
Average
Below Average
Unsatisfactory

Overall rating:

Good
Above Average
Average
Below Average
Unsatisfactory

Comments ------------------

Interview------- **Sign**------- **Date**--------

Verification of Information:

Verification of information given by the candidate is done in the following ways:

1. By contacting references given in application forms.
2. By contacting earlier employers.
3. By contacting customers.

It is becoming very important to check the information for all levels of staff. Many times the candidates have done financial frauds with earlier company's or with their customers which have repercussions on their efficiency. The best way is to ask the candidates to produce relieving letter/resignation acceptance from the previous employer. You can give the candidate an offer letter and ask him to produce the relieving letter before joining the company.

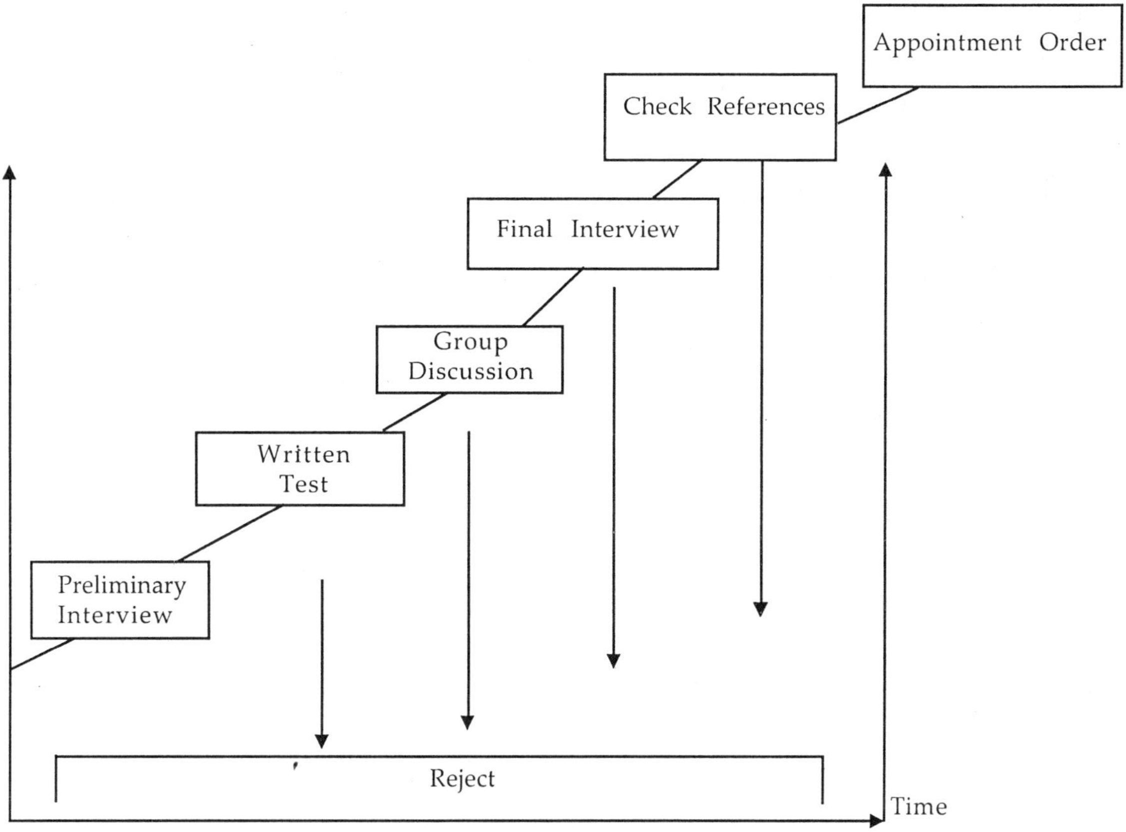

Fig. 3.1: Selection Process

Finalization of Wage Structure

Many good candidates will ask for higher salary than your scale being offered, this creates problems like:

(a) Existing employees objecting to higher salary to new people.

(b) Existing employees will also ask for similar salary levels (if higher).

Appointment Order

Specific appointment order needs to be given according to the job descriptions, so that problems of refusing any posting or job do not arise.

Specimen Job Descriptions

1. **Sales Officer/Executive:**
   Job description will have the following areas:

Sales

- Make regular calls (specify minimum number if required).
- Sell the products/product range.
- Give demonstrations.
- Achieve sales target both primary (to distributor/agent) and secondary (to retailer/consumer)
- Maintain adequate stock levels with all channel members.

Service

- Install product displays and merchandise
- Handle product related complaints
- Make credit notes, etc., for claims by consumers/channel members.

Territory Management

- Arrange route for best coverage.
- Increase width and depth of distribution.
- Look for development of new customers/areas.

Sales Promotion

- Train distributor staff for regular coverage and higher sales.
- Maintain high stock levels and its rotation.
- Prepare sales promotional schemes and submit proposals.
- Execute sales promotional plans.

Reporting:

- Send daily/weekly/fortnightly/area/monthly reports in time.
- Collect information on competitor's activity and report in time.

3.1.5 Compensation of sales staff

Compensations of sales force is done in different ways in different companies. Compensation related to achievement of quota is very popular mode of compensation in Western countries where efficient people want to get paid more than others. In India because of the cultural and financial condition of masses most of the people prefer to **SECURE** a job which may not be compensating the efforts well. Also the Indian work force is happy with compensation at subsistence level and tries and earns higher income through-

(a) Sycophancy

(b) Illegal/amoral means

Most of the people believe that EFFICIENCY and GOODWORK cannot lead to higher compensation package and prosperity. The belief is not ill placed as even in many multinationals people are able to get positions of responsibility through sycophancy. But this is the fault of

Indian culture where everyone thinks of becoming 'King' in his own right so that he can do what he thinks is right and not necessarily what is actually right.

The animal principle of MIGHT IS RIGHT still hold true in civilized societies of India, the might (position of power) make you always right. So, the compensation based on achievement of quota exists only where the job is done as ADDITIONAL SOURCE OF INCOME and not as main source of income e.g. Insurance policy sales person, financial instruments sellers (small scale saving certificates, UTI, company deposit mobilization etc.)

Sales staff needs to be compensated properly to ensure they remain motivated enough to work properly and achieve the given targets. There is no point in replacing sales staff every time someone is found to be working unsatisfactorily. The reasons for better compensation are as follows

- They are required to spend time outdoors everyday
- They are required to eat outside food everyday which is expensive and not good for health
- They may be required to travel at odd hours
- They may be required to stay away from family for long duration of time
- Working hours are not specified, may be required to work long hours many times without any over-time pay
- Required to stay smartly dressed requiring extra expenses on clothing
- More wear and tear for shoes and cloths requiring frequent change
- Work pressure is higher due to target orientation of job which is not so for office staff.

Sales staff compensation is done under following heads

I. **Salary**: Salary to sales staff can be paid in various ways depending on the organization's condition (start-up, established), product condition (start-up in competitive market, established in commodity type market, established in brand market etc.). The salary can be paid as follows:

   - **Straight salary**: A fixed salary as per the market conditions can be fixed with annual increments depending on the achievements during the year. The salary can be in consolidated form or can be bifurcated as basic + dearness allowance + house rent allowance + local conveyance etc.

   - **Salary + commission**: A fixed salary at very low level taking care of basic needs plus a commission based on achievements can be decided. In this method the incentive starts at a minimum achievement level and goes on increasing as per the higher achievements, the slabs of incentives are worked out in such a way that the sales person is motivated to achieve higher and higher level of sales as the higher the slab of achievement higher the rate of incentive, e.g., if the salary is fixed at ₹ 3000/-PM + incentive, the incentive can be for say 10 units @ ₹ 100/- per unit, next 10 units (11-20) @ ₹ 200/- per unit, next 10 units (21-30) @ ₹ 300/- per unit and next 10 unit or more (31 onwards) can be @ ₹ 500/– per unit. If the sales person achieves 10 units he gets ₹ 3,000+ 1,000= ₹ 4,000 but if achieves 30 units he gets ₹ 9,000/- which is very attractive and after 30 units he starts getting ₹ 500 for every extra unit which is more than attractive. Because of this the sales person remains always on his/her toes. In India sales persons are not interested in salary + commission and prefer straight salary even if it is low.

II. **Allowances**: Different types of allowances are paid to sales staff to take care of their various requirements they are as follows:

- **Daily allowance/HQ allowance**: This is paid for every working day spent in the field (not illegible when in office) in the sales persons base town (headquarter of his area of working). His allowance takes care of his expenditure on local conveyance for visiting the route he/she is working plus his need for tea/coffee snacks. The allowance varies from company to company, it may start at ₹100/- per day and can be up to ₹ 250/- per day; higher allowances are paid to sales person at higher level of hierarchy. Some companies pay only the petrol allowance and nothing for tea/coffee snacks, in such companies' sales staff turnover is very high.
- **Up-country day allowance**: When a sales person travels out of his/her base town (HQ) for a day returning by evening/night he is paid this allowance. This allowance is normally 1.5 times the HQ allowance paid to sales staff and can take care of tea/ coffee snacks and one working meal plus the local conveyance of the town visited.
- **Up-country night away allowance**: When a sales person travels out of his/her base/ HQ town and is not returning same day and is required to spend the night away he/ she is paid this allowance that is normally three times the base town/HQ allowance. This allowance takes care of the lodging boarding and local conveyance needs of the sales person away from his/her base town. Senior staff is allowed actual expenses with varying upper limit per day that allows them to stay in three/four/five star luxury as per their position in hierarchy.
- **Travel expenditure**: Most of the organizations pay actual travel cost when travelling away from base town (not paid in case of salary + incentive scheme). The travel is allowed in different mode of travel and class of travel as per the organization norms, e.g., some organizations pay ordinary bus travel up to 100 kms and after that they pay for luxury buses, similarly up to 100 kms they pay ordinary rail fare and after that they pay sleeper class fare. Good organizations ask their staff to travel in style and luxury and always pay luxury bus travel and three tier or two tier (second class) a/c fares. Senior people travel by air and top brass travels by executive class air.
- **Incidental allowances**: incidental expenses like telephone charges, stationery charges etc. are paid at actual through claim procedure requiring bills and vouchers for the same.

III. **Incentives**: Incentives are paid to straight salary sales staff also but not as a regular feature but as motivational schemes. These incentives are for short or long-term target achievements and mostly on slab system that keeps increasing after a minimum level of achievement. Some organizations add a dimension of best/star sales person award to it to create competition among the high achievers for top spots that can be defined as regional/national best/star with first second third rankings. Most of the good organizations give these awards in kind rather than cash to avoid sales person paying higher amounts in taxes due to the incentives earned, cash awards then become unattractive as it all goes in taxes. The incentives can start with gifts like TV/fridge/

music systems to holidays inland or to foreign locations for two (husband and wife)

Some organizations pay a small amount as target incentive/bonus every month to all sales staff for achieving a minimum level of sales target.

IV. **Insurance**: All the sales staff is insured under two heads:

- **Health/medical insurance**: Under this the sales staff gets benefit of reimbursement of medical expenditure inclusive of hospitalization etc.
- **Personal belongings insurance**: Under this the sales staff is required to give declaration as to how much is the total valuation of personal belongings (cash, mobile, cloths, bag, ornaments, company property, credit/debit cards etc.) while travelling on company duty and is insured for the entire amount. In case of loss of belongings during the travel the sales staff is reimbursed with the entire amount, this ensures his/her safe worry free travel.

V. **Bonus**: Sales staff is paid bonus as per the bonus act along with other staff.

3.2 Training of Sales Staff

Training of sales staff is the most important aspect of recruitment, without training the selected candidates may not be able to give their best as they will take their own time to understand their proper responsibility and what the organization is expecting from them. Training will consist of following:

1. Induction training
2. On job training
3. Training for improvements in skills
4. Training for higher responsibility

Let us look at all these areas one by one.

3.2.1 Induction Training

This is very important aspect of training; it is found that many organizations do not carry out induction training and sales staff is left to find their way around. The sales staff may learn or may not learn every aspect of the organizational structure, the culture of organization and the procedures leaving them open to making mistakes which can be very well be avoided by giving induction training. Induction training will consist of following:

- **Explaining organizational structure and position of the new person joining the organization:** The new recruit can be taken around the office and be introduced to each and every staff member of the organization. The new recruit can be given all the information brochures, write-ups, etc., about the organization that can familiarize him/her to the organization. A senior staff member or the head of the branch/regional office should then talk to the new recruit and explain the hierarchy and the cultural expectations from the new recruit.

In Induction Training the sale personnel are made aware of:

1. Their position in hierarchy.
2. Their relationship with other departments and the key contact persons for coordinating sales function.
3. Production and dispatch points.
4. Product knowledge/visit to factory.
5. Reporting formats and frequency of reports.
6. Allowances and reimbursement of expenses procedure.
7. Administrative rules and regulations.

- **Explaining the procedural aspects:** The new recruit should be given the procedure manual to read and understand the procedures to be followed by him/her while working in the organization. Explain all the forms and formats and importance of filling them properly and what is the information expected in all the columns. Many times it is observed that the new employees do not give proper information just because they have not understood the importance of the information sought. Many companies prepare Sales Manual which will give all details to the Sales personnel and which will remain handy to him all the time. Following details are given in a Sales Manual:

1. Rules and Regulations.
2. Leave Rules.
3. Allowance Rules.
4. Daily Sales Report. (DSR)
5. Weekly Sales Report.
6. Stocks and Sale Report. (SSR)
7. Credit Investigation Report.
8. Distributor Details.
9. Customer Details.
10. Retail Universe.
11. Permanent Journey Plan (PJP).
12. Tour Itinerary (program).
13. Leave Application.
14. Expense Report.
15. Claims Report.
16. Eyes and Ears Report (Competitors Activity).
17. Sales Analysis Format.
18. Monthly Report.
19. Addresses and Telephone Numbers of Sales Depots.
20. Addresses and Telephone Numbers for Sales Office.

Each and every company will have different types of formats for their own use, but the basic information collected and the reasons for it remain the same.

Table. 3.2: DSR Consumer Product

Daily Sales Report (Consumer Products)

Name of Sales Rep. -------- **Dt.** ---

HQ ------------ **Name of Route:** ---- **Last Visit on** --

Sr. No.	*Name of Retailer*	*Cat*	*Product*																		*Total*
1			S T	O R	S T	O R	S T	O R	S T	O R	S T	O R	S T	O R	S T	O R	S T	O R	S T	O R	Value
2																					
3																					
4																					
5																					
6																					
7																					
8																					
9																					
10																					
11																					
12																					
13																					
14																					
15																					
16																					
17																					
18																					
19																					
20																					
Total																					

ST = Stock available, OR= Orders received for execution
SO/Reps. Signature | Distributor
Categories: GM – General Merchant GR – Grocery | Stamp & Signature
Ch – Chemist Co-operative

Table. 3.3: Daily Calls Report (Ethical)

Daily Calls Report (Ethical Sales)

Name of M. Rep . ________________ **Dt.**____________

HQ ______ **Name Route** __________ **Last visited** _____

Sr. No.	*Name of Doctor*	*Type*	*Samples & Gifts Details*									
1												
2												
3												
4												
5												
6												
7												
8												
9												
10												
	Signature of MR	Opening Balance										
		Receipts										
		Given Today										
		Closing Stock										

Table. 3.4: Daily Sales Report (White Goods)

Daily Sales Report (White Goods)

Name of Sales Ex. ______________ Dt.________________

HQ ____________ Name of Route ____ Dt. Last visited____________

Sr. No.	*Name of Retailer*	*Class*	*Display*		*Demonstrator Working*		*POP Material*		*Order*
			Yes	No	Yes	No	In Place	No	
1									
2									
3									
4									
5									
6									

Self **Competition**

Market Operating Prices (MOP): Fridges

Washing Machines

TVs

Competitive Activity: ....

....

Service Problems ....

Sign of S. E. ....

Table. 3.5: Daily Report Industrial Products

Daily Report (Industrial Goods)

Name of Sales Ex. __________ Dt. ____________

HQ ______________ Town ____________

Sr. No.	*Name of Industry*	*Person Contacted & Designation*	*Phone No.*	*Stage of Call*			*Next Contact*	*Action to be taken*
1				Proposal	Demo	Quote		
2								
3								
4								
5								
6								

Detailed Notes

Signature

Benefits or Daily Report:

1. Daily report makes a person work daily. Human tendency does not allow anyone to write 100% fictitious report everyday.
2. Daily report provides control point to Sales Manager on the sales person. A Sales Manager can CHECK BACK on any daily report to verify the information.
3. To fill up the columns of the daily report the sales persons is required to FIND all the required information. This puts him in a habit of making enquiries. This improves his working.
4. Daily report is a source of lot of information to Sales Manager. A Sales Manager can add specific information collection columns on a Daily Report to get the information whenever required.

Table. 3.6: Stock and Sales Report

Stock and Sales Report

Name of Sales Representative _ _ _ _ _ _ _ _ **Period: from** _ _ _ _ _ _ _ _ **to** _ _ _ _ _ _

H.Q. _ _ _ _ _ _ _ **Town** _ _ _ _ _ _ _ **Name of Distributor** _ _ _ _ _ _ _ _ _ _ _ _ _

Sr . No.	*Details*	*Products/Packs*							*Remarks*
1	Opening Stock of the month								
2	Receipts till date								
3	Total Stock (1 + 2)								
4	Sales till date of visit								
5	Sales during visit								
6	Total Sales (4 + 5)								
7	Closing Stock (3 – 6)								
8	Estimate for the month								
9	Target for the month								
10	Difference + – (9 – 8)								
11	Plan for next month								
	Sales for Previous Three Months								

Payment Position Clear/Not Clear

Pending Bills dt. **Exp. Payment dt.** **Dist.**

1. _ Stamp
2. _ and Sign.
3. _ S. Reps. Sign.

Benefits or Stocks and Sale Report:

Stocks and sale reports if filled judiciously is beneficial to both, the sales person and the sales manager. The benefits are as follows:

1. Gives a clear picture at distributor point on stock and sale.
2. Shows distributors participation. If the participation is below expectations, action can be planned for it.
3. Shows Sales representatives efforts *vis-à-vis* distributor.
4. Estimates of months sale is available for planning purpose.
5. If shortfalls are expected timely actions can be taken.
6. Payment remains under control.

Low stocks/high stocks at distribution point can be avoided

Customer's Details:

Customer's details are collected for industrial customers and for sale of white goods or sale of chemicals, etc., on a regular basis. These details will help in keeping the relations with the customers.

Table. 3.7: Customer Details

Customer's Details

Name of Customers ....

Address: ....

....

Telephone No. .... Fax : ....

E-mail ....

Contact Person for Orders .... Phone direct .... Ext.

Contact Person of Billing .... Phone direct .... Ext.

Contact Person for Payments .... Phone direct .... Ext.

Important Persons:

1 . Name Designation ....

Direct Phone................. Ext .... Residence ....

2 . Name .... Designation ....

Direct Phone .... Ext .... Residence ....

3 . Name .... Designation ....

Direct Phone .... Ext. .... Residence ....

Other Suppliers 1. ph.

2. ph.

3. ph.

Retail Universe

Retail universe is the term used by consumer companies to denote number of retailers stocking their products. By keeping this record they know the increase or decrease in customer base and can monitor it. When competitor companies retail universe is compared, one knows their position vis-à-vis competitor's retail universe and can plan to increase the retail base to improve availability and distribution. For companies other than consumer companies retail universe shows current position in comparison with potential customer base. In consumer form the category of retailers is shown and in industrial or other forms. Category of customers can be mentioned.

Table. 3.8: Retail Universe

Retail Universe

Name of Sales Person ------ **Period:** **from---to------**

HQ ------

Sr. No.	*Details/Town/ Route*	*Freq. of visit*	*This year*					*Last year*					
			CH	GM	GR	Super Co-op	Total	CH	GM	GR	Super Co-op	Total	Remark
1													
2													
3													
4													
5													
6													
7													
8													
9													
10													
	Total												

Permanent Journey Plan (PJP): To maintain control over visits of the sales person to all the customers (minimum visits to all customers), Permanent Journey Plan (PJP) is used. There are many benefits of PJP like.

Benefits of PJP

1. Each and every customer gets visited with predefined frequency.
2. Planning of sales and dispatches becomes easy.
3. Collection of payments can be streamlined.
4. Gives regularity to visit, increasing the output and reducing the problems.
5. Expenditure budgets can be planned and controlled well.
6. Manpower planning becomes easy. Available man power gets utilized to fullest capacity.

Table. 3.9: Permanent Journey Plan

Permanent Journey Plan

Name -- ------ HQ --- -- Period: Jan --- to Dec. ---

Sr. No.	*Town/ Route*	*Freq*	*Duration*	*Jan*	*Feb*	*Mar*	*Apr*	*May*	*June*	*July*	*Aug*	*Sept*	*Oct*	*Nov*	*Dec*	*Remark*
1	Nagpur	EJC	12													
2	Bhandara	AJC	1													
3	Gondiya	AJC	1													
4	Chand-rapur	EJC	3													
5	Warora/ Wani	QJC	1													
6	Yavatmal	AJC	1													
7	Wardha	AJC	1													
8	Amravati	EJC	3													
9	Akola	EJC	3													
10	Buldhana	QJC	1													
11	Malaka-pur	QJC	1													

Leave Application

Leave Application is a standard format in most organization showing available leave balance, leave asked for and the authorization signature. This is a disciplinary format which makes people take prior permission before going on leave.

Table. 3.10: Leave Application

Leave Application							
Name							Date.....................
HQ..........................		type of leave asked AL/CL/SL/RL					
Leave asked for		days..................		from..................	to..............	(both inclusive)	
Type	*Opening Balance*	*Add this year Provision*	*Total*	*Leave availed till this date*	*Balance*	*Leave asked now*	*Balance*
AL							
CL							
SL							
Checked by						**Signature of Applicant with name**	
Authorized by							
OK/Not OK						**Signature of Authorizing Person**	

Tour Itinerary (Tour Program)

Tour itinerary is a periodical program generally for period of a month prepared on the basis of PJP shows actual plan. The program is prepared by the person who intends to travel and is authorized by his superior. It is a very useful document if used judiciously and properly.

Benefits of Tour Itinerary

1. Planning of tour becomes systematic and allows one to make bookings in advance for hotel rooms and trains etc.
2. All the distributors can be informed well advance to remain present on the date of your arrival and keep all the information ready for you.
3. Availability of stock for sale can be arranged for the date of visit.
4. Promotions can be planned according to your date of visit.
5. Sales office can get in touch with the sales person according to tour itinerary at distributor point of the hotel.
6. Messages can be diverted to reach the sales person wherever he is present.
7. Relatives of sales person can contact him at various places in emergency
8. Other distributors can also relay messages to sales person wherever he is present.
9. Days are not lost due to weekly closing days of different towns.
10. Back tracking on same route is avoided. So additional expenditure is also prevented.

Table. 3.11: Tour Itinerary

TOUR ITINERARY

Name ___________________ Month ________

HQ ____________ Tour itinerary No______

Date	*Days*	*From*	*To*	*Mode of Travel*	*EDD*	*ETA*	*Night Halt at*	*Contact Tel. No.*
1								
2								
3								
4								
5								
6								
7								
8								
9								
10								
11								
12								
13								
14								
15								
16								
17								
18								
19								
20								
21								
22								
23								
24								
25								
26								
27								
28								
29								
30								
31								

Prepared by

Date

Authorized by

Date

Claims Report

A sales person may be required to make claims report for various customers due to various reasons like, transit damages, quality complaints, withdrawal of samples, discounts offered , display charges or promotional charges etc. All the companies have different types of the formats. Many companies have different formats for different types of claims. Some samples are shown in Table. 3.12 to 3.16.

Table. 3.12: Transit Damages Report

Transit Damages Report

Name of customer: .... Dt. ....

Address: ....

Prepared by ....

Sr. No.	*Invoice number*	*Date*	*RR/LR Number*	*RR/LR Date*	*Name of Product*	*Pack size*	*Qty. Sent*	*Qty. damaged*	*Certificate of transporter*
1									
2									
3									
4									
5									

Stamp and Signature of Customer **Name and Signature of Company Person**

Expense Report

Expense Report is also a also a control document. The expenditure of the sales person is controlled through this. A sales person will not be paid in excess of what is allowed to him and will not be paid less than what is allowed to him. Some sales managers use it for giving punishment by deducting the allowances for the days the sales person has not worked satisfactorily. But since a sales manager is not authorized to pay in excess on the days the sales person has worked excessively well, using expense statement as punishment tool is not good. A sales person may be forced to recover the deduction at a later date through unscrupulous means which will turn out to be **HABIT FORMING** and means to earn extra money and will lead to MALPRACTICES and loss of revenue to the company.

Expense reports can be of weekly/fortnightly or monthly types. The imprest/advance amount payable increases if the expense report is monthly type. Weekly types increase work load to office staff and accounts staff. Fortnightly statements are ideal and manageable. Table 3.12 shows Fortnightly expense statement format.

Table. 3.13: Expense Statement

Expense Statement

Name .... Exp. Statement for the period

HQ .... From .... to ....

Date	*Day*	*From*	*To*	*Mode of Travel*	*Kms.*	*Departure*	*Arrival time*	*Fare Time*	*Conveyance ₹*	*Other exp. bills*

Allowance details:

Total number of days HQ Allowance × ₹ _ = Total

Total number of days Ex HQ Allowance × ₹ _ = Total

Total number of days Night Allowance × ₹ _ = Total

Others Include: Stationery, Telephone, Postage etc

Total Fares

Total Local Conveyance

Total Others (attached bills)

Imprest Account :

Opening Balance ₹————————

Received during the period ₹——————

Total available ₹————————

Grand Total

Less: this statement ₹——————— Balance closing Signature

Checked by ——————————————

Authorized for ₹ ——————

Authorized by —————————————

C/h/D/D sent on date ————

Benefits of expense report: Expense statement can also be used as control report on a sales person as he has noted all his movements in it and are verifiable. Payment of expenses on time is an hygiene factor for sales persons, many people leave a job only because their expenses are not paid on time by the organization. A sales manager can decide a process by way of which all the expenses statements are paid every week/fortnight or month on a particular day to avoid demotivation caused by it.

Table. 3.14: Stock Withdrawal Report

Stock Withdrawal Report

Name of Customer ————————————— dt —————————————

Address ———————————————————— Prepared by ——————————

Sr. No.	*Product/Pack*	*Stock Withdrawn*	*MRP*	*Total*	*Reasons for withdrawal*
1					
2					
3					
4					
5					
		Total			

Checked by ———————————————

Authorized by ——————————————— Signature of Sales Person

Table. 3.15: Claim Report

Claims Report

Name of Customer————————— dt——————————

Address —————————————————— Prepared by —————————————

Sr. No.	*Details (Attach details and bills)*	*Amount*
1		
2		
3		
4		
5		
	Total	

Checked by ———————————

Authorized by ——————————— Signature of Sales Person

Eyes and Ears Report

Keeping tab on activities of competitors is a prime responsibility of field sales people. Sales people must inform their offices **IN TIME,** activities of competitors so that activities can be planned to counter them. It can so happen that **false information** may be planted by competitors on gullible sales people giving **FALSE ALARM**. To avoid this a proper format helps check the information authenticity.

Table. 3.16: Eyes and Ears Report

Eyes and Ears Report

Name .... HQ .... dt......................... Station from where sent ....

Information received from .... Credibility of Person High/Avg/Low

Supporting documents attached/not attached

Affectivity of Activity: High/Avg/Low

Details of Activity:...

....

Copies – Sales Office - Head Office - Marketing Dept.

- Self. Signature of Sales Person

Importance of eyes and ears report can be understood by reading the case of MILO (see box 3.1)

Box 3.1 Countering Competition

Case of Milo (white powder) launch Tamil Nadu

HMM Ltd. the subsidiary of UK based Horlicks Ltd. sold two products in India that are Horlicks (with two variants plain and elaichi) – most trusted health drink and a locally developed brown powder Boost a milk additive for health. Horlicks was sold in three SKUs 800gms, 450 gms and 200 gms jars and Boost was also sold in three SKUs 500 gms jar, 500 gms refill and 200 gms jar. 85% of total sales was plain Horlicks and rest was coming from elaichi variant and Boost. Horlicks had virtually no competition as the other product Complan was priced at double the rate of Horlicks and was out of most consumers reach.

Nestle' the company holding more than 80% of branded coffee market at that time had equally good distribution set up as that of HMM Ltd. was planning to enter the white powder-health drink in India and they had completed all the consumer and market research formalities for the same. They decided to enter India from the strong health food market of Tamil Nadu that accounted for 25% of Horlicks market in India (996 people out of every 1000 people in Tamil Nadu drank Horlicks everyday). The launch details were being kept completely under wraps and no one new when the product would be launched.

Mr. Anup Chib the then Marketing manager and MR. AR Sarker the then GM sales (all India responsibility) had made all the plans of countering the Milo launch. The plans were to offer 1kg and 500 gms Horlicks in place of 800 gms and 450 gms to consumers without extra charges and bring in the metric packs along with that, the retailers were being offered one jar free with every purchase of one dozen jars. The offers was to be launched just one week before the actual launch of MILO.

The opportunity came due to **"Eyes and Ears"** report filed by Gorakhpur based HMM sales officer who had a common distributor selling both Horlicks and Nescafe. The Gorakhpur sales officer learned from the distributor that the sales staff of Nestle will not be operative from a particular date as they were travelling down south to Chennai, he sent in the eyes and ears report saying Nestle has planned some major activity in Chennai from the particular date. HMM launched the counter attack exactly one week in advance of the Nestle plan and loaded the market so much that many retailers refused to buy MILO even in small quantities. Milo launch was complete flop and Nestle has not launched it till today (they launched the chocolate variant later).

Sales Analysis/Format

A sales person must keep records of sale regularly for him to understand the trends and analysis the sales for future planning etc. Without timely and properly maintained records a sales person will not understand the results of his efforts over a period of time. A person should keep records for all the products/packs on monthly basis for each town/ route/customer being covered. This will give correct information. Where the growth/drop in sales are coming from and what action one should take for it.

Table. 3.17: Sales Analysis

Sales Analysis

Name of Town/Route Customer ------ Name of Sales Person ----------

Months	*Products*						*Products*					
	This Year	Last Year	Tgt	This Year	Last Year	Tgt	This Year	Last Year	Tat	This Year	Last Year	Tat
January												
February												
Cumulative												
March												
Cumulative												
April												
Cumulative												
May												
Cumulative												
June												
Cumulative												
July												
Cumulative												
August												
Cumulative												
September												
Cumulative												
October												
Cumulative												
November												
Cumulative												
December												
Total												
Average												

Monthly Report: All the Sales personnel are required to write monthly report every month. The monthly report will be informative giving information about the individual sales areas. To avoid differences in information giving pattern, a standard format may be prepared by a Sales Manager. An individual may write other matters separately if he feels that they should be reported and are important enough. Each Sales Manager may have his points of emphasis and he would like to get them stressed and reported. It is always better to device individual formals. Specimens are shown for reference.

Table. 3.18: Monthly Report Part "A"

Monthly Report

Name HQ Months

Prod	*Sale this month*		*Target this month*		+ - %		*This year*		*Tar get*		*Last year*		+-% *Sec. Sale*	
	Pri	Sec	Pri	Sec	Pri.	Sec.	Pri.	Sec.	Pri.	Sec.	Pri.	Sec.	Pri.	Sec.

Table. 3.19: Monthly Report part "B"

Working Record

	No. of days worked	*No. of calls made*	*Average*	*No. of Productive calls made*	*% of Productive calls*	*STR*in the in days*				*Rmarks*
						Prod. x	Y	Z	R	
This Month										
Cumu. This Year										

*STR = Stock Turnover Ratio expressed in days

Table. 3.20: Monthly Report part "C"

Expenses Record:

	Travel	*Allowance*	*Conveyance*	*Telephone*	*Postage*	*Total*	*Budget*
This month							
Cumulative this year							

Giving product knowledge: Product knowledge is very important aspect of training, without proper product knowledge a sales person will not be able to do proper brand talk, and objection handling in the call procedure.

(a) **Product knowledge in industrial products:** Many industries make their sales engineers/ executives visit the factory and understand the production process of each and every product. This helps them understand the intrinsic strengths of the products, their raw materials used, the quality standards etc. it has been observed that some organizations selling OEMs (original equipment manufacturers) ask their sales engineers/executives dismantle the product and reassemble it several times to understand the product and its components in detail.

(b) **Product knowledge in pharmaceutical products:** In pharmaceutical products it is critically important for the medical sales officer to know the composition of the products as well as its effect on the various parts of the body of the patient as he or she is required to pass it on to the physicians or specialists properly and convincingly. In this category the molecule or the compound as they refer to the product has effect on various parts of the body of patient immediately or with a delayed effect depending on how the medicine is administered to the patient. The medical sales officer must know whether product is an oral dose (liquid, tablets or capsules) or an injection or a cream to be applied on the surface. If it is an oral dose what is the frequency (once/twice or thrice a day) of its consumption and whether it is suited for children (pediatric) or for all ages. If it is an injection how it is to be administered, is it intravenous (in the vain), or subcutaneous (under the skin) or intramuscular (in the muscle). In addition to this the medical sales officers are required to know the physiological effects of the medicine also. Most of the pharmaceutical companies conduct proper classroom training programs and refresher programs for their medicines regularly.

(c) **Product knowledge in consumer products:** In consumer products is also very important, many FMCG companies send their sales officers to visit the factories and gain proper knowledge of the product. In this case the sales officer must gain knowledge of the product to know the products features, benefits and advantages over the competition. Many companies prepare a feature, benefits and advantages chart for their every product and pass it on to the sales officer as a ready reckoner.

3.2.1 On job training

Next step is on job training, in this step the sales manager sends the new recruit along with the experienced senior and asks the new recruit to observe and learn the practical part of the job from the experienced senior. At the end of the on job training period which can be as short as a week to as long as three months depending on the urgency of the new recruit joining his/her designated territory. Some sales managers may give the new recruit some assignment to understand his/her efficiency and enthusiasm in the job. These assignments can be off research or developmental activity for the territory.

Care needs to be taken by the sales manager that the senior assigned to give on job training is career-oriented and ambitious and not the ones happy with their current position and want to retire in same position. The career oriented people train the new recruit on positive sides of the job and company culture and try and guide them to become career oriented themselves. The happy in the same position train the new recruits in negative sides of the job and all the dirty tricks they do to keep their job intact. The new recruit can get spoiled early with the happy in the position types.

3.2.2 Training for improvement of skills

many organizations as part of motivational activity and as activity towards improving sales volumes through better selling skills hold training programs in improved selling skills. Selling skills can be classified as basic selling skills, advanced selling skills and professional selling skills. Let us look at all these categories in detail.

3.3 Organizing Distribution Network

Organizing distribution network is a very important part of sales manager's responsibility. Without proper distribution network a sales manager cannot achieve his targeted sales. Following activities are very important is this direction

Appointment of new distributors for area not under coverage

Appointment of distributor for area not properly covered by existing distributor

Replace distributors that are not working as per the company norms

Let us look at all these aspects one by one

3.3.1 Appointment of new distributors for area not under coverage

Because of rapid urbanization of many areas demand for various products increases in such areas. The retailers in such area are satisfying this demand by bringing the products from nearby wholesalers. These areas may not get coverage from existing distributors due to logistical problems. A sales manager can always send his sales officer for scouting the area and if he finds that a new distributor can be appointed in the area that can do business and earn profit (distributors will not work unless they have opportunity to earn profits at reasonable level) the sales manager should look for parties who can fit the company requirements and appoint a new distributor.

Appointing new distributor before competition does that can give you added advantage of being first and can help convert loyal customers of competitor to your side (this happens because your product availability is higher and stockouts are absent due to local supplies).

3.3.2 Appointment of distributor for area not properly covered by existing distributor

Any area which a sales manager finds not being properly covered even after repeated requests to the existing distributor, needs a new distributor. Normally speaking a distributor neglects a particular area only when it is financially nonviable. An area becomes financially nonviable when the volumes are low and/or transportation costs are more (distance is too far). Many a times distributors neglect areas because of shortage of manpower and infrastructure. The expected business at that time may not justify the additional investment in infrastructure, and manpower. Distributors mostly think in short-term basis and are not looking at long-term benefits, which a sales manager cannot afford to do, he must look at long-term gains and should be prepared to invest for it.

3.3.3 Replace distributors that are not working as per the company norms

Many times the distributors stop working as per the company norms and are not willing to change even after telling them repeatedly, e.g.,

- They will not give the coverage frequency as decided by the company leading to out of stock situations with various retailers
- They may not offer any credit facility to any retailers as decided by the company
- They stop giving replacements as per the company norms
- They keep lesser inventory with them than the stipulated norms
- They default on payments to the company
- They start working as distributor to the competitive product
- They do not have required staff and infrastructure to take care of increasing business
- They start misbehaving with the sales officers

In such conditions the sales manager is forced to take action to change the distributor.

3.3.4 Steps in appointing a new distributor

Following steps are necessary in appointing a new distributor,

3.3.4.1 Search for a good distributor

A good distributor must have following qualities

1. He should be financially very strong
2. He should be enthusiastic and interested in your product
3. He should be ambitious and try to increase the business
4. He should have good infrastructure
5. He should be honest
6. He should give good service to retailers

7. He should have good reputation in the market
8. He should not be involved in to competitive products distribution

Normally speaking one should enquire about good distributor with prominent good retailers. If a retailer gives good report about a distributor that means his service to the retailers is good. Such distributors when appointed are found to be giving good service to the retailers and good business to the company.

3.3.4.2 Do credit investigation

Credit investigation is a very important step in appointment of a distributor; some companies call it due diligence formalities. Every organization plans to grow at the minimum rate of ten percentage points every year, some companies who are ambitious and are introducing new products every now and then can expect their business to grow at even more than 25 to 30 per cent per year in addition to this the inflation increases the prices of all the products by 4 to 5 per cent every year. This growth and effect of inflation needs the distributor to have additional investment capabilities every year. Following are the formats for doing credit investigation of a probable distributor.

Table. 3.21: Credit Investigation Report

Credit Investigation Report

Name of Party ---------- dt. Of Preparation

Address ---------- --------------

Phone No. (Office) ---------- (Key Man) **Residence** Fax -------

E. mail Address --

Partnership/Proprietary Organization

Sr. No.	*Names of Partners*	*Relation with Key man*	*Phone*	
			Office	**Residence**

Details of Finances:

Sr. No.	*Name of Bank*	*Branch*	*A/c No.*	*Fixed deposits*	*Overdraft limit*	*Today's Balance*
	Total					

Loans/Overdraft Details:

From whom	*Purpose*	*Period*

Property Details

Sr. No.	*Name of Partner*	*Address of Property*	*Free/ Mortgaged*	*Estimated Value*	*Remark*
1					
2					
3					
4					
5					

Other Deposits:

Sr. No.	*Name of Company*	*Amount*	*Interest rate*	*Period from to*	*Remarks*

Turnover Details

Sr. No.	*Company Name*	*Turnover*	*Working since*	*Average Stock level*	*Credit period*
1					
2					
3					
	Total				
	Expected Turnover of Company				
	Total Turnover				
Remarks					
Stamp and Signature of Party				Signature	

Benefits of Credit Investigation Report

Credit Investigation Report is helpful in many ways. Some of them are explained as follows:

1. In a hurry of appointing new distributors the sales people will not appoint a person who does not have real finances. Many people make a big show to impress the company representatives with borrowed funds. Their idea is to earn after winning the agency. This may lead to their prosperity but will restrain the company's growth prospects as enough finance will never be available.
2. If a party is OVERTRADING on available finances it is dangerous situation and will DEFINITELY lead to unrecoverable debts to the company.
3. In case of company stock and money is getting struck, the company can MOVE COURTS with knowledge of ATTACHABLE PROPERTIES.

Credit Investigation Report is prepared for existing distributors also periodically (say 2 to 4 years) and while appointing new distributor along with distributor details.

3.4.4.3 Collect distributor details

The distributor details are collected to find out suitability of a particular distributor (potential distributor) before considering him for appointment. It has following benefits:

Benefits of collecting distributor details:

1. It tells you about the current strengths of distributor in terms of:
   (a) Financial turnover
   (b) Staff strength
   (c) Delivery vehicles
   (d) No. of retailers being serviced
   (e) Warehousing capacity

2. The firm will also tell the distributors willingness to invest in your business.
3. Currently which are the companies he is operating with? (competitors should not be present).
4. What are his financial resources? Is he operating with own funds or borrowed funds?
5. What is his reputation in market?
6. How long is he in business?
7. What kind of records is he keeping?
8. What type of communication facilities does he have? (fax, e-mail, telephones, Internet etc.)

All these points become useful for comparison between the short listed distributors for selection of RIGHT distributor.

Table 3.22: Distributor Detail Form

Distributor Detail Form

Name of Organization ---------------- **Phone Nos.**-------------

Address: --

Any other firm being operated from same place

1. 2.

3. 4.

5 6.

Name of Key Person Residence Phone No.

Key Person Residential Address:--

Proprietary or Partnership Organization: --- If Partnership names of Partners:

Sr. No.	*Name of Partners*	*Relation with Key man*	*Residence Phone*	*Occupation*

Distributor details Form (Contd.).

Companies Operated:

Sr. No.	*Name of Company*	*Average paid up Stock ₹*	*Turnover PM*	*Marked Outstanding ₹*	*Under which firm name*	*For how long*	*Area for which being operated*
1							
2							
3							
4							
5							
6							
7							
8							

Expected turnover for the company ₹------------ P.M.

Area for which being considered --

FACILITIES

1. Godowns: No.s. ---- Total area --------- sq. ft.--------------
2. Vehicles: Cycles ---- Three Wheelers ---- Four Wheelers ---------
3. Salesmen: ------------ Delivery men ----- Office staff -------------
4. Retailers under coverage

   Chemist ------------

   Co operative ------------

   Bakeries --------------

   Semi w/s ------------

   General Merchants

   Grocers --------------

   Super Markets -----------

   Total ---------
5. Coverage pattern

   Weekly routes------------------

   Fortnightly routes-------------

   Monthly routes-----------------

Finances

Sr. No.	Book Name	Branch	A/c No.	Balance on this date	Term deposits ₹
1					
2					
3					
4					
5					

Remarks____

____

Suitable/Not suitable

Name and Sign of Sales Person

3.3.4.4 Discussing company expectations and explaining the norms

The sales manager before formally appointing new distributor should discuss all the expectations from the distributor and explain the company norms to him nothing should be kept to assumptions. It always pays to be honest and clear in all the dealings and avoids misunderstandings and complications latter. The norms can be of following type.

- **Minimum paid stock to be held all the times:** most of the consumer organizations offer some credit period to their distributors. Paid stock is the stock for which the payment is already made to the company. Some companies insist on advance payment in such case the distributors try and not keep enough inventory of stock in their warehouses/godowns which leads to stock out situations with the retailers.
- **Expected visit frequency to retailers:** each company may have different visit frequencies to their retailers, it may be twice a day, every day, twice a week, once a week, fortnightly or monthly. It is better that it is decided before you appoint the distributor.
- **Stock delivery norms:** some companies insist on ready delivery method and some companies expect the delivery to be done within 24 hours of the order taken.
- **Stock stacking norms:** when the containers of the product are fragile the cartons holding the product cannot be stacked in high quantity, as this can lead to breakages in the lowest cartons because of the load above. Most of the distributors neglect this because of space shortages and keep claiming credit for breakages. Some sales managers also do not give importance to this thinking that the breakages are already covered under transit damage insurance. One must always remember that the insurance companies increase the insurance premium if the damages claimed are high.
- **Procedure of claiming damages and breakages:** every company may have different norms for claiming credit for damages and breakages from the company. It should be clearly explained to avoid clashes afterwards.
- **Sales reporting procedure:** every company may have different method of reporting sales by distributor to the sales office. It can be daily, weekly or monthly reporting in a specific format. The procedure should be explained while appointing the distributor.

- **Ordering stocks from the company:** some companies allocate stock directly based on the closing stocks reported by the distributor at the end of the month, while some companies take order every week from the distributor based on the weekly sales reported by him. The procedure should be explained to avoid clashes latter.

3.3.4.5 Appointing distributor

A distributor may be given a detailed appointment letter or it all may be oral agreement, it all depends on company to company but has no effect on the working of distributor, distributor will work well as long as he is earning good profits out of the business, the moment the profits stop coming he will stop working properly or opt out of business.

3.4 Selection and Appointment of CFAs (Clearing and Forwarding Agents)

Most of the companies appoint CFAs in every state sometimes even more than one CFA in a state. The reasons for appointing CFAs are as follows

- Avoids central sales tax reducing the cost burden
- Reduces transport cost to large extent. Cost saving is the major benefit in appointing a CFA.
- Small loads can be effectively sent to distributors without damages
- The response time is shorter as the goods are sent from a point closer to distributor
- Inventory can be managed at low levels at various CFA points to reduce inventory carrying cost.
- The reduced response time allows the distributors to hold lower pipeline stock (inventory at distributor level) so they are willing to work at lower % of margin.
- Low inventories and pipeline stocks increases stock rotation so consumers always get fresher stock and reducing damages due to dating.

The same can be done more efficiently by opening up a depot of the company, but operating company owned depot works out to be very costly and increases labor problems. Companies open their own depots only when it is cost effective.

Why CFA cost can be lower?

- CFAs operate for various companies from the same campus with separate warehouses for each company.
- The clerical staff, coolies and the security staff, etc., are common in most of the cases.
- In addition to this the CFA himself acts as the manager of the operation reducing the cost substantially.
- Even if the companies ask for separate staff for their operations the cost of CFA is lower as the salaries and wages paid by him are much lower as compared to the salaries and wages paid by the companies.

- Most of the time the CFA owns the warehouse complex and he is willing to consider lower warehouse rent for himself in CFA operations

The cost savings can be explained better through examples.

Example 3.1 With following conditions will you appoint a CFA or not?

- Manager salary ₹ 25,000/-PM
- Clerk's salary ₹ 10,000/-PM
- Helper's salary ₹ 5,000/- PM (requirement 2 helpers)
- Other expenses ₹ 15,000/-PM
- Turnover 15000 boxes PM
- Warehouse Rent ₹ 20,000/-
- CFA asking rate ₹ 7/- per box

Answer

Let us work out expenses of the company in operating the warehouse

Manager's salary ₹ 25,000/- PM +

Clerk's salary ₹ 10,000/-PM +

Helper's salary ₹ 5,000/- PM x 2= ₹ 10,000/- +

Other expenses ₹ 15,000/-PM +

Warehouse Rent ₹ 20,000/- PM = ₹ 80,000/-

Cost of operating company warehouse is ₹ 80,000/- PM

Let us now find out cost of operating warehouse through CFA

Turnover 15000 boxes × ₹ 7/- box fee PM = 1,05,000/-

We will not appoint CFA as the cost of operating the warehouse is less than CFA fees.

3.4.1 Qualities of a good CFA

1. He will have a good infrastructure like warehouse, communication systems, security etc.
2. His reputation is good
3. He is experienced in handling CFA work
4. He has good staff
5. He is interested in increasing business
6. Company is saving money by appointing this CFA.

3.4.2 Terms of business with CFA

The terms of business with CFA needs to be leading to be big saving. The terms are negotiated in various ways as explained below.

1. Rent of warehouse + salary of staff +commission
2. Handling charges only
3. Rent of warehouse + handling charges
4. Rent of warehouse + handling charges + salary of staff
5. Commission only
6. Rent of warehouse + commission

The transportation costs and telephone, stationery cost, etc., are either paid at actual or at fixed rate. There is no fixed system of deciding the remuneration of CFA. A good Sales Manager will negotiate them for getting good savings to the company.

The cost saving by appointing a CFA can be achieved in following areas

1. Central sales Tax (CST) can be saved in interstate operations, as the CFA is technically company premises and stock sent to CFA does not become sale and hence, no CST
2. The staff appointed by CFA is always at lower salaries than what company may pay to its own employees reducing the cost and also does not create liability.
3. The CFA is willing to negotiate the warehouse rent at lower level than the going market rate, as he is trying to get returns on idle assets and trying to win the agency for himself against the competition.
4. The CFA works as depot manager and is not paid salary but the commission earned by him is treated as his salary, saving cost to the company totally.
5. If the CFA is operating as transporter also, he gives you the most economical transportation rates.

3.4.3 Decision on location of CFA (logistic interface)

Decision on location of CFA is again taken on the basis of saving cost that can be generated by appointing one or more CFAs in one state. The decisions are based on following points

1. **The volume of business:** If the volume of business is very high a company can appoint more than one CFA in same or different location
2. **Cost of transportation:** The business in various states can be divided in two or three hubs, from these hubs the transportation cost can be low as compared to transportation from single point, e.g., In Karnataka companies use Bengaluru and Hubli as two CFA points
3. **Time taken for transit:** If transit time from one place to other from one CFA point is high it defeats the purpose of appointing CFA, i.e., reduced response time. In such cases more than on CFA points are opened, e.g., in Uttar Pradesh Ghaziabad, Lucknow and Gorakhpur/Varanasi are chosen as CFA points

Example 3.2

For following details where will you appoint the CFA if the warehouse required is of 5000 0sft area?

Detail	*Sale in the area*	*Mumbai*	*Pune*	*Nagpur*
Warehouse rent p/sft ₹		75/-	20/ -	15/-
CFA charges p/c		12/-	8/-	6/-
To-Mumbai	4500	10	15	30
Pune	900	15	10	40
South Maharashtra	400	25	15	55
Konkan	200	25	30	60
Marathwada	400	30	30	30
North Maharashtra	750	20	30	40
Vidarbha	200	30	40	25
Nagpur	600	35	45	10
Gondiya/Bhandara	50	40	55	20
Total	**8000**			

Answer: We have to calculate the expenses at each place and decide the locations

Cost at Mumbai

1. Warehouse cost = area x rate = 5,000 x 75 = ₹ 3,75,000
2. CFA charge = sale x rate = 8,000 x 12 = ₹ 96,000
3. Transportation cost= area sale x cost

Mumbai	4500 x 10	₹ 45,000
Pune	900 x 15	₹ 13,500
South Maharashtra	400 x 25	₹ 10,000
Konkan	200 x 25	₹ 5,000
Marathwada	400 x 30	₹ 12,000
North Maharashtra	750 x 20	₹ 15,000
Vidarbha	200 x 30	₹ 6,000
Nagpur	600 x 35	₹ 21,000
Gondiya/Bhandara	50 x 40	₹ 2,000

Total-- ₹ 12,500

4. Grand total-----₹ 5,96,000/- PM

Cost at Pune

1. Warehouse cost = area x rate = 5,000 x 20 = ₹ 1,00,000
2. CFA charge = sale x rate = 8,000 x 8 = ₹ 64,000
3. Transportation cost= area sale x cost

Mumbai	4500 x 15	₹ 67,500
Pune	900 x 10	₹ 9,000
South Maharashtra	400 x 15	₹ 6,000
Konkan	200 x 30	₹ 6,000
Marathwada	400 x 30	₹ 12,000
North Maharashtra	750 x 30	₹ 22,500
Vidarbha	200 x 40	₹ 8,000
Nagpur	600 x 45	₹27,000
Gondiya/Bhandara	50 x 55	₹ 2,750

Total -- ₹ 1,60,750

4. Grand total ----- ₹ 3,24,750/- PM

Cost at Nagpur

1. Warehouse cost = area x rate = 5,000 x 15 = ₹ 75,000
2. CFA charge = sale x rate = 8,000 x 6 = ₹ 48,000
3. Transportation cost= area sale x cost

Mumbai	4500 x 30	₹ 135000
Pune	900 x 40	₹ 36000
South Maharashtra	400 x 55	₹ 22000
Konkan	200 x 60	₹ 12000
Marathwada	400 x 30	₹ 12000
North Maharashtra	750 x 40	₹ 30000
Vidarbha	200 x 25	₹ 5000
Nagpur	600 x 10	₹ 6000
Gondiya/Bhandara	50 x 20	₹ 1000

Total -- ₹ 2,59,000

Grand total ----- ₹ 3,82,000/- PM

Since the cost of CFA is lowest at Pune the CFA should be located at Pune

3.5 Selection and Appointment of Super Distributors

Many companies with product with low consumer loyalty and unable to sustain selling expenses as their products have not yet established in market prefer to appoint super distributors initially. Once the market is set and the brand is established they go in for CFA and distributor system. Companies can appoint any number of super distributors by demarking areas for them in a state. Super distributor appointment gives following advantage

- Super distributor pays for the stocks he is buying reducing inventory cost of the manufacturer
- Super distributor appoints own sales force reducing the cost of selling for manufacturer
- Super distributor appoints distributors and pays them commission from his earnings
- Super distributor spends on transport cost from his warehouse to distributor point
- If the product remains unsold the super distributor loses his money involved in it, so he ensures that the product does not remain unsold.
- Responsibility of transit damages in super distributor's warehouse and market returns is borne by super distributor
- Local level advertisements and promotions are done by super distributors

3.5.1 Qualities of good super distributor

A good super distributor will have following qualities

- All ready working as a super distributor for some other companies
- Have good warehousing facilities
- Have good infrastructure to handle super distributor working
- Should have good sales staff
- Should be financially very strong

3.6 Mother Depots and their Locations

An organization having manufacturing facilities at more than one location may require having a mother depot located centrally to service the markets without incurring high inventory costs for their slow moving products. Mother depot appointment is done in similar way as that of CFA.

3.7 Exercise

1. Visit any warehousing area near your town and visit any warehouse to see how the products are stored. Talk to the warehouse operator to find out how many different manufacturers are storing their products in the warehouse. Ask the warehouse operator how is he being compensated for the warehousing service he is providing.
2. Visit any transport office and find out how they accept goods for transportation. Ask the transport operator what are the rates charged for different locations and how he decides to charge that rates. Find out if he gives rate contract to various companies.

3. Check different newspapers/job portals for advertisements of recruitment of sales personnel and analyze the basic qualifications and experiences demanded by various companies.

3.8 Questions for Practise

1. You are a sales manager of a company that has planned a new range of products to be launched; you need to appoint around 20 sales officers under you at a time. What recruitment method will you use and why?
2. You are a sales officer of Indore which is growing with leaps and bounds, you have two distributors working for you in the city and you find that the sales are not increasing to your satisfaction as the distributors are unable to give proper service to new areas. What action you will take and why?
3. You want to appoint a new distributor what qualities will look for in the prospective distributors before you appoint them?
4. Draw a daily sales report for a pickle manufacturing company.
5. Prepare an expense statement for a sales person who does not travel out of his headquarters and works locally.
6. You want to appoint a CFA what qualities you will look in the prospective candidates?
7. You want to appoint a transport contractor what steps will to take to do so?
8. What is the difference between operations of CFA and a super distributor?

Case Study 3.1 Extending Distribution

Mr. Paranjape the regional manager of the western region was planning for the next year's sales volumes which were coming to be only 10% higher than the current years expected sales volumes. He was planning for higher positions in the company hierarchy and so he wanted to grow by at least 20% which was much ahead of the other regions expected growths. Since he believed firmly on the growth formula

MORE customers buying

MORE number of times

MORE quantity of products

He was looking for the distribution width and depth currently, he came to the conclusion that the depth of distribution at current level was good and there were not many gaps but the width could be definitely increased. He found that the current distribution was restricted to all towns above population strata of 50,000 and there were about 150 more towns that can be brought under coverage in the population range of 20,000 to 50,000. If all the 150 towns were brought under the coverage and all the towns could give ₹50, 000/- worth of business in the coming year he will be able to achieve 30% more business than the expected current year business.

Mr. Paranjape has called a regional review meeting on first of February and has asked all his ASMs to come with their next year plan, he wants to prepare a plan to ensure that the ASMs accept his plan for extension of distribution. Can you help Mr. Paranjape in doing that?

Case Study 3.2 Choice of Distributor

Avinash Khakkar was looking for appointment of new distributor for expected turnover of around ₹ 15 lakh in Panvel; he had shortlisted two parties with following details

	Mahaveer Agencies	*Gokuldas and Co*
Current turnover	₹ 25 Lakhs	₹20 lakh
Fixed deposits in the bank	₹ 5 lakh	₹20 lakh
Own funds invested in business	₹ 10 Lakh	₹20 lakh
Bank overdraft	₹.20 lakh	₹ 40 lakh
Godown	Rented, just the right size for current business	Owned and in excess of requirement
Office	Rented	owned
Residence	Rented	Owned
Delivery vehicle	On contract	Two three wheelers

Avinash has already promised Mahaveer agencies that he will ensure his appointment, but the ASM Mr. Dave has rejected the candidature of Mahaveer agency and has favored Gokuldas and company.

Do you accept the decision of ASM? Give reasons for your views either Yes or NO.

Case Study 3.3 Transfer of CFA Location

SKACO Company is operating its CFA from Vikhroli area in Mumbai with following details

Monthly average turnover Mumbai plus Maharashtra	12,000 cartons
Monthly average turnover Mumbai only	8,000 cartons
Average value of one carton	₹ 2000/-
Octroi paid for entire consignment	@ 7% of value
Octroi refund claimed per month for	4,000 cartons
CFA rate Mumbai	₹ 6 per carton
CFA rate Pune	₹ 3 per carton

SKACO regional manager Subbarayan wants to shift all its operations outside Mumbai as they are required to claim octroi refund for the consignments sent out of Mumbai and the refund comes only after 12 months from the date of claim. An octroi agent is required to be paid for doing process of stamping all the incoming consignments "for export out of Mumbai" without which the refund claim cannot be made when the stock is sent out of Mumbai. The octroi agent will do the loading and unloading operation at the octroi post for stamping/showing stamping of the incoming and outgoing consignment, the octroi agent charged 2% of the value of refund claim for the process.

CFA rates at Pune are at 50% of the Mumbai rates with transport cost ex-Mumbai and ex-Pune being same for rest of Maharashtra excluding Pune and Mumbai where the Mumbai to Mumbai, and Pune to Pune rates are ₹ 8/- carton and Pune to Mumbai and Mumbai to Pune rates are ₹ 20/-carton.

The ASM for Mumbai Mr.Punekar has suggested that a separate CFA be appointed for rest of Maharashtra in Pune and Mumbai CFA should only cover Mumbai area.

Whose decision do you agree with and why?

Case Study 3.4 Choice of Distribution Channel

"Super tasty" brand of condiments were planned to be launched and the sales manager Mr. Purandare was thinking of the possible distribution channel to be selected. He had following options

1. Appoint CFA-distributor-retailer channel with company ASMs and sales officers
2. Appoint Super-distributor-distributor-retailer channel with salesmen of super distributor

The difference two methods was as follows

In CFA – distributor with Company ASMs and sales officers the cost of sales team was coming to be 18-20% initially gradually coming down to around 10% in 3 years and around 7% in another 3 years depending on the acceptance of the products. If the product was not accepted entire product would come back to the company as the product will be sold on credit with all the expenses on sales team going down the drain. Since the condiment market is not brand loyal and very price sensitive, success was very difficult to come by. The advantage was that the sales team would be dedicated to one product range and will work hard to achieve targets.

In super distributor set up the cost of sales force could be negotiated between 2 to 5% with complete purchase by super distributor on advance demand draft, so product once sold will remain sold and no fear of return of goods. The sales team of super distributor will be selling product range of two or three companies and their concentration on "Super tasty" was doubtful.

Can you suggest the best method to Mr. Purandare with reasons behind it ?

CHAPTER 4

SALES MANAGEMENT – DIRECTING THE SALES EFFORTS

Learning Objectives:

- Directing sales staff—Various types of meetings – JCM/Monthly meeting, weekly meetings, field visit meeting, travelling meetings, telephonic meetings, internet meetings etc. Finding training needs, counseling the sales staff.
- Motivating sales staff – Theories of motivation and their practical use in sales management
- Directing channel partners – Distributor visits, physical verification of stocks, warehouse check, feedback about the sales officer, motivation of channel partner.

Part I - Directing Sales Staff

Directing sales staff is done through various means like sending memos, circulars but it is best done through various meetings. Meetings can be of following types:

- Journey cycle/Monthly meetings
- Weekly meetings
- Field visit meetings
- Travelling meetings
- Telephonic meetings
- Internet meetings

Let us look at them one by one in detail

4.1 Journey Cycle/Monthly Meetings

The word Journey cycle was used in case of travelling sales persons for many years. Earlier the organizations like Hindustan Lever (now called as Hindustan Unilever ltd.) used work in a four week journey cycle, i.e., a sales territory in-charge will start working from his headquartere town on first day of the four week cycle cover his entire area in the four weeks and report back to headquartere on the last day of four weeks to restart his next tour of his area in the fifth week. This way he used to visit his area thirteen times in a year. At the end of every four week journey cycle he will have one day meeting with his supervisor/area sales manager for submitting reports. Though the system has been long discontinued the name journey cycle is still being used as a sales person is currently finishing the visits to his area in a month so the journey cycle is now one month and not four weeks but it is still a journey cycle. Some organizations call it monthly meeting.

Journey cycle/monthly meetings are very important events in sales managers and sales officers working. This is an opportunity where the sales manager can give directions to his entire staff collectively about the company expectations and plans and can also reviews the performance of each and every sales officers which collectively becomes his own performance. He can take stock of happenings in the market place (his area of operation) and decide course of actions that will lead to achievement of his monthly and yearly targets. To make journey cycle/monthly meeting successful the sales manager should create a standard agenda for these meetings and ask his staff to come always prepared for the items on this standard agenda. The variable agenda can always be informed to everyone well in advance from time to time. (See Table 4.1)

Table. 4.1: Standard Agenda JC/Monthly Meeting

STANDARD AGENDA JC/MONTHLY MEETING
TO **Sales Officers Rest of Maharashtra** JCM for the month of March will be held on 28th March at RSO (Regional Sales Office). Meeting will start sharp at 9.00 AM, make your travel arrangements so as to reach RSO in time for the meeting. Following points will be discussed along with the standard agenda
Standard Agenda 1. Review of sales for the month of March 2. Targets for the month of April 3. Issues faced during the month by sales officers/distributors 4. Any other topic with the permission of ASM
Special points 1. Effectivity of promotions carried out during February-March period 2. Review of sales for quarter ending March 3. Plans for the quarter April-June

Since the meeting can get prolonged make your return arrangements for 29th March and not on 28th March.

Signed

Ivan De'souza

Area Manager

Cc: RSO for information and actions

It is very important for the sales manager to do his home work before the JCM starts. Ideally he should prepare charts/tables for the information he seeks to collect from the sales officers so that he will not forget to collect information and discuss on any particular issue during JCM. He should fill up all the information which is readily available with him through the accounts, dispatch departments and also from the previous records; this will give him more time to discuss the issues. Some examples are given below

Table. 4.2 JCM Primary/Secondary Review Format

Product/Pack(SKU-Stock Keeping Unit)

Name of Sales Officer	*This Month Secondary Sales*					*This year Secondary Sales April - to -*				
	Target	**Actual**	**% of target**	**Last Year**	**% Of Last year**	**Target**	**Actual**	**% of target**	**Last Year**	**% Of Last year**
Prakash										
Milind										
Ajit										
Kiran										
Vivek										
Total										

It is very important for a sales manager to ask for reasons for not only the drop in sales but also rise in sales. It is possible that the sales officer concerned is reporting false achievements by hiding the actual sales thereby increasing the pipeline stock (stocks in the distributors warehouse) pressures at the distributor end reducing his profit margins and so the ROI (returns on Investment). It is also possible that the sales officer may be running some promotions at his end unscrupulously (see Box 4.1)

Box 4.1 Raman's Magic in Vadodara

Raman's Magic in Vadodara

Raman was a sales officer working in south Gujarat territory. He was achieving unbelievably high sales in his territory. The area manager was very happy and was not suspicious about the achievements. Once area manager of Mumbai happened to be in Vadodara for his personal work, during this time he visited the Vadodara distributor as that distributor was appointed by this area manager earlier and was a friend. The Vadodara distributor complained to the Mumbai area manager that the credit notes are not getting settled in time and he was not understanding why the company suddenly started running various consumer and trade promotions the cost of which is to be adjusted through credit notes prepared for transit damages.

The area sales manager for Mumbai was shocked, though he did not show any reaction to the distributor and assured him that all the credit notes will be shortly settled. He had a discussion with the area sales manager (ASM) of Gujarat and asked him to stop the thing immediately. The Gujarat ASM was not ready to believe this first so he visited the entire south Gujarat territory and found that Raman was at this trick everywhere. Raman was not only achieving high sales for the company but also making money for himself on the side.

Raman was summarily dismissed from the services and it was a blemish on the Gujarat ASM's career and changed the company later to avoid repercussions on his career.

A sales manager is required to keep check on the stock pressures at distributor level, if the stock pressure at distributor level is high the distributors will not give primary (company to distributor) orders and the sales manager will fall short of his achievements in primary sales. A sales manager should keep pressure of secondary sales (distributor to retailer/Consumer) on the sales officers because the real sale. If secondary sale is good primary sale is automatically good. To check closing stocks, he can use following two formats

Table. 4.3: Closing Stocks in the Area (Pipeline Exercise)

Product/Pack (SKU)

Name of SO	*Opening stock*	*Receipts during the month*	*Total*	*Secondary sales*	*Closing stocks*	*Secondary sale Avg. of previous three months*	*Primary Target next month*
Prakash							
Milind							
Ajit							
Kiran							
Vivek							
Total							

The pipeline exercise format for the territory given below helps the sales officer plan his primary as well as secondary sales achievements equitably. In the organization which do not believe on taking orders from the distributors for making supplies and allocate the stocks (as a regular practice or during the shortages) this pipeline exercise becomes guideline to allocate stocks to various distributors according to their secondary sales achievements and equitable proportions.

Pipeline exercise helps the sales officer do range selling also as he is required to the exercise even for slow moving products/SKUs.

Pipeline exercise becomes a good record with the sales officer for tracking the stock movements and calculating ROI of the distributors.

Table. 4.4: Closing Stocks Sales Officer's Area (Pipeline Exercise)

Product/Pack (SKU)

Name of Distributor/ town	*Opening stock*	*Receipts during*	*Total*	*Secondary sales*	*Closing stocks*	*Secondary sale Avg. of previous three months*	*Primary Target next month the month*
Thane							
Dombivli							
Kalyan							
Ulhasnagar							
Ambernath							
Badalapur							
Neral							
Karjat							
Khopoli							
Pen							
Alibaug							
Panvel							
Navi Mumbai							
Bhivandi							
Shahapur							
Titwala							
Kasara							
Total							

These Tables will ensure that the sales officer is planning his sales properly and evenly at all the distributor points; the sales manager can take JCM as an opportunity to train the sales officers in planning activities.

JC Meetings should be used for building team spirit; the sales manager should encourage team members to help each other in achievements of their respective targets as the market conditions have their own compulsions and it becomes difficult sometimes to keep achieving all the targets of all the SKUs. In such conditions sales officers helping each other in achievements of respective targets helps the sales manager keep achieving his overall targets.

JC Meeting is also a time when sales manager can motivate his team members. Simple gestures are found to be very motivating, e.g.,

- Referring to sales officers as the kings of their respective territories, or your right and left hands
- Asking the team members to clap for the highest performance by any sales officer in any one SKU
- Congratulating team members for their individual achievement in the meeting
- Asking the highest performer to decide the lunch menu during the lunch break
- Ordering sweets or ice cream if the team has done well etc.
- Inviting senior manager in the meeting to congratulate the team or individual for their achievements.

JC Meeting is also the time when a sales manager can explain organizations new policies, plans and how they have to be implemented.

JC Meeting is the time when the tour itinerary of the sales officers is finalized. The guidelines for tour itinerary is the PJP (permanent journey program) which we already seen in Chapter Two, care should be taken that the sales officer is not doing back tracking and following the route set in the PJP.

JC Meeting is also the time when the sales officer can sort out his problems with the accounts department and sales manager should ensure that all these problems related to their expense statement reimbursements and salary related problems are sorted out. These problems are demotivators/hygiene factors and can lead to decreased performances.

Sales manager can arrange for some motivational presentations during the JC Meeting by self or by inviting some expert to do so. It is also a good idea to ask one of the sales officers to narrate some incidence that is interesting and useful as learning out of it with your own commentary for it. This motivates the narrator to a large extent.

Communication process in sales meetings

Communication process in all sales meetings is always two-way type. If the communication is one way the meeting is waste of time, energy and money. The one way communication can be sent on paper also.

How to make sales meetings meaningful and useful

To make sales meeting or for that matter any meeting successful, wholehearted participation by each participant is a must. Each and every participant should be awarded enough time to express his views and give facts and figures to substantiate his views. Each and every participant should listen carefully to other person's views and express his own views only with clear facts and figures. No one should be criticized without any reason. The leader of the meeting should be impartial and understanding. He should not behave authoritatively. To make the meeting more meaningful following precautions should be taken.

1. Date, time and venue of the meeting should be communicated to each participant well in advance for him to make his travel arrangements.
2. Agenda of the meeting should be circulated well in advance to participants to allow them time for preparation.
3. Method of presentation should be communicated well in advance so that everyone is prepared to make presentation using proper tools (OHP, slide projectors, CDs, pen drives etc.).
4. For gathering information in standardized format, the formats should be forwarded well in advance to bring the information in the format only.
5. Arrangement of night stay should be made if the meeting is going to take more than a day's time.
6. Place of meeting should have comfortable sitting, ventilating, air conditioning facilities with adequate toilets, etc., for convenience.
7. Drinking water, tea, coffee, snacks, lunch and dinner arrangements should be proper to avoid loss of time.
8. Flow of agenda should be properly adjusted to take up issues one by one
9. Time schedule should be strictly adhered to.
10. Personal matters should not be discussed in group meeting.

Handling sales personnel during the meeting

Some sales personnel may behave differently in a sales meeting creating problem of discipline. The leader of the meeting should not tolerate such behaviors and admonish the person strongly. The leader must remain the boss of the group and handle the meeting as planned and should not allow waste of time at any cost.

People with personal grievances or grievances against each other should be asked to discuss the matter separately at the end of the meeting, so that, time of other participants is not wasted.

4.2 Weekly Meetings

In large metropolitan cities the sales manager calls for a weekly meeting. Generally these meetings are held on first day of the week, i.e., Monday and the sales for the previous week are discussed. Since these meetings are held in the evenings after working in the field they are short and only held to take review of the sales so far and corrective actions required ensuring the target achievements at the end of the month.

The sales manager may ask the sales officers to keep coming one by one as they finish their field work and take review of their territories.

4.3 Field Visit Meetings

It is important for the sales managers to pay field visits to their sales officers to take firsthand knowledge of what is actually happening in the market place. It is observed that many sales officers rely upon their sales officers to give them market feedback and get cheated.

Field visit meetings are also beneficial for the sales manager for assessing the training need of the concerned sales officer.

Training needs development

(a) A Sales Manager will come to know about the training needs of a sales person only by observation. This is the prime reason why ASM works with Sales Officer. To find training needs of the subordinate the ASM should carry a format as illustrated in Table 4.5.

Table. 4.5: Training Needs Investigation

Training Needs Investigation

Name of Sales Officer ----------------- Date -------------------

Place --------------------------- Route -----------------

Sr. No.	*Call Procedure/ Remark*	*Good*	*Above Average*	*Average*	*Below Average*	*Needs Corrections*
		Pts. 50	40	30	20	Pts. 10
1.	**Planning and Preparation** (a) Day plan with targets (b) Stock check at distributor (c) Organizer up to date (d) Samples					
2.	**Approach** (a) Key men names known (b) Key men salutation proper (c) Waits for key men to become free (d) Key men relations good					
3	**Stock check** (a) Physical (b) As per key man (c) Not done					
4.	**Brand Talk**					
5.	**Objection handling**					
6.	**Close of call**					
7.	**Detail work**					

This format can be printed on a small pocket dairy size page and made into a pad for ease of carrying. The ASM can keep noting his observations while working with the Sales Officer ; and can discuss with him during the day or at the end of the day and give him tips to correct the procedure . When the ASM starts doing this regularly the Sales Officers make the calls properly first in front of him and then by habit in his absence also as they understand the benefits of the proper call procedure.

(b) Training needs can be in relation to relations with distributor and handling the matters at distributor place. Following things need to be observed by ASM.

1. Distributors stock checked physically or not.
2. Distributor stock verified with monthly report sent by distributor and the stock register.
3. Distributor payments checked or not.
4. The check clearance checked and verified with bank pass-book.
5. Stock levels high/average/low.
6. Reasons of stock levels being maintained at high/average/low levels.
7. Distributors interim coverage (in absence of company person) pattern checked and verified with norms.
8. Motivation of ISRs (Interim Sales Representatives appointed by distributor which may be or may not be subsidized by company and their reporting).
9. Claims position. How frequently are they settled?
10. Transportation problems if any.

In whatever are the Sales Officer is falling short of expectation ASM should give him training inputs to correct the situation.

(a) Training needs can be relation to report writing and submission. The ASM should give feedback on report quality and required) improvements.

(d) Training needs can be in relation with record keeping requirement for the sales achievement ASM can devise good format to maintained record of past achievements which are useful in planning process.

A Sales Manager will train his subordinates in call procedure and will ensure that they are following it religiously

4.3.1 Field visit FMCG product

For FMCG (fast moving consumer goods) the sales officer's call procedure is very important for achievement of sales targets. In FMCG the higher achievements in sales are generally through eating in to market share of competition and not by market expansion. If the call procedure of sales officer is right he will be able to put higher quantity per retailer that in turn pushes the products to consumers to gain profit by faster turnover of money. It is important to make sure that the sales officer understands the principle of high sales achievement which is as follows

More customers buying

More quantity of products

More number of times

The sales manager can correct the deficiencies in sales calls by observing the sales officer and should give him feedback and if necessary practical training of that point. (See Box 4.2). While doing the field work the sales manager should take break for tea/coffee and during the break give feedback to sales officer about his work and possible corrections.

Box 4.2 Training Needs for Prakash Deshpande

Training Needs for Prakash Deshpande

Prakash Deshpande started working in Aurangabad territory and sales of some routes started falling. ASM Sunil Apte was unable to understand why this was happening even Prakash was unable to explain the thing. ASM Sunil Apte decided to work with Prakash in one of these routes; while they were working together Sunil noticed that Prakash's body language was awkward while talking to the retailers and he was not properly checking the stock position and arranging display before taking the order. Since the route was sensitive, display and constant stock pressure only could give required sales volumes.

Sunil gave feedback to Prakash about it during the tea break they took; Prakash said that he was reluctant to do the stock check and display fearing that the retailers may say something to him. Sunil understood the problem, Prakash was tall, handsome, fair skinned person with a post graduated diploma in management and was actually shy to call himself a sales officer.

Sunil understood the problem properly and had counseling session with Prakash wherein he advised Prakash that as long as he worked as sales officer he must do his calls properly and achieve his targets. He also advised Prakash that "if a retailer says something and even abuses while doing the call the retailer is doing it to the company sales officer and not to Prakash Deshpande individually, so he should take it as a feedback from the retailer and pass it on to the higher authorities in form of report".

Sunil then did next three calls himself showing that the procedure is simple and results better. Prakash did well afterwards and then moved on to become sales manager in another equally good organization.

Field visit observations normally throw up sales officer's shortcomings in following area

- **Recognition of key person in retail shop:** A sales officer not recognizing the key person shows that he is not working the route regularly and so does not know the key person in the retail shop. Sales manager can take up this issue with the sales officer during the break and tell him in no uncertain terms that he will be watched and similar incident will not be tolerated again.

If the sales person does not know the key person it is advisable that he enquires about it and talks to the key person only, talking to people other than key person is waste of time because that person will not be in a position to take any decision about buying your products. Many times persons other than key persons just tell you "product does not sell enough or they do not want it as lot of stock is already there" both these answers are misleading and lead to call failure.

- **Recognizing the behavioral type of retailer:** Every retailer will have his behavioral type and needs to be tackled in that way to get the results. A sales manager should train the sales officer in recognizing these behavioral types and deal with them in proper style. Some of the behavioral types are given below

(a) **NO man:** says No to every thing

(b) **Know it All:** Knows everything and shows off

(c) **Friendly customer:** Behaves in very friendly manner

(d) **Frustrated fighter:** Fights with every one because his business is not doing well

(e) **Positive thinker:** Is very positive in outlook, understands business well

(f) **Indecisive:** Find taking decisions very difficult

(g) **Tough customer:** Bargains very hard and very difficult to please

(h) **Low reactor:** Not interested in anything

We have discussed the method of handling various types of customers in part -II of this book personal selling.

• **Physical stocks not being checked:** It is important for every sales person to check physically the stocks available at the retailer, this basically tells you how much order you can expect and if you want to sell more you can plan your brand talk accordingly. This also helps you save your time in arguing about the quantity you want to sell and the retailer is objecting. This also helps you win respect and trust of the retailer as he knows that you are not overselling or underselling to him.

• **Overselling:** By overselling the sales officer loses the trust and respect of the retailer and the retailer starts feeling that you are always trying to oversell and starts objecting to the quantity you are trying to sell every time. By overselling you also reduce your chance of getting order from the retailer next time and your call becomes unproductive. The retailer may get in to a habit of you going back without any order which is not good. One should put a habit in to all retailers that every time you visit you must get a good order.

• **Underselling:** Underselling is also a bad habit, underselling will lead to stock outs at the retailer point giving entry to the competition to grow and displace you.

• **Getting emotional while handling objections:** Sometimes the sales officers get emotional while handling objections to quantity or the display or the service being provided. The sales manager should train the sales officers to remain calm and listen to objections, it is possible that the objections are true and you may have to take them seriously and act upon them. Getting emotional does not help anyone; an emotional person cannot take rational decisions while under influence of emotions.

• **Giving false promises:** Giving false promises is like digging your own grave. It always pays to be honest and talk truth. One can boldly explain your own position on any issue, a sales person can always tell the retailer certain things are not possible as they will lead to loss to the organization and while he does not want any loss incurred by the retailer his prime duty is to protect the organization he is working for. This always increases the respect for him in the eyes of retailers, it is always said "the person who cheats his employer can cheat anyone".

• **Not arranging displays:** Arranging display ensure that your product gets sold it is said "visibility of products leads to sale" or in Hindi "Jo dikhta hai woh bikta hai". By ensuring that the product gets sold you ensure that you will get good order next time.

• **Not doing any friendly gestures:** It is important for a sales officer to create friendly atmosphere with the retailer, remember the retailer is facing various customers during the day and mostly none of them is friendly. If you show friendly gestures it helps you develop business and also avoid tensions during objection handling.

Field visit meetings are also used for doing counseling of the sales officers for his shortcomings. A good sales manager will always praise his juniors/subordinates in public and do counseling and reprimand sessions in isolation.

4.3.2 Field visit – Industrial products

In industrial products the sales manager looks at the sales officer's customer relations and the negotiation skills. If the industry is using distribution channel the sales manager can use the opportunity to discuss the potential of various customers in the area and steps required to be taken for increasing the numbers of customers and their order quantities in presence of the sales officer and can monitor the progress later.

The sales manager will also take this opportunity to find out the training needs of his sales officers.

4.3.3 Field visit – Service products

In services the sales manager observes the call procedure of the sales officer and gives him feedback for the same. Sales manager also looks for training needs of the sales officer and give him required suggestions. The field visit will also be used to find out specific needs of the customers and make changes in service delivery system.

4.4 Travel Meeting

Sales manager travels with his sales officer many times out of which some journeys can be for longer durations. This time the sales manager should use for familiarizing himself with the sales officer as a person and know about his family background, details of his family, his interests, ambitions etc. This helps him understand the personality and behavioral trends of the sales officer and thus, handle him and motivate him better.

Sales manager can talk to the sales officer about the distributors in his territory and their strong and weak points, which can give the sales manager the correct picture of the territory and its potential.

Sales manager can ask the sales officer to do his SWOT (strength, weakness, opportunities and threat) analysis and help him find the right path for his career growth. Discussing SWOT analysis of the sales officer gives the sales manager opportunity to give inputs in improvements of the sales officer and also opportunity to motivate him.

4.5 Telephone Meetings

Telephone meetings are basically for discussing urgent matters, care should be taken to avoid discussing unrelated matters before discussing the urgent matter for which you are calling the sales officer. Sales manager should decide the objective of the call before he dials the number and ensure that the objective is fulfilled. This helps in giving out a signal that you mean business and will not tolerate nonsense.

4.6 Internet Meeting

With advent of internet most of the sales persons have access to net and many possess laptops with them. One always gets connected online and chat on the internet. Chatting on internet is much cost effective as there is no additional cost involved in internet connection other than your fixed monthly outgo. Same principle applies to internet meeting as that of telephonic meeting of objectivity.

4.7 Memorandums (Memos)

Memos should be used as sparingly as in can be used; use of memo is only done when you want to make something official record for future use. One must follow all the rules of the classic communication while writing memos; they should be short, to the point and focused. For different subjects different memos should be written and subjects should not be clubbed together in one memo. Clubbing different subjects makes the issues lose their importance. Memos can be used as circulars by marking copies to other recipients.

4.8 Circulars

Circulars are used when you want to make the subject matter non personal. Circulars are always authentic official documents and give explanations and details of policy matters.

4.9 Motivating Sales Staff

Sales staff gets de-motivated for following reasons

- Monotony of work for sales staff working in one city
- Missing friend circle due to touring
- Missing family due to touring
- Not getting adjusted to outside food
- Low allowances forcing to stay at unhygienic places
- Low allowances forcing to eat at cheap joints
- Chances of getting promoted low
- Places to be visited not properly connected by rail/road transport service

A sales manager must keep track of the motivation level of his staff and must ensure that they are highly motivated. A sales manager should always remember that "MONEY" is not the answer to every problem, and one cannot satisfy the need for money ever. So to motivate the sales staff he should find non monetary benefit ways. To understand non monetary methods he must learn as many motivational theories as he can.

4.9.1 Herzberg's two factors/hygiene theory

Herzberg conducted various experiments in some manufacturing units and came up with findings that

1. There are motivators that keep the workers motivators in their job. These motivators can be job satisfaction, good group of workers, training opportunities, growth opportunities, good bosses etc.
2. There are demotivators that de-motivate the workforce. The demotivators commonly are no toilet facilities, no proper drinking water, dark place of working, improper ventilation, no canteen facilities, transport to and fro to working place not goods, long working hours, no holidays and leaves available etc.

Since the demotivators are mostly connected to individual hygiene the theory is also known as hygiene theory.

Herzberg says that as long as the demotivators are present the motivators cannot motivate the work force and if the demotivators are absent the work force remains motivated at varied degree of motivation.

This is very important theory for all the managers, by ensuring the absence of demotivators a sales manager can maintain motivation level of his staff and with motivational process can increase to higher and higher level.

Use of Herzberg's theory in sales management

A sales manager can remove the demotivators as follows

- Ensure that every sales person gets at least 6 to 8 days every month to be with his/her family
- Ensure that the night stay is planned in good towns
- Ensure that good transport service is available at places of visit.
- Ensure that sales staff does not travel for more than 3-4 hrs everyday
- Ensure that the staff has enough money to travel (many organizations give imprest float to their sales staff)
- Ensure that the expense statements are cleared on time
- Ensure that the sales staff is not required to visit disturbed areas where their life is in danger.

4.9.2 Maslow's need hierarchy theory

Maslow came out with a theory that every individual has certain strong needs at every stage of their life cycle (not related to life cycle), these needs can be arranged in to a hierarchy of needs with ascending order shown in Fig. 4.1 below. Maslow professes that a person keeps climbing the need ladder after satisfying each level.

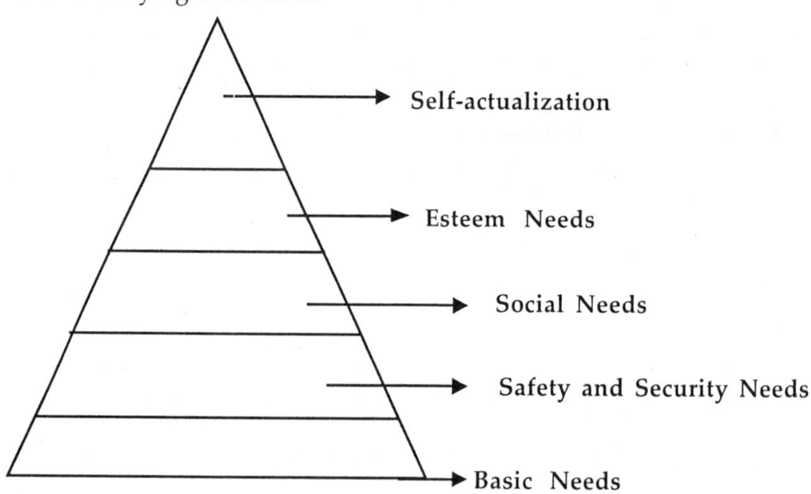

Fig 4.1 Maslow's Hierarchy of Needs

Maslow classified these needs in five distinct classes as follows:

Basic needs: these are basic requirements like food, clothes and shelter, a person whose these needs are not satisfied can do anything to satisfy these needs, e.g., to satisfy basic needs a person can beg, borrow or steal, sometimes even commit grievous crimes.

Safety and security needs: A person starts looking for safety and security after satisfying his basic needs. If the basic needs are not satisfied the person is not worried about the safety and security as he does not have anything to lose other than life which he thinks is worthless. Examples of safety and security needs are job guarantee, bank account, safe and strong house in better location, medical facilities etc.

Social needs: Once the person feels safe and secure he starts feeling the need for social contacts like friends, family members etc. A person whose safety and security needs are not satisfied does not care about family and friends, e.g., if someone is new in job and his job is not secure he will miss all family functions and friends gatherings.

Esteem needs: Once the safety and security needs are satisfied, a person gets in the level of satisfaction of esteem needs; examples of esteem needs are membership to organizations, higher and better titled job, expensive clothes, electronic gadgets at home, ownership of vehicles etc.

Self-actualization: Most people stay in the level of esteem need satisfaction as the expectations of esteem keep modifying and one keeps aspiring for higher and higher esteem. When a person reaches the highest esteem level in his/her mind and is satisfied with material needs satisfaction, the person seeks spiritual or inner self-satisfaction and starts concentrating on various hobbies that he/she might have neglected while trying to satisfy social and esteem needs.

Use of Maslow's hierarchy of needs in sales management

A sales manager can use Maslow's hierarchy of needs in motivating his staff very effectively, for that the sales manager must know following about the sales officers

(i) Family background

(ii) Number of people in the family and earning members in the family

(iii) Place of stay and size of house

(iv) What he/she aspires to be

Once the sales manager have these details he can decide at what level of satisfaction is the sales officer is currently and provide him/her with need satisfiers in that level, e.g.,

- If the sales staff is in safety and security level one can assure him/her that the job is safe till the time you work hard enough to get the results
- If the sales staff is in social needs level ensure that he/she gets leave of absence whenever there is an important family function or social gathering. Sales manager can arrange get-together of staff and families or a picnic for staff and family.
- If the sales staff is in esteem need the sales manager can arrange star sales officer contest and give tags or ties bearing "STARS" and give special treatment to achiever of STAR status. The stars can start from one can become five with "Five Star" sales person getting higher allowances and chance to get promoted faster.

- Esteem needs can be satisfied by various other methods like allowing stay in three/four star accommodation while on tour, allowing travel by First A/c in railway or allowing to fly by air etc.

4.9.3 Motivating through leadership styles

Leadership style has direct impact on motivation level of the sales staff, following leadership styles are common

- **Autocratic leader:** Autocratic leadership style is the oldest style of leadership, in this type the leader thinks that his knowledge is supreme and he knows everything that is required to be known and so he never takes anyone in confidence and decides all the plans himself and forces everyone to follow him without any questions. This type of leadership is not accepted by all the literate people and not advisable in sales management.

- **Democratic leader:** Democratic leader takes opinion of all his staff in most of the decision making, if the leader is highly respected for his achievements and knowledge he is able to control his subordinates in democratic style. In sales management a combination of autocratic and democratic leadership (democracy up to a level after that "boss is right") works well.

- **Fatherly leader:** In this style the leader is known to be and accepted to be the "Mr. Right" and everyone looks to him for advice as to what should be done to avoid any mistakes. This type of leader does not get angry with the subordinates but explains the reasons for the mistakes committed and tells how to avoid them next time. His motto "a person who works makes mistakes, but same mistake should not be repeated". This type of leader does not like people who repeat the mistakes and takes punitive action against them. In sales management if one can adapt this position his staff will always be highly motivated.

- **Free rein leader:** In this style the leader gives tasks to all his subordinates and allows them to do what they want, failures are punished severely but successes may not be immediately rewarded. This type of leadership is not good for sales management.

Part II - Directing the Channel Partners

Directing channel partners (distributors, clearing and forwarding agents, CFAs and transporters) is also very important part of sales manager's duty. Inefficient channel partners can lead to low sales achievements. Let us look at the directions to be given to the channel partners in detail.

4.10 Directing Distributors: Distributors Need to be Directed in Following Matters

- **Coverage of the area of operation:** Distributor gives interim coverage to all the retailers in absence of company sales officers. Many companies insist on appointment of exclusive interim/distributor's sales representatives (ISRs/DSRs) by the distributors. Sales manager should give proper directions as how he wants the interim coverage to be given, i.e., at what frequency and through what route plans. These directions must be given in presence of sales officers who can then monitor the performance of the ISRs.

  Some organizations organize selling skills training for the ISRs which help generate high sales volumes continuously and maintain high market STRs (stock turnover ratio). The trained ISRs can also keep watch on competitive activity and send periodic reports.

- **Timely delivery of orders taken:** If the distributor is not operating ready delivery (salesman travels with the van loaded with products and delivers the orders immediately) then the distributor should be advised to deliver the orders taken within twenty-four hours. This ensures that the retailers do not face "OUT OF STOCK" position and customers do not shift to competition.

- **Minimum stock holding at the warehouse:** The distributor should be made to hold a minimum inventory of fifteen days at his warehouse for all the SKUs of the company; this ensures that no orders go without supplies.

- **Stacking of the products at the warehouse:** Many times it is found that the distributors do not stack the cartons holding the products properly; this leads to breakages/damages to fragile packaging. If the stacking is not proper maintaining FIFO (First in first out) becomes difficult and some products may reach their expiry without getting sold.

- **Replacements of products from retailers:** Replacing products at retailer's place which need replacements as per the company policy should be done by the distributor immediately; if it is not done the retailers become unhappy unnecessarily which affects the product sale.

- **Maintenance and reporting of routine information:** The distributor should be trained to maintain sales records properly, which may include daily sales records, stocks and sale register etc. You may also ask him to send the weekly/monthly sales records to the company office on a fixed date. Nowadays with advent of internet it has become easy and the distributors can be given formats which they can e-mail to you regularly.

- **Giving feedback on competitive activity:** Distributor should collect information on competition through their ISRs and keep giving feedback to you on it.

- **Advising distributor on good and safe business practices:** Sales manager should advise the distributors on goods and safe business practices like not to accept checks at the distributor point and insist on cash only (see Box 4.3), not to trust anyone while dispatching goods from warehouse or receiving the accounts of the delivery of goods (see Box), not to keep more than one bill pending with any retailer, etc., these safe practices helps avoid bad debts to the distributors.

Box 4.3 The Bombay Sales Agency Story

The Bombay Sales Agency Story

Bombay Sales Agency (BSA) was a distributor in Santacruz west in Mumbai and was dealing in HMM Ltd. (Horlicks, Boost etc.), Ahmad Omar Mills (Postman oil), HMT bulbs and tubes etc. He had a practice of distributing stocks on a weekly basis and the routes were fixed. If any retailer faces out of stock situation during the week they could give telephonic order which will be supplied within two days or the distributor should send someone to collect the goods if urgently required. Goods supplied at the counter needed to be paid immediately but at the retailers place the BSA people even gave credit and took a signed bill copy as receipt. Retailers sent their helpers with signed checks to BSA with orders for urgent requirements.

One day a person from large retailer came with a blank check and asked BSA to supply a large quantity of Postman oil and gave the check against the bill. Next day when the check was banked it was returned by the bankers saying there was a stop payment order by the retailer. When enquired it was found that the person who came to purchase Postman had left the job and had stolen signed checks from the drawer of the retailer, so the retailer had requested bank to stop payments for stolen checks and lodged Police complaint but had not informed any of the distributors about it. BSA lost the amount unnecessarily.

This can happen anywhere and all the distributors should take care for it.

Giving all these directions always helps the sales manager to create better relationship with the distributors and helps in motivating them. If possible one can also give them suggestions to improve their ROI by advising them on their warehousing and distribution set ups.

Box 4.4 The DD Shah Story

The DD Shah Story

DD Shah was distributor in Ghatkopar east in Mumbai dealing with HMM ltd. (Horlicks, Boost), Glaxo (Farex, Nycil), Godrej (Key detergent) and Balsara (Promise tooth paste, Odopic). His office was on Ghatkopar Mahul Road and he had two warehouses, one behind his office and second at Vidyavihar. For HMM Ltd., the system was ready delivery and so the stocks used to be loaded at warehouse office, but for all the other products it was next day delivery. DD Shah had no help from his family as his daughter was going to school and sometimes his sister used to come and relieve him for any urgent work.

DD shah had some delivery men who were working with him for many years and he trusted them. In those days Nycil sandal used to be always in short supply and wholesalers were ready to pay premium on it. DD Shah had ordered a large quantity and was keeping it in his Vidyavihar warehouse for opportunity to cash on the demand when it peaks. He used to send his tempo driver to Vidyavihar warehouse with a stock withdrawal slip to remove stock from there and seldom used to go and check it himself.

When he finally got an order from a wholesaler to supply three hundred cartons of Nycil at a good premium (his stock holding according to stock register was five hundred cartons) he called a bigger vehicle and went to the Vidyavihar warehouse he was shocked to see only two hundred cartons there. It was then found that his delivery men used to take out four to five extra cartons and keep them nearby with a saloon owner. These cartons were then sold and money distributed amongst them.

Similar stories have been happening in many places and many distributors have gone bankrupt.

CASE Study 4.1 The Case of R.V. Raman

R.V. Raman was recruited by ABC Company from another company on the basis of his earlier experience of 3 years in that company. The Regional Sales Manager S. Thiruvenkat put him in the territory directly under Mr. Dinesh Valavalkar without giving any induction or field training. ABC Company was professional company and had proper call procedures in use. Top brass of ABC Company always insisted that the sales force follow the proper sales call procedure. Mr. Dinesh insisted on proper induction and field training of Raman before putting him in the area ; but the request was turned down by the RSM who was transferred to sales from marketing department (as he was a failure there) to Sales department. The RSM felt that the sales procedures are very easy and anyone can follow them and the marketing department is the most important department which can bring success without even having a sales department (Sales Department had made strong protests against sales promotion devised by Thiruvenkat which was biggest flop).

During the second month of Raman's service in ABC Co., the Sales Director and Managing Director decided to visit the market in Raman's area. (The town was tourist attraction and the directors had come for some conference). During the market visit, the Sales Director pointed the call procedure mistakes of Raman to Dinesh and questioned why he is not aware of the call procedure. Dinesh said he was not formally trained. The RSM Thiru blamed Dinesh for improper training and assured the Sales Director that Raman will be trained properly before he is confirmed in the services.

The RSM placed Raman under another Area Manager Deshpande where he was given training for a month. Raman was found to be average person but he picked up the procedures and was confirmed in the services and started giving good results. RSM Thiru-Venkat then concluded that sales procedures from one company to another are different and the induction and field training is very important even to experienced new recruits as it makes lot of difference in the results.

Case Study 4.2 The Case of Ram Krishnan

Ram Krishnan was recruited by SBM Foods in 1988 and was posted in Kolhapur. Ram Krishnan had previous experience of 4 years and he had left the earlier job due to his family problems (his grandmother was hospitalized due to terminal illness and he was not given leave to visit her and stay besides her in her last days). Ram Krishnan was appointed on recommendation of Subbarayan who was Sales Admin. Manager, Ram Krishnan had not submitted his experience certificate and had no copy of resignation letter showing acceptance by previous company.

Within short period Ram Krishnan started giving good results and high sales volumes were generated. Mr. Subbarayan started showing-off about how he has brought a STAR Salesman to the company. The area Sales Manager B. Bhaskar was also praising Ram Krishnan and even recommended his early confirmation with higher salary raise. Mr. Bhaskar and Ram Krishnan had become very close friends in short span of period.

Mr. Kulkarni who was a devotee of Goddess Mahalaxmi of Kolhapur went to Kolhapur when there was a holiday on one Saturday to enjoy his long weekend (he took leave for Friday) and pray to Goddess Mahalaxmi. As usual, he enquired about the sales of SMB products in Kolhapur. He found that the Sales booming due to various promotions being operated by the company in Kolhapur. Mr. Kulkarni was surprised as their company was not in habit of promoting the products. To collect details of the promotions and show them to his ASM Mr. Mahadeokar, he went to the local distributor and asked for the information. Mr. Kulkarni knew the distributor well as he had worked this area earlier. The information received by him was shocking. Ram Krishnan was operating the promotions not only in Kolhapur but also in Sangli and Ratnagiri. The funds were generated through false claims and partly used for promotions; remaining part was shared by Ram Krishnan, Bhaskar and Subbarayan. The distributors were keeping quite as their turnover had gone up.

Mr. Kulkarni come back to Mumbai and handed over the details with Xeroxes of claims to his superior Mahadeokar. Mahadeokar in turn, informed RSM Mr. Malhotra. The RSM questioned both Subbarayan and Bhaskar about the information. Both Subbarayan and Bhaskar claimed that Mahadeokar was jealous of their achievements and as Shiv Sena sympathizer was anti South Indian (Shiv Sena is a political party fighting for sons of soil policy in Mumbai) so he was creating story which is not true.

Mr. Malhotra went into the claims register in detail and analyzed the claims against:

(a) Previous claims of same area.

(b) Claims of other areas in same period and concluding that the claims were really high and so summoned the various distributors to Regional Office. The distributors spilled all the beans leading to ouster of Ram Krishnan and Bhaskar. Subbarayan was admonished but was not punished as the link could not be proved. Mr. Malhotra decided not to recruit any one without checking with earlier company as it so turned out that Ramakrishna was sacked from the earlier company for fraud.

Case Study 4.3 Case of Subhash Patil

Subhash Patil joined RHS Ltd., from a small company. His salary doubled after joining RHS Ltd. The only problem was, he was now required to work a larger area and was on tour for almost 10 to 15 days a month. Subhash Patil's wife had completed studies for BA externally. (Subhash and Asha got married before completing their studies). It was a love marriage and Asha had now secured admission for B.Ed. Course in SNDT University. The first year went well. Mr. Agavekar the ASM was very happy as Subhash Patil had increased the sales volumes in short time and was having very good distributor and retailer relations.

In the second year the situation changed. Subhash Patil's area started showing drop in sales regularly. Mr. Agavekar thought that after high growths in earlier year the market was stablising at actual potential and the sale will show upward trend or stable sale. But, it was not so, the sale kept on declining Mr. Agavekar made a trip to Subhash Patil's area along with him. All the distributors and retailers were all praise to Subhash Patil. Mr.Agavekar did not understand the reasons. He started analyzing Subhash Patil's sale town wise and he found the reason. Subhash Patil's HQ town was not showing any drop at all, only the town where he was required to stay and work for 3-4 days were showing drop. The problem was in these towns, which he could not find while visiting them with Subhash Patil.

Mr. Agavekar decided to give surprise check to Subhash Patil's area (upcountry towns). All the towns he contacted where he was supposed to find Subhash Patil working he could not contact Subhash Patil. The distributors said he was there on earlier date and has revised his tour program to be with his ailing daughter. Mr. Agavekar said he was trying to contact Mr. Subhash Patil for the same reason and there was no other tour itinerary and no deviation was reported. Mr. Agavekar did not confront him about it and decided to investigate further.

Next month he made surprised visit to Subhash Patil's area and on not finding him where he was supposed to be, confronted the distributors. The information he got was shocking. Subhash Patil had requested distributors help as he was not able to spend enough time with his sick daughter and was actually spending only one day or half a day with them instead of 3 to 4 days he was required to spend with them. After getting this information Mr. Agavekar went to Ashok Patil's HQ town and visited his home to enquire about his daughter's health and advise Ashok Patil to request readjustment of territory instead of false reporting. At his home, he could not find Subhash Patil. Asha, his wife, told him a strange story, Ashok was suspecting his wife to be unfaithful and as having affair with her professor at SNDT college. So, he was returning from tour but was staying in a garage owned by his friend and spying on his wife. As the suspicion was ill placed he was unable to catch them together.

In next JCM Mr. Agavekar confronted Subhash Patil about his false reporting and low sales and advised him to correct himself or leave the job Subhash Patil left the job and started his own business which did not require touring.

Case Study 4.4 Case of Ulhas Salvi

After rearrangements of routes and visiting days Ulhas Salvi started to report low sales in Bazaar road, Chapel road Bandra (W) route. He was unable to reason why the sales volume was dropping when most of the retailers were buying good amount of stock. Mr. Purandare his ASM asked him to do analysis on retailer to retailer basis and get back to him. The analysis showed that Al Acsa bakery and stores and Karachiwala department stores had not purchased any stock during his visit and had purchased stocks by ordering for it over the telephone from the distributor.

Mr. Purandare asked Mr. Ulhas Salvi why was this happening and Ulhas said that when he reached the shops the key men were found to be absent every time. Actually, it was his normal practice to reach these shops by 1230 to 1 O'clock and spend enough time with these retailers as they were the super 'A' class outlets. Mr. Purandare asked Ulhas to check the problems and report back.

Next week Ulhas came to office happy as he had found the reason and the solution for his problem. With rearrangement of working the area was being visited on Friday instead of Wednesday as earlier. On Friday's both these key men of Al Axsa bakery and Karachiwala dept. Stores went for afternoon NAMAZ and were not available. Ulhas changed his visiting pattern and started visiting these shops before noon to avoid the problem.

Case Study 4.5 The Case of Nilesh Working Ready Stock Operation

Nilesh used work his territory on order booking earlier, when he started working with ready stock he found that one of his routes, *viz.*, Sakinaka started showing decline in sales. When he did the situation analysis he found that the STRs in the route have dropped steadily from 40 days earlier to 10 days now. He was alarmed and tried to find reasons for the same but was unable to do so; he approached his ASM Mr. Vasishtha for help, who agreed to do so.

Mr. Vasishtha visited the route on the day and as was his habit he started walking the route from the reverse direction talking to various retailers before he met Nilesh. On his way he found that a vehicle carrying HUL products was making deliveries to all the retailers and collecting cash from them.

When he met Nilesh he asked whether he was aware of the fact that HUL van moves ahead of him on the route, Nilesh said yes but it cannot be the reason as it was happening earlier also. Mr. Vasishtha asked Nilesh can he change the day of visit to that area one day prior to or one day later of the current weekly visit day. Nilesh's answer was negative as that would affect his working in the other routes; Mr. Vasishtha asked Nilesh if he could reach the route earlier than HUL vehicle, the answer was again negative as the HUL had a distributor in nearby area and Nilesh's distributor was five kms., away.

Mr. Vasishtha told Nilesh to start working the route from the reverse direction and the sales were restored. The reason for drop in sales was very simple the HUL salesman was taking the cash away from the retailers before Nilesh reached so they reduced their purchases to bare minimum

4.11 Exercise

1. Meet any sales person and ask him about the meetings he/she is required to attend and the meetings frequency. Try and find out what the purpose of various meetings is and what preparations are required to be done.
2. Observe the behaviour of the shopkeepers with the salesmen present in their shops, and also observe how the sales person handles the shopkeeper.
3. Observe the behaviour of the shopkeeper when he/she is receiving goods from a distributor.

4.12 Questions for Practise

1. What are the different types of meetings held by a sales manager?
2. What is the standard agenda of a JC meeting?
3. What are the different purposes of field visits by a FMCG sales manager?
4. What are the different purposes of field visit by industrial sales manager?
5. What are the different purposes of field visit by a services sales manager?
6. What are the different methods of directing the sales staff?
7. "It is important for the sales manager to discuss the sales and working of sales officer with the distributor in presence and in absence of the sales officer", do you agree with the statement? Explain why you agree or disagree with the statement.
8. "Sales manager should always make field visits", do you agree with the statement? Explain why you agree or disagree with the statement.
9. Explain following terms (a) Back checking, (b) Physical verification of stocks, (c) Primary, secondary sales and consumer off-take
10. "Training needs development and is an important part of sales manager's responsibility", do you agree with the statement? Explain why you agree or disagree with the statement.

CHAPTER 5 SALES MANAGEMENT – CONTROLLING THE SALES EFFORTS

Evaluating Sales Force Performance through Performance Measurement, and Controlling Sales Activities (Sales Records and Reporting Systems), Improving Sales Productivity Diagnosis and Corrective Actions

Controlling is the most important activity in sales management, this can be done very easily if the planning is done faultlessly and the directions about the plan have been given to the sales staff properly through monitoring the activities of the sales officers and the distributors. In this chapter we will look into the monitoring the activates of the sales officers through the control documents we have already discussed in earlier chapters.

5.1 Evaluating Performance of Sales Officers

Control is normally done through measuring and monitoring performance of sales officers in different areas which point out his overall performance. While monitoring the performance in these areas the sales manager can also give the sales officers feedback on their performance and direct them towards better performance. Some sales manager only tell their sales officer that their performance is not up to the expectations but unless the sales manager tells the sales officer what is going wrong and how it can be improved. Controlling sales officers is done on following areas for FMCG sales officers

5.1.1 Working everyday

Sales manager must ensure that all his sales officers are working every day. It is a major problem in many organizations more so in organizations that pay their salesmen/officers low salaries and allowances that they do not work every day (see Box 5.1). To ensure that every sales person is working every day the sales manager should do surprise checks on the sales officers by visiting the route they are supposed be working or supposed to have worked without alerting the sales manager, if it is found that the sales officer is not working regularly he should be caught red handed and severe punishment must be meted to the sales officer and should be made known to all others so that they are prevented from doing the same (see Box 5.2).

Box 5.1 Checking of Sales Officers

Arun Gandhi worked Gujarat territory came out with an idea to save trouble of travelling and still earn salary and allowance. He started sending reply paid post cards to all his distributors and asking them to inform the closing of the day and the order to be supplied to them in the month. On the basis of these closing stocks he used make false reports (daily calls report and stocks and sales) of market working in those towns and send them to the company along with order forms which were pre stamped and signed by the distributors when Arun Gandhi used to visit once in three four months. Arun Gandhi also started a retail shop in his home town to augment his income and spend his spare time.

Arun Gandhi was caught doing this by his sales manager in surprise check and was dismissed from service

Box 5.2 Checking Sales Officers

Mr. Suresh Abhyankar while working with one his clients suspected that the sales officers were not working regularly, so he asked the clients sales manager to arrange market working with the sales officers. The very first sales officer they worked was found to be avoiding some retailers and was found not visiting them, so Mr. Abhyankar made that sales officer visit some of these shops avoided by him. The sales officer who was supposed to be visiting these retailers every week was not recognizing the key persons of the retailers and the retailers were asking him which company he represents.

When questioned it was found that the sales officer was running a van for school going students and would visit few main retailers everyday and submit false reports based on the distributors, sales. The sales officer was dismissed from service.

5.1.2 Working at places as per plan

Many sales officers are found to be working at any route at will and send false report of working as per plan. This problem can also be controlled by surprise check.

5.1.3 Number of calls made

Every organization has a policy for the sales officers that they should make a minimum number of calls per day. Now when the organization says that sales officer should make so many minimum calls per day they expect it to be on an average but sales officers are found to be making that many calls at maximum and do less call wherever the calls available are less than the stipulated number. The sales manager should insist that if they do less calls on any particular day they should make extra call some other day to reach the required average. The average number of calls made can be found by following formula

Total number of calls made during the month/number of working days = average number of calls made

5.1.4 Productivity per call

A sales officer should ask his sales officers to meet productivity benchmark again on an average. The productivity can be benchmarked at anywhere above 60% of calls made. Productivity can be calculated by following formula

(Total number of orders collected/number of calls made) x 100 = percentage productivity

5.1.5 Range selling

Every organization has many products, some are selling fast and some of them are selling at a slow pace. Since it is easy to get orders for fast moving products the sales officer takes orders for these products and move on. This will not give any chance to these slow moving provides many of which may be newly launched one to grow and establish. Every company should ensure that they have more than one fast moving product that can keep earning good profits for the company.

To ensure that the sales officers do range selling, the sales manager should insist on the sales officers that they achieve minimum productivity level for every product. The benchmark for every product can be decided differently depending on the market opportunity and company targets.

Sales manager should direct his sales officers that they sell difficult/slow moving first and fast moving products at the end of each call. This will help the sales officers achieve range selling objectives

5.1.6 Business per call

Sales manager should insist on a minimum average business generated per call in rupee value, this will ensure that the sales officers are not underselling to achieve required productivity level every time. Business per call can be fixed in various ways some of them can be as follows

Based on the average business per call achieved by the best sales officer: In this method the benchmark for business to be achieved can be set at 80% of the average business in rupee value achieved by the best sales officer and all the other sales officers are asked to achieve the same level; the bench mark can be raised subsequently higher and higher. E.g., if the best sales officer books orders valued at rupees ten lakh and make 40 calls everyday with 25 working days in a month the average business per call can be arrived at as follows

10,000,00/40 x 25= ₹ 1,000

Based on the territory target: In this method the monthly volume target is converted in rupee value and this value is divided by the average number of calls made by the sales officer in a month; this value can then become minimum business to be achieved per call where the entire sale is supposed to be achieved by the sales officer. In case the sale is not achieved by the sales officer alone a percentage of this value can be fixed for the sales officer as a benchmark. E.g., if the volume target per month is 10,000 unit and the product value is ₹ 100 and the sales officer makes 40 calls per day for 25 working days a month the business per call can be arrived at as follows

10,000 x 100/40 x 25 = ₹ 1,000

In case the sales officer is working only thirty per cent of the total time required to cover the entire area and rest of the time the market is covered by the interim sales representative (ISRs) the sales officers per call average business will be 1,000 x 30% = ₹ 300

5.1.7 Achievement of targets

Achievement of target can become a major performance measure of the sales officer, care should be taken that the targets are based on proper market opportunity assessment and should not be overambitious or less than the opportunity. A SMART target is the best way to judge the performance of every sales officer where SMART means

S - Stretchable

M - Measurable

A - Achievable

R - Ratable

T - Time bound

If a sales officer is achieving sales more than the previous year but falls short of achieving target, the sales manager should first check that there is no mistake in setting the target and then should pull up the sales officer for not achieving target.

5.1.8 Punctuality in sending reports

The sales officers must send their reports in time to the sales office; this can be done by issuing circular to that effect saying that the reports if posted should reach office on fourth day from the date of report and if e-mailed should reach next day. This way the sales manager reduces the chances of false reporting and also increases the chances of making mistakes if there is false reporting. A false report made in haste always leads to mistakes which can be easily detected on scrutiny.

The sales officers should not get the opportunity to say "why push us to send reports in time when nobody reads them", a simple method is to read reports of every sales officer randomly and send comments on those reports to him. This way everyone feels that you are reading all the reports and all the borderline cases of false reporting are stopped. If sales manager has doubt about anyone's report then sales manager should investigate that sales officer thoroughly till the time doubt is gone or the sales officer is caught making a mistake.

One way of making sales officers send their reports in time is to stop payment of expense statements if the reports have not reached.

5.1.9 Cost consciousness

Cost consciousness has to be imbibed in all the sales personnel, most of sales persons think that what happens if I spend some money when company is spending so much on many unnecessary things. This attitude of sales officers is mostly due to lack of perception about the company's intentions behind spending. Best way is to start using budgetary controls on everyone.

In budgetary control every sales officer is given financial budget on every expense head and asked to remain in the limit, one can give awards for getting good results without crossing the budgetary limits. These budgets can be monthly basis leading to annual budgets. It is found that when budgetary control is started sales officers try and spend less and try to win accolades from the seniors. Sales manager must declare results on budgetary control every month in the JC Meeting and congratulate sales officers for their budgetary control.

Cost Analysis: Cost analysis is partly controlling activity and partly activity for future planning. Following types of cost analysis and sales analysis are done.

1 Cost to sale analysis.

2 Cost of call and sale per call analysis.

3 Transport cost to sales analysis.

Let us look at all the types individually.

Cost to Sale Analysis: This type of analysis will give the effectivity of the sales person. The cost of the sale will include:

(1) Allowances (2) Conveyance (3) Travelling cost.

The analysis will be $\frac{\text{Sales Revenue}}{\text{Sales Cost}}$ = Sales per rupee cost.

The cost can be compared with standard performance to take corrective action. Table 5.1 will illustrate the same

Table. 5.1: Cost to Sales Analysis

Name of Sales Person	*Kolhatkar*	*Dhore*	*Sapkal*	*Phadke*	*Total*
Sales Turnover	1.50 lakh	2. 25	3.20	1.80	8.75 lakh
Expenses					
Allowance	1500	1500	2000	2000	7000
Conveyance	600	600	600	600	2400
Travel Cost	400	400	1000	1000	2800
Total Expenses	**₹ 2500**	**2500**	**3600**	**3600**	**12,200**
$\frac{\text{Sales Turnover}}{\text{Total Cost}}$	$\frac{1.50 \text{ lakh}}{2500}$	$\frac{2.25 \text{ lakh}}{2500}$	$\frac{3.20 \text{ lakh}}{3600}$	$\frac{3.20 \text{ lakh}}{3600}$	$\frac{8.75 \text{ lakh}}{12,200}$
= Sale per rupee cost	60	90	89	50	72

Dhore and Sapkal have done well (if standard is set at 80) and Phadke and Kolhatkar have performed badly. A look in there working is on card. The performance standards can be set differently for different sales personnel depending on the territory being covered. It is possible that Phadke is covering difficult terrain (cost of travel is high) with low sales potential. In such case standard for Phadke can be set even for 50. In case of Kolhatkar the terrain is easy and performance is low. The Sales Manager must investigate the working of Kolhatkar.

Cost of call and sales per call analysis

Cost of call is calculated on the basis of sales expenses to number of calls. Table. 5.2 will illustrate the same.

Table. 5.2: Cost Per Call Analysis

Name of Sales Person	*Kolhatkar*	*Dhore*	*Sapkal*	*Phadke*	*Total*
Sales Expenses	2500	2500	3600	3600	12,200
Number of call made during the month	750	1000	1200	1200	4150
$\frac{\text{Sales Turnover}}{\text{Number of calls}}$	$\frac{2500}{750}$	$\frac{2500}{1000}$	$\frac{3600}{1200}$	$\frac{3600}{1200}$	$\frac{12,200}{4150}$
Cost per call	= 3.33	= 2.50	= 3.00	= 3.00	= 2.92

Kolhatkar's cost per call is also higher than others.

Sale per call will give other aspect of the performance of sales person. Table 5.3 will illustrate the same.

Table. 5.3: Sales Achieved Per Call

Name of Sales Person	*Kolhatkar*	*Dhore*	*Sapkal*	*Phadke*	*Total*
Sales Turnover	1.50 lakh	2.25 lakh	3.20 lakh	1.80 lakh	8.75 lakh
Number of Sales made	750	1000	1200	1200	4150
$\frac{\text{Sales Turnover}}{\text{Number of calls made}}$	$\frac{1.50\text{ lakh}}{750}$	$\frac{2.50\text{ lakh}}{1000}$	$\frac{3.50\text{ lakh}}{1200}$	$\frac{1.80\text{ lakh}}{1200}$	$\frac{8.75\text{ lakh}}{4150}$
= Sales per call	= ₹ 200	= ₹ 225	= ₹ 267	= ₹ 150	= ₹ 211

All these analysis will give the Sales Manager, the performances of the sales personnel. If the compensations are linked to performance, the low performers will be paid less. If the compensation is not linked to performance the Sales Manager must take action against non-performers.

Cost Reduction Exercises

A Sales Manager can reduce the cost of selling in the following ways without reducing the sales staff.

1. Reduction in allowances paid.
2. Reduction in conveyance paid.
3. Reduction in travel cost.
4. Reduction in transport cost.
5. Reduction in warehousing cost.

Let us look at all of them one by one to understand them clearly.

Reduction in Allowances Paid

As discussed earlier the Sales Personnel are paid allowances in three ways:

1. HQ allowance
2. Ex. HQ allowance
3. Night away allowance

Care should be taken to reduce the number of days a sales person is paid Ex. HQ or night away allowance. Let us see Case 5.4 to understand the situation.

Example of Reduction in travel cost and allowances in Shri Balaji Foods, Bengaluru:

A Sales Manager of Shri Balaji Foods, Bengaluru Mr. Venugopal was facing problem of excessive selling expenditure and was being asked to reduce the selling cost continuously by the Superior Manager. He had sales staff located as follows:

1. Bengaluru - 3 Sales Reps.
2. Mangalore - 1 Sales Reps.
3. Hubli - 1 Sales Reps.

With following area demarcation as shown in Table 5.4

Table. 5.4: PJP Summary of Karnataka Sales Person

Sr. No.	*Parthsarthi*	*Days*	*Venkatesh*	*Days*	*Bhaskar*	*Days*	*Kamath*	*Days*	*Deshpa-nde*	*Days*
1	Bengaluru HQ	12	Bengaluru HQ	21	Bengaluru HQ	6	Manga-lore HQ	14 1	Hubli HQ	6
2	Bangarpett	1/2	Chinta-mani	1	Mandya	3	Karakal	2	Dharwad	2
3	KGF	1/2	Chikman-glur	1	Chanap-atna	2	Udipi	1	Dandeli	1/2
4	Tumkar	2			Mysore	1	Bhatkal	3	Yellapur	1/2
5	Tiptur	1/3				1/2	Chikm-anglur	3	Karwar	2
6	Ariskere	1/3	Gauribi-dnur	1	Manjan-gud	1	Hassan		Kumta	1/3
7	Bhadravati	1/3			Chamra-jnagar	1/2			Sirsi	1/3
8	Shimoga	1			Gundul-pet	1			Haveri	1/3
9	Chitradurga	1			Vijaypet				Belgaum	5
10	Davangere	1			Krishna-rajpet	1			Gadag	1/2
11	Harihar	1/3			Madikai	1			Bijapur	1
12	Bellary	2							Wadi	1/2
13	Hospet	1							Gulburga	2
14	Sindhnur	1/3							Bidar	1
	Tip		1/2 day = AJC one day,					1/3 day = QJC one day		

The expense bill of Kamat and Venkatesh was lowest with maximum HQ allowance. The expense bill of Parthsarthi was higher than Kamat and Venkatesh with 12 days spend outside Bengaluru he did 7 days night away and 5 days Ex. HQ for towns in Bangalore district like Tumkur, Tiptur, Arsikere, Bhadravati, Bangarpett and KGF the highest bill was Bhaskar and Deshpande who spend maximum time away from their families and the Sales Manager Venugopal sympathesised with them. He was unable to find how the sales expenditure could be curbed . He was unable to find how the sales expenditure could be curbed. He went to his General Manager Mr. Karandikar for help. Mr. Karandikar gave him the following tips.

1. A sales person should spend maximum time in his HQ.
2. A sales person should not travel in same direction twice.
3. For ex-towns the total travel time should not exceed 4 hrs. to and fro.
4. A sales person should not spend more than required time in any place.

When Venugopal looked at the expenses travel plans of each person. He found the following:

Table. 5.5: Expenditure Analysis of Parthsarathi

Name of the Sales person - Parthasarathi

Name of Sales Person	*Town visited*	*Days*	*Freq.*	*Travel Time hours*	*Amount spent*	*HQ @ ₹ 60/- @ ₹ 90/-*	*Ex. HQ All*	*Night allow ance @ 15 p/-*	*Total*	*Total*
Parth-sarathi	Bengaluru	12	Ejc	-	-	720	-	-	720	720
	Bangarpet	1	Ajc	2	40	-	90	-	130	65
	KGF	1	Ajc	3	60	-	90	-	150	75
	Tumkur	2	Ejc	5	200	-	180	-	380	380
	Tiptur	1	Qjc	7	240	-	90	-	330	110
	Ariskere	1	Qjc	8	260	-	-	-	350	117
	Bhadravati	1	Qjc	2	340	-	-	150	180	60
	Shimoga	1	Ejc	5	150	-	-	150	300	30
	Chitradurg	1	Ejc	2	50	-		150	200	200
	Davangeri	1	Ejc	1	30	-	-	150	180	180
	Harihar	1	Qjc	2	60	-	-	150	210	70
	Bellari	2	Ejc	6	150	-	-	300	450	450
	Sindnur	1	Qjc	3	60	-	-	150	210	70
	Siriguppa	2	Qjc	3	60	-	-	150	210	70
	Return to Bengaluru			Over Night	250	-	-	-	250	250
					1360	720	540	1200	1260	3117

As per the rules:

1. Suggested by Mr. Karandikar Parthsarthi was spending maximum time at HQ. As per 2 and 3 Parthsarthi's visit to Tumkur, Tiptur, Arsikere were objectionable, as he was traveling the same route 5 times in same direction and the travel time was exceeding 4 hours every time. By Correcting the plan following saving was achieved.

Table. 5.6 : Expenditure Saving of Parthsarthi

Correcting the plan following saving was achieved.

Town	*Days*	*Freq.*	*Travel Time hours*	*Amt spent ₹*	*HQ allo-wance @ ₹ 60/-*	*Ex. HQ allo-wance @ ₹ 90/-*	*Night allo-wance @ 150 p/day*	*Total*	*Effective*	*Saving*
Tumker	2	Ejc	21/2	100	-	-	300	400	400	(20)
Tiptur	1	Qjc	1	30	-	-	150	180	60	50
Arsikere	1	Qjc	1	30	-	-	150	180	60	57
Shimoga	1	Ejc	1	30	-	-	150	180	180	120
Total				**190**	**-**	**-**	**750**	**940**	**700**	**207**

Table. 5.7: Expenditure Analysis of Venkatesh

Name - Venkatesh:

Town	*Days*	*Freq.*	*Travel Time*	*Amt spent ₹*	*HQ @ allo-wance ₹ 60/-*	*Ex. HQ allo-wance @ 90/-*	*Night allo-wance @ ₹ 150/- p/day*	*Total*	*Expenditure*
Benga-luru	2	Ejc	-	-	1260	-	-	1260	1260
Chinta-mani	1	Ejc	3	60	-	90	-	150	150
Chikm-anglur	1	Ejc	3	60	-	90	-	150	120
Gaurib-idnur	1	Ejc	4	80	-	90	-	170	180
Total				**200**	**1,260**	**270**	**-**	**1,730**	**1,730**

No rule was being violated in case of Mr. Venkatesh.

Table. 5.8: Expenditure Analysis of Bhaskar

Name - Bhaskar

Town	*Days*	*Freq.*	*Travel Time*	*Amt spent ₹*	*HQ Allow @60/-*	*Ex. HQ Allow. @ ₹ 90/-*	*Night Allow. @ ₹ 150/-*	*Total*	*Effective Total*
Bengaluru	6	Ejc	-	-	360	-	-	360	360
Mandya	3	Ejc	5	450	-	270	-	420	420
Chanapattan	2	Ejc	5	300	-	180	-	480	480
Mysore	8	Ejc	4	130	-	-	1200	1330	1330
Nanjaangud	1	Ajc	3	60	-	-	150	210	103
Gundulput	1	Ejc	3	60	-	-	150	210	210
Virajpet	1	Ajc	4	80	-	-	150	230	115
Krishnaraj-peth	1	Ejc	5	150	-	-	150	300	300
Madikeri	2	Ejc	3	120	-	-	300	420	420
Return to Bengaluru	1	Ejc	5	150	-	-	150	300	300
			4	130	-	-		130	130
				1,500	**360**	**450**	**2,250**	**4,390**	**4,170**

Following rules were broken

Rule No. 1: HQ should be Mysore instead of Bengaluru.

Rule No. 2: Travel in same direction was done more number of times in case of Mandya and Chanapatna.

Rule No. 3: Ex-towns travel time was more than 4 hours in case of Mandya (5 times), Chanapatna (5 times), Virajpet Ex- Mysore (5 times), Madikeri Ex- Mysore (5 times).

By correcting the deficiencies the saving achieved was as illustrated in Table 5.9.

Table. 5.9: Effective Saving Bhaskar Area

Town	*Days*	*Freq.*	*Travel Time*	*Amt spent ₹*	*HQ allow. @ ₹ 60/-*	*Ex. HQ allow. @ ₹ 90/-*	*Night allow. @ ₹ 150 p/day*	*Total*	*Effective Total*	*Saving*
Bengaluru	6	Ejc	4	130	-	-	900	130	130	470
Mandya	3	Ejc	2	120	-	270	-	390	390	30
Chanapatan	2	Ejc	3	120	-	180	-	300	300	180
Mysore	8	Ejc	3	120	480	-	-	480	480	850
Nanjangud	1	Ajc	3	60	-	90	-	150	75	30
Gundulpe	1	Ajc	4	80	-	90	-	170	85	30
Chamrajnagar	1	Ejc	3	60	-	90	-	150	150	60
Virajpet	1	Ejc	12/2	75	-	-	150	225	225	75
Madikeri	1	Ejc	11/3	60	-	-	150	210	210	90
Krishnarajpet	2	Ejc		120		180	-	300	300	120
Return to Bengaluru				130	-	-	-	130	130	-
Return from Madikeri			75	-	-	-	75	75	175	
Total				**1030**	**480**	**900**	**1200**	**3610**	**3450**	**720**

Analysis of Kamath area and Deshpande area did not show any breaking of rule; so no saving was achieved. So total saving Sales Manager Venugopal could achieved was ₹ 207 + ₹ 720 = ₹ 927/- per month which worked to be ₹ 11,124/- per annum; which was an substantial saving for Mr. Venugopal.

Exercise 5.1

1. A Sales Manager has the following area with 5 Sales Representatives working under him. He wants to prepare PJP for them with all of them having Pune as HQ. All the 5 must work at least 4 days outside Pune city and total no. of working days in field should not exceed 24 days a month. All the routes in all the towns must be visited at least once in two months. All routes with average monthly sale of ₹ 20,000/- per month should be given one full day every month. All routes with ₹ 40,000/- as average monthly turnover should be visited twice a month and all routes above ₹ 80,000/- as average monthly turnover should be visited every week. The details are as shown in the Table 5.10 and solution in Table 5.11

Table 5.10: Details of Sales

Town/City	*Number of routes*	*Average monthly turnover of the routes*	*Town/City*	*Number of routes*	*Average monthly turnover of the routes*
Pune	10	80000	Baramati	1	10,000
Pune	26	40,000	Nagar	4	10,000
Pune	6	20,000	Junnar	1	10,000
Satara	2	20,000	Lonavala	1	10,000
Karad	2	10,000	Chiplun	1	10,000
Sanglli	2	20,000	Kankavali	2	10,000
Sangli	2	10,000	Kudal	2	10,000
Kolhapur	4	20,000	Sawant	2	10,000
Solapur	2	20,000	Wadi		
Solapur	4	10,000	Ratnagiri	2	10,000

Table. 5.11 Total Number Days Available = 24 × 5 = 120 days

Solution: Total number of days required can be calculated as in Table 5.12

Town/ City	*Number of returns*	*Days per month*	*Total days*	*Town City*	*Number of returns*	*Days per month*	*Total/ days*
Pune	10	4	40	Baramati	1	½	½
(Alternate							month)
Pune	26	2	52				
Pune	6	1	6	Nagar	4	½	2
Satara	2	1	2	Junner	1	½	½
(Alternate							month)
Karad	2	½	1				
Sangli	2	2	4	Lonavala	1	½	½
Sangli	2	½	1	Chiplun	1	½	½
Kolhapur	4	1	4	Kankavali	2	½	1
Solapur	2	1	2	Kudal	2	½	1
Solapur	4	½	2	Sawantwadi	2	½	1
				Ratnagiri	2	½	1
				Total			**120**

Since days required in Pune are 98 it can be allocated as 20 days to 4 Sales Representatives and 18 days to 5th Sales Representative and other towns will be allocated to complete 24 days per month as shown in Table 5.12.

Table 5.12: PJP Summary

1	2	3	4	5
Pune 20 days Satara 2days Karad 1day Baramati ½ day Junnar ½ day	Pune 20 days Sanghvi 3 days Lonavala ½ days Chiplun ½ days	Pune 20 days Kolhapur 4 days	Pune 20 days Kankavati 1 day Kudal 1 day Sawatandi 1 day Ratnagiri 1 day	Pune 18 days Nagar 2 days Solapur 4 days
Total 24 days	**24 days**	**24 days**	**24 days**	**24 days**

Tip Baramati, Junnar, Lonavala and Chiplun should be visited alternatively.

Exercise 5.2

In a territory of Salesman he has the following towns with number of days required for coverage as follows:

Narayanpur 5 days Rampur 6 days Lakanpur 1 day

Kishanpur 2 days Sitapur 1 day Janakpur 3 days

Lavnagar 4 days Kushinagar 2 days

Allowances are as follows:

HQ - ₹ 60/- per day

Ex HQ - ₹ 90/- per day.

Night allowance - ₹ 180/- per day.

Travelling time between Narayanpur and Rampur, Narayanpur and Lavnagar and Rampur and Lavnagar is 8 hours. All other towns are nearer to Lavnagar and it requires 2 hours travel, e.g., Lavnagar. The entire Salesman stays at Lavnagar and covers these towns. Currently Salesman'S Head Quartered is at Rampur. The Sales Manager is doing cost saving exercise. Suggest way to save expenses to Sales Manager without making any change in current rates of bus fare and allowances.

Solution

Cost of travelling and allowances currently is

Table. 5.13: Current Cost of Travelling and Allowances

	Bus fare	*Allowance*	*Total*
Rampur to Narayanpur	40 + 40 = 80	5 x 180 = 900	980
Rampur to Lavnagar	40 + 40 = 80	4 x 180 = 720	800
Rampur to Lakhanpur	10 + 10 = 20	1 x 180 = 180	200
Rampur to Krishanpur	10 + 10 = 20	2 x 80 = 540	560
Rampur to Sitapur	10 + 10 = 20	2 x 180 = 360	380
Rampur to Janakpur	10 + 10 = 20	1 x 180	200

Rampur to Krishn-nagar	10 + 10 = 20	2 x 180	380
Rampur to Rampur	------		
		Total	**3500**

The cost will not change by relocating HQ to Narayanpur as the traveling and the allowance will go up (Narayanpur requires one day less than Rampur). The relocation to Lavnagar will have difference as follows:

Table 5.14: Cost of Travelling and Allowances after Savings

	Bus fare	*Allowance*	*Total*
Rampur to Narayanpur	40 + 40 = 80	5 × 180 = 900	980
Rampur to Lavnagar	--------	4 × 80 = 240	240
Rampur to Lakhanpur	10 + 10 = 20	1 × 90 = 90	110
Rampur to Krishanpur	10 + 10 = 20	2 × 90 = 180	200
Rampur to Sitapur	10 + 10 = 20	1 × 90 = 90	110
Rampur to Janakpur	10 + 10 = 20	3 × 90 = 270	290
Rampur to Krishnnagar	10 + 10 = 20	2 × 90 = 180	200
Rampur to Rampur	40 + 40 = 80	6 × 180 = 1080	1160
		Total	**3290**

5.1.10 Display levels in the area

Display is major concern of sales manager, good product displays in most of the retail outlets always helps growth in sales volumes. With new generation of retail shops, the retailers are reluctant to use of POP (point of purchase) materials in their shops as it destroys the glaze of furniture. A good sales officer can always get good display for his products through good customer relationship.

A good display is always at eye level of consumer and should be visible while entering the shop and should also be visible from outside the shop. Many consumers purchase many products on impulse and good display induces impulse purchases. Good display also works as reminder to the consumer and he/she does not forget to purchase the product that is visible.

5.1.11 Growth in retail universe

As said earlier the sales volumes of any products can grow only when "MORE customers buy MORE quantity MORE number of times" to ensure that more customers get more opportunity to buy your product more number of times the products must be made available at more and more retail shops. Retail universe of any product is the number of retailers selling that product in a given area.

Sales manager must do the exercise of recording details of each and every retail shop in each area and compare this list of retailers with the previous year record to find whether the retail universe is growing or shrinking. The sales manager will note that if the retail universe is not growing the sales do not grow substantially, if the retail universe is shrinking the sales volumes will fall and if the retail universe is growing the sales volumes will show good growths.

5.1.12 STRs in the markets

STR (stock turnover ratio) is indicative of the stock pressure of any product in the market place. Ideally the STRs in the market should be one and half times (1.5 times) the frequency of coverage. STR is always in number of days, it can be calculated as follows

Total quantity of product available in the market (route)/average sale of the market for a month = STR days

Total quantity in the market/route is available from the daily sales report (DSR) of the sales officer and average sale can be calculated on the basis of average orders received from the market/ route.

If the STRs are high the competition never gets chance to enter the market in a big way and the product shortage is never felt by the consumer.

5.1.13 Control on distributors

Sales officer must have good control over the distributors in his area of operation and should be able to get many activities done through without spending any additional cost to it.

Control on distributor is directly proportionate to the ROI (returns on investment) the distributor is generating from your business. ROI is dependent on the amount of paid stock held by distributor, the amount of outstanding payments with the retailers and the expenses incurred in distribution of the products. All these elements can be controlled by the sales officer with proper planning. To understand this properly we must learn to calculate the ROI. As said earlier ROI means returns on investments which can be denoted mathematically as follows

(R/I) x 100= ROI where

Some people call ROI as ROCE i.e. Return on capital employed

Whatever you call it is one and the same.

Returns = Gross earnings less gross expenditure

Gross earnings = Total turnover × margin + earnings from other sources (incentive, interest on deposit etc)

Gross expenditure = all expenditures on business (interest on borrowed capital not to be included)

Investment = Money blocked in paid stock + market out standings + security deposit paid

Investment in warehouse, vans etc is not included if rent on it is included in expenditure.

Once we understand the elements of ROI, we can now know that

The ROI will go up if the --- Turnover is high

--- Margins are high

--- Investment is low

--- Expenditure is low

A sales manager can control the three elements except the margin by increasing the sales volumes Reducing the paid stock (giving supply more number of times, or giving credit),

Reducing the market outstanding (increased frequency of coverage, and not giving credit), Reducing the expenditure (subsidizing market coverage, delivery cost etc.).

Some manufacturers even go further to guaranteeing a fixed ROI by giving credit note for the shortfall.

Example 5.1

Maganlal Damjee is covering part of Mumbai. His monthly turnover is ₹ 6 lakh

He has following monthly expenses

1. Office rent ---------------------------------- ₹ 1,000/
2. Warehouse rent------------------------------- ₹ 500/
3. Office staff----------------------------------- ₹ 2,000/
4. Office expenses---------------------------- ₹ 1,500/
5. Salesman----------------------------------- ₹ 1,500/
6. Delivery man ---------------------------- ₹ 1,000/
7. Van charges ------------------------------ ₹ 1,500/
8. Discounts and incentives --------------- ₹ 2,500/

If the paid stock is 20 days and market outstanding is 10 days and margin is 5% what is his ROI

Solution

If we total the expenditure it is ₹ 11,500/

The gross earnings are ₹ 6 lakh × 5% = ₹ 30,000/

So earnings = (30,000 – 11,500) × 12 = 2,22,000 PA

Investment is 20 days paid stock = ₹ 4 lakh (6 lakh for 30 days is 4 lakh for 20 days) + 10 days market out standings ₹ 2 lakh = ₹ 6 lakh

ROI = R/I= (2,22,000/6,00,000) × 100=37%

Example 5.2

In above example if the turnover is₹ 3 lakh what will be the ROI.? Will any distributor agree to work for the company? What measures can you suggest to increase ROI to 36%+

Solution

The earnings will be (15,000 – 11,500) × 12 = 42,000

Investment will be ₹ 3 lakh

ROI = (42,000/3,00,000) × 100= 14%

No distributor will agree to work at this ROI

Any one of following measures can be taken to increase ROI to 36%+

1. Increase margin to 10% (gross earnings becomes 2,22,000)
2. Give 20 day credit (Investment becomes 10days i.e. ₹ 1 lakh)
3. Subsidize the cost of salesman, delivery man, discounts and incentives and rent of warehouse (expenses reduced by ₹ 7,000/)
4. Give guarantee of 36% ROI and give credit note for the shortfall

5.1.14 Claims analysis

Claims analysis should be done by the sales manager regularly as many sales officers have this habit of preparing false claims for benefit of distributors and retailers. Many sales managers and sales officers think that by making false claims for benefit of the distributors or retailers they are not leading any losses to their company as insurance pays for it, but it is wrong the insurance companies immediately increase the insurance premiums next year for getting compensated for their losses.

5.1.15 Relationship with major customers

It is very important for a sales officer to have good relations with the major customers in the market. Law of 80:20 is applicable in the business and it is observed that 20% of the customers give you 80% of the business and if the relations with these 20% customers are good a sales officer secures his 80% business and achieving 100% target becomes easy for him.

5.1.16 Team spirit

Every sales person is individualistic and does not like any interference in his work, but for the sales manager to achieve his targets he needs consorted efforts of his team and so he must build team spirit within the team. Some sales managers play one sales officer against the other which may give them short-term benefits but in the long run it is harmful. One should encourage healthy competition within the team but must show team spirit also.

5.1.17 Relationship with colleagues

The competitive spirit amongst the sales officers should not lead to enmity that can harm the team spirit and harm collective interest of the team and the sales manager. The sales manager must take care that the competition does not lead to infighting.

5.2 Performance Appraisal of Sales Officers

Performance appraisal means telling/informing or appraising the performance of someone to him/her objectively. Since performance appraisal is informing a person about his/her performance it cannot be done without the full knowledge of that person, some manager fill up performance appraisal forms themselves (after taking signatures of the subordinates on blank forms) and send it to the higher authorities for further action. Performance appraisal is the best way to have control on the sales officers and keep them motivated by giving inputs on their shortcomings and opportunities for development. But performance appraisal can be dangerous if the sales officers are not receptive and are biased against the sales managers; in such case they can take the criticism wrongly and start behaving in frustrated manner (see Box).

Procedure for performance appraisal (objective-based)

MOST of the companies in both Indian and MNC sector have started giving importance to performance appraisal. It is a key management tool for monitoring, controlling and improving the performances of the subordinates. It also helps in preparing second line of managers for future use.

Box 5.3 Ravikumar's Frustration

Ravikumar's frustration (performance appraisal)

Ravikumar was working in the company SKACO, his sales achievements were much below expectations. His sales manager Mr. Vasishtha checked on to his working and found following

1. He submitted false reports many times,
2. He reached market late (He was fond of Gym. So he reached the market at noon after doing workouts in Gym.)
3. Many routes were never covered by him

During the annual performance appraisal these issues were pointed out to Ravikumar by Mr. Vasishtha and was informed that unless he improves his behaviour he will never get promoted and his career path will be blocked. Ravikumar talked with Mr. Venkat (sales admin. Manager) and Mr. Mohan (regional accounts manager) both were jealous of Mr. Vasishtha who was a Maharashtrian. They (all three Tamilian) planned a scheme against Mr.Vasishtha and sent a unsigned letter to Mr. Ghosh who was Bengali saying Mr. Vasishtha is communal and is purposefully denying right full promotions to non Maharashtrians, they also falsely reported some derogatory remarks about Mr. Ghosh as uttered by Mr. Vasishtha.

Mr. Vasishtha who was due for next grade promotion making him senior to Mr. Venkat and Mr. Mohan lost it that year

Performance appraisals if not done systematically can lead to lot of frustrations, grumbling, reduction in performance levels and high turnover of manpower. What are the common mistakes done by the appraisers?

5.2.1. The appraisal is based on the performance of 2 - 3 months preceding the appraisal

This is a common mistake found in all the companies. The appraiser makes his decision on the performance of previous 2-3 months only. The high performances during the first half or three-fourth of the year go unrewarded. So we see efficiency levels going up during the appraisal period in most of the companies the subordinates suddenly become more obedient and subservient. They are ready to do anything and spend lot of extra hours without any compensation for it. But, you cannot blame the people for understanding the wrong method being adopted by the Manager in appraisal them with a short memory period. They are at a liberty to take full advantage of situation; it is for the appraiser to correct his mistake.

5.2.2. Appraisal based on personal bias

This is another common mistake. The appraiser prepares the appraisal based on his personal impressions about the subordinates and not on the hard facts. Since, he is not discussing the appraisals with the subordinates, they never come to know what is happening and why they are left out everytime.

The appraiser is neglecting a fact and possibility that his impressions are based on his encounters with the subordinates on very few occasions and that too many a times not in work situation. This writer knows some incidences where a very good salesman lost his chance of getting higher increment because he did not wish the manager properly in the men's room during the appraisal period, and many such reasons. The manager must give the subordinates fair chance of proving themselves.

5.2.3. Appraisals based on hearsay

Sometimes the appraisals are based on the opinions expressed by others about someone you are appraising. This is totally unfair. The people who are passing the judgment may not be qualified to do so. It is also possible that they have their own grudges and scores to settle.

After looking into common - mistakes let us look into methods followed for appraisals

1. Actual achievements *vis-a-vis* previous year.
2. Profits generated during the year by every subordinate in absolute terms
3. Growth in percentage terms achieved by every subordinate.
4. Appraisal against set standards decided at beginning of the year.

Since the method based on standards set at the beginning of the year has no inherent flaws and gives equal opportunity to every individual we recommend the same. This method has following steps.

(a) Setting objectives at beginning of the year: At the beginning of the year you must choose 5 - 6 common parameters against which you wish to appraise the performance of your subordinates. The parameters can be any of the following:

(i) Achievement of set targets

(ii) Adherence to budgeted expenditure.

(iii) Sending reports on time as decided.

(iv) Personal appearance and grooming.

(v) Behavior with the colleagues.

(vi) Behavior with the distributors.

(vii) Behavior with the retailers.

(viii) Behavior with the distributor sales staff.

(ix) Punctuality in work

(x) Planning and preparation for the work

(xi) Enthusiasm

(xii) Merchandising and display standards

(xiii) Increase in retail universe

(xiv) Development of new markets, etc.

Give weightages to each parameter and fix performance standards at say POOR, FAIR, GOOD, VERY GOOD, EXCELLENT etc., levels. Discuss these parameters and performance levels and their respective weightages with your subordinates and take their acceptance to all the parameters.

(b) Self-assessment by the subordinate: At least a month before the appraisal interview sends blank formats of appraisal (see Annexure) to all the subordinates for self-assessment. Inform the subordinates that the performance interview will be held on so and so date at so and so place, at so and so time and the subordinate should come prepare with his self-assessment and supporting documents/facts to prove his point view. This gives them time for preparation so that the discussions at the time of performance interview becomes meaningful.

(c) Fixing appraisal interview: It is very important that appraisal interview is fixed well in advance. If possible it should be fixed in some neutral area with absolutely no tension of work load. The atmosphere should be free, possibly a secluded restaurant where you can have lunch/ breakfast without much disturbance and talk with each other without interruptions.

Advise the subordinate to talk freely as this is very important opportunity he has which is available once in a year and he should not waste it. Also advice him that in case he could not prove his point , your opinion prevails. There should not be any heated discussions and loosing temper will go against the subordinate, with this background start showing him your view and ask him to prove his point if he does not agree to your view-point and not *vice versa.* You can on your own give him the facts on the basis of which you have made your views and opinion. To help you do that keeping a diary of events both good as well as bad for each member of your team throughout the year proves very useful.

After the interview is over it is advisable to take the subordinates signature on the points as accepted.

(d) Discussion on appraisal with your superior: It is very important to have discussions with your superior on the appraisals you have made. Your report along with the appraisal forms may not be accepted by your superior, so it is better to have personal discussions on this important issue. It is advisable that you show the appraisals to your superior before holding appraisal interview so that you can take your superior approval before you commit yourself in front of your subordinate. You can also get his views about your subordinates which will be helpful for future planning.

If the appraisals are carried out in this manner there is very little room for disagreements and ill-feelings. The shortcomings pointed out about the subordinate can very well be termed as training needs and a plan can be made to act upon it.

ANNEXURE – 17

Table. 5.15: Appraisal Format

FORM OF PERFORMANCE APPRAISAL (SPECIMEN)

(To be submitted in duplicate at the time of appraisal interview)

Objectives:

(To be decided and agreed upon at start of appraisal period)

Standard objectives **Your rating for self** **Agreed rating**

(i) To achieve agreed sales targets

(ii) To achieve agreed reporting standards

(iii) To achieve agreed retailing standards

(iv) To achieve agreed merchandising standards

(v) To achieve budget adherence levels

Special Individual objectives:

(i) To improve distribution in Pune

(ii) To appoint distributors in all district/taluka places

(iii) To increase retail universe by 20%

RATING CAN BE IN PERCENTAGE OF SET STANDARD OR ON FIVE POINT RATING SCALE

(AGREED ACTION POINTS)

S. NO.	*Point for action*	*By whom*	*By date*

NAME OF APPRAISEE : ....SIGNATURE................

DESIGNATION : ....

H.Q. : ....

DATA OF INTERVIEW : ....

CONDUCTED BY : ....SIGNATURE................

DESIGNATION : ....

5.3 Counseling of Sales Officers

When a sales manager finds that the sales officers under him are under performing or not following rules and regulations the first thing he has to do is to confront the person with list of irregularities found in his/her work. Many times it is found that the person concerned is to doing the mistakes out of ignorance, in such cases a mere warning to improve is sufficient to effect changes in behaviour and performance. Sometimes the sales manager may be required to give training inputs to the erring sales officers so that the understanding of the procedural aspects is clarified.

If the erring sales officers is found to be doing the mistakes with purpose there can be three reasons for it

(a) He/she has some personal problems which are hampering the work or

(b) He/she is unhappy about the work conditions/career prospects

(c) He/she is doing it due to attitudinal problems

In all the above cases the sales manager should give the sales officer a chance to improve, so he should find out the reasons behind the erroneous behaviour and take appropriate action against it. The fact finding exercise for erroneous behaviour and suggesting the remedy to improve is called as counseling.

5.4 Reprimand

If counseling fails to get improvement, the sales manager is required to reprimand the subordinates. Reprimand is a punishment meted out to the subordinate at varying degree. The degree of punishment will change with the seriousness of offence; it is not right to ask a person to resign from the job for a occasional delay in reporting as it is not so serious offence to warrant such severe punishment.

Methods of Reprimand/Punishment

Following methods are normally used to punish a person

- Ask the concerned subordinate to report (in person or over telephone) both in the morning and in the evening.
- Write a memo to subordinate with copy to senior managers, warning him/her of severe action if change in behaviour/working style is not noticed within a specified period.
- Write a show cause notice with copy to senior management asking the subordinate why serious action should not be initiated/taken for the offences listed.
- Take appointment of senior manager and ask the subordinate to be present with his/her explanations for the offenses listed.
- Disallow expenses for the period of suspected working
- Suspend from job for a period
- Ask him to resign or else face removal from job.

One must remember that removal of staff is not a solution of problems as there is no guarantee of a new person working better and not creating problems, "A known devil is always better than an unknown person". Care should be taken to counsel/train the existing sales staff and give them chance to improve before the final decision of removal is taken.

5.5 Exercise

1. Observe how your parents control your behaviour and ensure that you perform you/ your duties properly. Are doing your duties and completing your responsibilities? If yes or no try and explain the reasons behind it.

2. Observe how your mother controls the performance of the maids in the house; is she successful in doing so? What suggestions will you give to your mother in improving the performance of the maids?

3. Observe the behaviour of the subordinate staff in your institute; do you think they are aware of their duties? Are they doing their duties properly? What suggestions would you like to give to your management for improving the performance of subordinate staff?

4. Do you think your teachers are doing their duty of giving you knowledge of the subject properly? What will you do to ensure that your teachers do their duties properly?

5.6 Questions for Practise

1. Sanglikar who joined as ASM for Rest of Maharashtra wanted to understand the sales officer's efficiency objectively; he had following information to judge them. Will help him rate the sales officer on the basis of the information given below

	No. of working days	*Calls made*	*Productive calls*	*Sales generated Through calls* ₹	*Primary sales achieved* ₹	*Secondary sales achieved* ₹	*Target for the period* ₹
Chitnis	80	240	200	5,00,000	22,00,000	20,00,000	21,00,000
Kolhatkar	80	280	220	7,00,000	25,00,000	24,00,000	25,00,000
Dhore	75	260	220	5,00,000	20,00,000	15,00,000	21,00,000
Patil	66	220	170	3,00,000	20,00,000	12,00,000	22,00,000
Kulkarni	80	290	200	9,00,000	30,00,000	29,00,000	27,00,000

2. Mr. Phadtare the sales manager for industrial fasteners wanted to access the performance of the sales executives working under him objectively; he had following information to go by, you are requested to help him assess him

	Sales achieved ₹	*Target* ₹	*Cost of sales* ₹				
			Travel ₹	Phone calls ₹	Discounts ₹	Entertainment ₹	Total ₹
Phatak	20,00,000	20,00,000	5,000	2,000	40,000	2,000	49,000
Varma	20,00,000	20,00,000	7,000	3,000	1,00,000	8,000	1,18,000
Mutthu	20,00,000	20,00,000	9,000	2,000	1,00,000	10,000	1,21,000

3. Mr. Ajinkya ASM for Gujarat was going through problem of drop in sales in Saurashtra (HQ-Rajkot) and south Gujarat (HQ-Surat) areas, he suspected that both the sales officers are not putting in enough efforts in their working. Mr. Ajinkya suspected that both the sales officers are working all their markets ex-HQ so they reach the towns late and in a hurry to reach back home before night; he also suspected that the sales officers are working for shorter duration (one day instead of two or three days as planned). Suggest method for Mr. Ajinkya to catch the sales officers red handed and take appropriate action.

4. Plan a salesmen (ISR) + sales officer incentive scheme with following information available. The budget available is 2% of the sales in the promotion period which should be of three months.

Sales Officers	*Desouza*	*Ravikumar*	*Thakur*	*Phatak*	*Total*
No. of Distributors	6	10	12	8	36
No. of ISRs	20	15	16	12	63
Avg. salary of ISRs	8,000	6,000	6,000	6,000	26,000
Avg. monthly sales in the area Rs. In Lakhs	125.6	112	110	110	457.6

5. With following information plan a PUSH promotion, the budget for the promotion is 5% of the additional sales planned. The average sales in the area is ₹ 1,25,00,000/-

Retailers	*"A" class*	*"B" class*	*"C" class*	*Total*
Numbers	250	800	1450	2500
Contribution to sales %	45%	37%	18%	100

6. Kiran kulkarni a star sales officer has off late started showing drop in sales, his punctuality in reporting is also dropped. Suggest action against this problem to Mr.Deshpande (ASM) so that the situation improves.

7. Mr. Joshi the ASM for SKACO company found following while going through the records, suggest action against erring sales officers to him

Retail universe	*Kolhatkar*	*More*	*Hariraman*	*S.Sriram*	*Desai*
2007-08	1200	1800	1600	1700	1200
2008-09	1300	1950	1600	1720	1250
2009-10	1500	2100	1600	1750	1400

8. Natarajan is sales officer working in south Maharashtra territory, one day the accounts clerk came to Mr. Patil (ASM) with a observation that Natarajan claims railway first class fair from Pune to Mahabaleshwar when there is no train connection available to Mahabaleshwar. The accounts clerk also pointed out some other irregularities like purchase stapler pin box every second month, purchase of pens twice every month, purchase of stapler every quarter etc., the clerk said that this is happening for last two years and the earlier accounts clerk was passing the statements. Suggest action against Natarajan to Mr. Patil.

9. Calculate the ROI of Pioneer Distributor from following details, and give your comment whether the ROI is satisfactory or not giving reasons for the same.

Monthly sales turnover ₹	**Margin % of TO**	**Avg. Paid up stocks ₹**	**Avg. Market Outstanding ₹**	**Monthly Selling expenses ₹**	**Office/Godown expenses**
20,00,000	6%	8,00,000	4,00,000	20,000	10,000

10. Calculate ROI of Aarati agencies with following details

Monthly sales Turnover ₹	50,00,000	Avg. Market outstanding ₹	10,00,000
Margin %	8%	Avg. Discounts to retailers %	1%
Avg. Paid up stocks ₹	20,00,000	Monthly Selling expenses ₹	50,000
Deposit with the company @ 12% PA interest	15,00,000	Monthly office expenses ₹	10,000

Case Study 5.1 Counseling of Dave

Dave was sales officer working in south Gujarat area with base town (HQ) as Vadodara. He was newly married and his wife was from Borivili in Mumbai. Dave's last station on Maharashtra border was Vapi that was less than two hours journey from Borivili, Vapi was a AJC working town, i.e., Dave should visit it once in two months and the duration of visit was two days. The other place nearer to Borivili was Valsad which was little more than two hours journey and was AJC with two days working.

Mr. Manjarekar who was ASM Mumbai with additional temporary charge of Gujarat (Gujarat ASM had left the organization and suitable candidate was not immediately available) was a strict disciplinarian and used check the sales officer's working against the PJP (permanent journey plan). He found that the Valsad and Vapi markets are being visited on Saturday and Monday instead of Friday and Saturday as per the PJP. He also found that the sales in both these towns were on a decline even when the sales officer is present in these towns for three days (Sunday holiday being spent in Valsad or Vapi); the sales of south Gujrat area as such were also not showing any growth when rest of Gujarat was on a upswing. He also found that Dave has started claiming compensatory off for the Sunday spent in Valsad and Vapi.

Mr. Manjrekar sent a memo to Dave asking him why he has made the changes and what is the reason behind spending an extra day in towns like Valsad and Vapi when he can do so in important cities like Vadodara and Surat? Dave had no answer but next two months he adhered to the PJP.

One day while working with the sales officer in Borivili the sales officer said to Mr. Manjarekar that he meets Dave occasionally in Borivili and that Dave's wife is expecting a child. Mr. Manjarekar planned his visit to Vapi next month; Mr. Manjarekar asked Dave to start working the route and said he will contact him in the market. Mr. Manjarekar started working the route from the other end and checked with the retailers whether Dave visited them regularly or not and also the why the sales were not growing? The answer was same from most of the retailers that Dave was not visiting regularly and the service to the market by the distributor was poor. After meeting Dave both of them visited the distributor and informed him that the retailers were unhappy with the service, the distributor said that his claims with the company were pending for many months and Dave has not prepared fresh claims in last six months.

Mr. Manjarekar asked Dave to make fresh claims and both of them went to Valsad in the evening. Next day Mr. Manjarekar found the situation in Valsad identical to Vapi; so after lunch Mr. Manjarekar invited Dave to his hotel room and confronted him with the situation and said that he has a doubt that Dave is not working both these markets properly and spending his time in Borivili instead. He asked Dave if there was any problem at home or was there any problem with his wife's health? Mr. Manjarekar also offered to sanction leave of absence for a week if it was needed.

When all the answers to Mr. Manjarekar's querries were negative, then he said that he should start working properly and should not bunk the markets or else Mr. Manjarekar will be required to take action against Dave.

Do you feel Mr. Manjarekar took right action against Dave? Explain your answer with suggested action against Dave if any.

Case Study 5.2 Launch of Promotion by Prakash Sahu

Mr. Chandawarkar reached Nagpur late as his train was delayed so asked his sales officer Prakash Sahu to drop him at the hotel and start working the route; Mr. Chandawarkar decided to join Prakash somewhere along the route. Mr. Chandawarkar had come to see the progress of the consumer promotion his organization had launched so he was keen on working the market and see the retailer's and consumer's reaction for himself.

After getting ready Mr. Chandawarkar started for the market and instead of going straight to the route Prakash was working that day he went to the route Prakash had worked the previous day. In the route Prakash had worked previous day he neither could see the promotional stocks on display nor could he see any promotional POP (point of purchase) material in the retail outlets. He inquired with the retailer's whether they had purchased the promotional stocks and why they were not displaying it? The retailers said that they had received the stocks that morning only and they will display it by afternoon. Mr. Chandawarkar was surprised to get such answer as his organization was paying special allowance to the distributors for arranging ready stock operation so that the sales officers could arrange proper display and merchandising for the promotional stocks.

Mr. Chandawarkar then went to the market where Prakash was working, he found that there were arrangements for ready delivery and Prakash had not done any display merchandising in the outlets already visited by him. When Mr. Chandawarkar caught up with Prakash he worked as per the required norms and did proper display and merchandising.

What action do you suggest that Mr. Chandawarkar should take against Prakash Sahu? Give reasons for your suggestions.

Part – II
Personal Selling

CHAPTER 1 PERSONAL SELLING

Learning Objectives:

- Basics
- Different selling situations
- Salesmanship–Definition of sale

Sales can be achieved by non personal selling and by personal selling. Personal selling methods are more effective than the non personal methods. Before we start talking about the personal selling methods, let's talk about the non personal methods and their advantages and disadvantages.

1.1 Non Personal Methods of selling

We can list some of the non personal methods of selling as follows:

1.1.1 Catalogue sales

Most popular form of non personal selling is catalogue sales. Catalogue sales is very popular today also in United States of America and Australia as many people in these countries are required to travel long distances to reach the nearest retail stores who may or may not be keeping the product variety the customer wants to buy, so the customers prefer to send mail order to different producers and wait for the delivery. These customers are willing to pay the delivery cost as even if they make a trip to the nearest retail shop they incur travelling cost. These catalogues are available on order and are charged to the customers.

Some manufacturers keep their catalogues with retailers and a customer can order products and collect the delivery from the retailer. In this method the customer is not required to purchase the catalogue but the cost of service by the retailer is charged either to manufacturer or the customer.

1.1.2 Print advertising sale

Manufacturer can advertise his products in print media of various types like newspapers and magazines or wall paintings and give instructions of sending the order. In this form the manufacturer is required to give separate advertisement for each product or product category.

1.1.3 Display sale

Marketer can display the products at locations frequented by the consumers like theatres, bus stands, railway stations or airports etc., and can display ordering information along with the product. In this method the customer can visualize the product as it is displayed in front of him.

1.1.4. Vending machine sale

Marketer can place vending machines for his products at various locations and make the product easily available to customers at these locations. The vending machines serve dual purpose (1) it creates display of products which creates awareness of products and (2) it allows customers to buy it whenever he desires to do so.

1.1.5. Internet advertising sale

This is similar to print media and the advertisements keep popping up on screen of customers at regular intervals. This form of advertising is much cost effective as compared to print media but with limited OTS (opportunity to see)

Advantages of non personal selling: Advantages of non personal selling can be listed as follows

- **No liability of sales force:** In non personal selling there is no sales force and so no liability of making payments to them. The expenses incurred on delivery of products are directly proportionate to the sale and if there is no sale there is no cost of distribution and sale.
- **Establishment cost is low:** Non personal sale can be handled through the production point and there is no requirement of opening up of warehouses and selling offices at various locations.
- **Gathering of customer information is easy:** Since all the customers are required to send their requirement to the marketer along with the details of forwarding address, it is easy to prepare list of users with their details. Marketer can always request the consumers to send their expectations from the products and any unsatisfied needs.
- **Launch of new products is easy:** Launching of any new product is easier in non personal selling as one can announce a new product first and start producing it once the orders start flowing in, reducing the risk involved in the launch of new products. The marketer can get product ideas from the customers and can do product testing very easily through existing consumer base.
- **Disadvantages of non personal selling:** Though we have many advantages of non personal selling there are more disadvantages of non personal selling also, they can be listed as follows

- **Reduced reach, reducing opportunity of sale:** Catalogues costs are high and so cannot be distributed free reducing the reach and availability of catalogues. The catalogues kept with retailers are also not displayed by retailers properly as the retailers prefer to sell products in their shops rather than products in the catalogue. All these reasons reduce the reach of the catalogues to limited consumer base and reduces the opportunity to sell the products to large number of customers i.e. mass marketing is not possible.
- **Vulnerable to competition attack:** Competition can set in very fast by making their products available with the retailers nearer to the consumers and reduce your consumer base further. Since the competition is launching a product you are selling successfully they do not have any risk of product failure.
- **Increases the cost of distribution:** The cost of distribution of consumer products gets reduced when a vertical marketing system (VMS) is used effectively. Since major part of distribution cost is the transportation cost it gets reduced considerably when goods move in bulk and not in units (see Box 1.1).

Box 1.1 Reduction of Distribution Cost by Using VMS

Distribution cost reduction by using VMS

Consider a product which is weighing say 100 gms., while the product sale is low and can be managed by hand delivery at convenient time to marketer, a delivery boy using a bicycle being paid say ₹100/- per day delivering 100 units (10Kg by weight) in a day can lead to a delivery cost of ₹1/- per unit.

If the product needs to be delivered to far away locations even locally through a courier service the cost will not be less than ₹10/- per unit. If the price of the product to consumer is ₹10/- along with the delivery cost it becomes ₹20/- and the distribution cost is 50% of the cost to the consumer or 100 % addition to original cost of ₹10/-. If the marketer uses distribution system (VMS) and passes on this amount to distributors and retailers (25% + 25%) his sale will be much higher as his reach and availability increases multifold. Actually most of the marketers of FMCG pay only 6 to 8% to distributors and 10 to 25% to retailers and incur about 25 to 30% cost as distribution margin. This reduces price of product to customer and increases profit margin to marketer.

Consider a Pune based manufacturer is selling 10 tons (10000 units) of same products in a month to Mumbai customers. Since the courier charges for 100gms product from Pune-Mumbai location will be ₹35/- the cost of distribution will be ₹3,50,000/- (₹ Three lakh fifty thousand) but if you use VMS and pay ₹ 10/- (50% of ₹ 20/- as selling price to consumer) as distribution margin per unit to distributor and retailer and pay ₹ 10,000/- to transporter using a truck the total cost comes to ₹ 1,00,000 (10 x 10,000 units) + ₹ 10,000 = ₹1,10,000/- which is lesser by ₹ 2,40,000/- (3,50,000- 1,10,000 = 2,40,000) than the non personal sale achieved.

All the mass marketers sell products all over India and the quantity is very large one can very easily understand the savings affected by using VMS by mass marketers

- **Difficulty in getting customer trust:** Catalogues can produce pictures of the products in two dimensions only and cannot give proper idea of the actual size and looks in three dimensions. Many a time customers get mislead (May be unintentional) and lose trust on the products being sold in mail order format. In countries like India where consumer protection laws are not stringent and the existing law enforcement ineffective and corrupt; many people take advantage of the situation and cheat many customers easily reducing the consumers trust on mail order organizations.

- **Difficult to persuade and convince customers:** In non personal selling persuading and convincing of customers cannot be done easily.
- **Cannot be used for high value products:** Customers buying high value products always prefer to actually see the products in physical format ask many questions and doubts about the products features and benefits before deciding to buy them. This is not possible in non personal selling.
- **Cannot be used for daily use/frequently bought products:** Daily use products and frequently used products cannot be ordered and kept at home all the time in large quantity as it will block customer's money. Consumers prefer to buy such products as and when required.
- **Cannot be used for low shelf life products:** Low shelf life products if ordered through mail order are left with still lower life of use and may become non usable before they reach the consumer.
- **Cannot be used for emergency pharmaceutical products needing prescriptions:** Life saving emergency drugs sold against prescription cannot be ordered and kept by any consumer; since these drugs and medicines are expensive even medical practitioners do not keep them in their stock, such products need to be sold through personal selling mode.
- **Cannot be used for products of impulse purchase:** Consumers buy many products on impulse such sale is not possible in non personal selling method.

Looking at the disadvantages of non personal selling one can always decide to go in for personal selling as it is more effective. Non personal mode of selling is useful for all products that are unique and do not have fear of being copied easily. Non personal mode of selling is also useful when the customers are spread geographically and trying to reach then personally is very costly. Since the cost of reaching customers, automatically gets added to the final cost of the products, non personal selling becomes useful in such cases. Examples of such products can be hearing aids, scientific microscopes and other specialty instruments etc.

1.2 Personal Selling Situations

In a day to day life we observe personal selling being done in various situations, some of the selling situations need less selling skills while others need higher selling skills. Let us look at different selling situations in detail.

Selling situations

Following selling situations are found:

1. Door to door sale. (Direct to consumer)
2. Network Marketing (MLM – Multilayer Marketing)
3. Stall owners to consumer (Roadside/Exhibition etc.)
4. Shopkeeper to consumer (Retailing)
5. Salesman to shopkeeper (Selling to Retailer – Retailing)
6. Salesman to distributor
7. Salesman to Purchase Manager (Industrial/Institutional Sale)

8. Telephone Sale
9. Teleshopping Network/Catalogue/Mail Order Sale
10. Missionary sale (Canvassing to medical professionals – Doctors)

Let us look at all these situations one by one.

1.2.1 Door to door sale

Many companies are taking this path of direct marketing (eliminating distribution network). The company who popularized it in India is Eureka Forbes. They pioneered into selling household appliances through direct sales, by successfully selling. First - Euro- clean (Vacuum Cleaner) then Aqua Guard (Water purifier). The other company to do so successfully was Cease Fire (Fire extinguisher). This concept was used by many small time manufacturers of eatables (salty snacks, sweets etc.) but in that the idea was to save selling expenditure to remain competitive and cheep.

Objectives in door to door sale

1. To offer products to consumers at lower rate than market and attract them to buy the product.
2. To reduce selling cost by eliminating distributors and retailers.
3. To eliminate liability of selling staff (everyone is paid commission only).
4. To eliminate advertising cost.

Advantages of door to door Sale

1. Direct contact with actual user.
2. It works out to be more convincing and persuasive.
3. Customer can see the product/product demonstration.
4. Sales persons are paid on commission only basis so no liability unless there is sale.
5. Area of coverage can be pre-determined and is controllable.
6. Different promotions can be tried in different areas through different or same sales Rep. Simultaneously.

Disadvantages of door to door sale

1. Quality of sales people is low as the turnover of sales person is high.
2. Productivity is very low (out of 100 calls made may be 40 are effective–you can talk to the consumer–and may be 15 - 20 are or even less are productive) leading to frustration among the sales personnel.
3. The sales personnel may vanish with demonstration kit and products taken for sale leading to losses.
4. Wear and tear of demonstration kit is more
5. Cost of Supervision in high.

1.2.2 Network Marketing (MLM) Multilayer Marketing

To remove the disadvantages of door to door of selling a different set up is evolved. In this the role of supervisor and stock point is eliminated. The sales personnel become supervisors/ distributors/stock point themselves. The loss of stock due to the sales personnel vanishing with demonstration kit and stock is also eliminated, the sales person pays in advance for everything. The problem of low productivity is also eliminated, the sales personnel do not visit the customer, but instead invite the customers to their own place or other convenient place and make sales call in front of all of them together (Reducing efforts). The customers buy at least the lowest price product, willingly or unwillingly. If the seller can create conducive atmosphere the productivity is high. Successful companies in Network (MLM) Marketing are Japan life, Tupper wear, Amway etc.

The system of Networking (Multilayers)

The company appoints sales personnel as distributors of the product with following conditions:

1. The product should be sold directly to customer.
2. The product should not be displayed at any kind of retail outlet.
3. The product should not be advertised through newspapers, radio etc.

These distributors are paid fixed commission (given discount on selling price) to avoid the possibility of distributor ordering for his personnel use instead of selling (As there is no minimum purchase level), the distributors are offered incentives for appointing more distributors (minimum number prescribed). On completion of minimum prescribed sub-distributors the distributor starts getting overriding commission on the sale of all the products made by the company to these sub-distributors and their sub-distributors. Since the growth of business is slow, the distributors take more interest in appointing sub-distributors to guarantee effortless returns on the sale of the sub-distributors. The network keeps growing as shown in Fig. 1.1

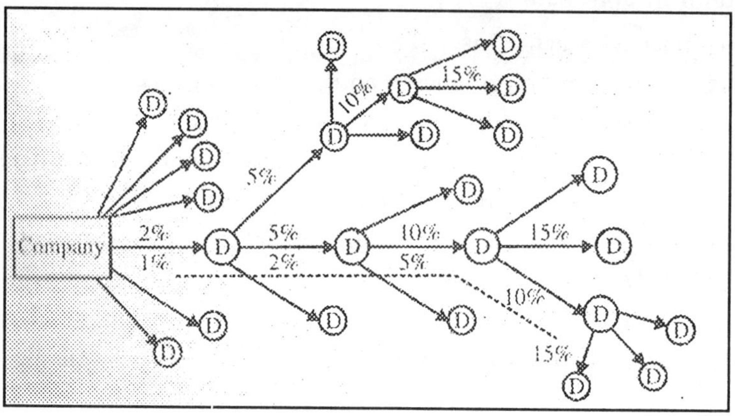

Fig. 1.1 Network Marketing

Advantages of Network Marketing:

1. A person joining this organization initially can earn good amount of money. Because of this only, the networks Multilayer Marketing is also called "MAKE LOTS OF MONEY (MLM)". But the possibility of earning money is only for those who RISK and join early. Subsequently it becomes difficult to make your DOWNLINE of sub-distributors which is the real source of income.
2. Company makes lot of money (MLM) through networking multilayer, without any expenses of supervision, advertising etc.

3. Works well where services of retailers are scarce. In USA, the nearest retail shop in many a times 30-40 or even 100 kms away (for people staying is villages or on their farms), so buying products through a nearest neighbor and having a good social outing is a welcome change.

Disadvantages

1. If a distributor is not able to create his own DOWNLINE of sub-distributors, his earnings are not good and he loses interest not only in the business but in the products also and many a times stop using the products.

2. The product is required to be priced high to accommodate the commission of the distributors and sub-distributors. The quality may not justify the end price, so the products may be used by first time consumers only and even the distributors and sub-distributors may not use them. Leading to piling of stock in pipeline (as inventory with distributors and sub-distributors) and not actual usage. So if the quality is not very high the system will fail.

1.2.3 Stall Owners to Consumers

We see lot of people selling their products either on pavement stalls or in exhibition stalls, though both the situations are technically same. The difference lies in the operations.

1. The roadside or pavement stalls are owned by independent owners who buy different products from different resellers. (People buying products from other person not for consumption but for selling to consumers for profit).

2. Stall at exhibition is operated by company people who sell the product for recovery of cost of exhibition stall etc., and not for profit. The motive is to make people aware of the product and induce trials.

In stall owner to consumer sale the consumers are attracted to the products by the display. So the stall owner can stand at one location (either in crowded area or in a area where crowd is attracted by exhibitors).

Advantages of stall sales

1. Consumer awareness is created without spending any additional money.

2. Product reaches to more places very fast.

Disadvantages of stall sales

1. Image of products is affected, consumers think that it is low priced because of cheap quality.

2. There is no control on selling price as it is decided by market forces.

Shopkeeper to Consumer

People get into business to provide different products to consumers by establishing a retail store (shop). The idea is to buy at low price and sell at high price. The selection of product depends on saleability of product in quantity and level of margin the shopkeeper can earn. High margin, low turnover or low margin high turnover both become acceptable. High margin with high turnover is most desirable but low margin low turnover is not wanted. The shopkeeper attracts customer by creating awareness of variety of products by displaying them suitably or by advertising about it.

Advantages of shop sale

1. Price can be fixed high giving good margin to shopkeeper; so that he pushes the product to consumers for high benefit.
2. Availability of products increases improving the chances of sale i.e. opportunity to get sold.
3. Awareness of product increases as it is displayed in shops. A consumer may notice the product and decide to buy during future purchases.

Disadvantages of shop sale

1. Product loses its exclusivity and is open to competition.
2. The competitor may give higher margin to shopkeeper forcing you to compete with him in margin and service. The shopkeeper may take advantage out of this.

1.2.4 Salesman to shopkeeper

Selling to shopkeeper is to ensure that the products are available in maximum number of shops (Retail stores) and the shopkeeper should get encouraged to sell the product to maximum number of consumers. As explained earlier the shopkeeper will be interested in all the products where he gets high margin and high turnover (good quality leads to high turnover). He is also looking for better service, so sales person should provide maximum of these things to get higher and higher sales.

1.2.5 Salesman to distributor

The objective in selling and distributor is to get maximum coverage in presence and absence to the sale person. The coverage is good only if the returns to the distributors are better. So the sales person should try to give maximum returns to the distributor.

1.2.6 Salesman to purchase manager

Purchase managers make decisions about purchases for the products required for their industry, institutions. Their objectives are:

1. Good quality at low price
2. Promptness of delivery

All those who can satisfy these conditions can get sale in that industry through the Purchase Manager.

1.2.7 Telephone sales

Potential customers are contacted over telephone by the Telemarketing team and they are persuaded for purchase of their products. The main important thing to remember in this are:

1. Right type of customers is contacted so that time is not wasted.
2. The telemarketing person should have proper training to persuade the customer.

1.2.8 Teleshopping network

In Teleshopping Network the customers are made aware of the product in detail, and are then persuaded to buy the product. Use of television is done to do selling in teleshopping, in this method the information about the product is required to be given in detail.

1.2.9 Missionary/Ethical sale (Sale through doctor-medical practitioners)

Sale through doctors is called as Missionary Sale because the Medical Representative canvasses about the product. (As missionaries canvass about religion) and is not involved in actual sales. Hence, the Medical Representative is required to be impressive and should be able to induce action from the Medical Practitioner.

1.3 Salesmanship

When a product is in high demand and does not require any efforts in selling it (customers are coming and demanding it) as the customer has no choice but to buy the product as sold by the seller and at the price he is selling, in such situation a salesman does not need any selling skills, e.g., when Maruti was not launched the sales people of PAL (Premier Automobile Ltd.) did not require any salesmanship consumers were forced to buy Premier Padmini after Maruti was launched the marketing department of PAL without having any selling/marketing skills could not sell Premier Padmini and the company closed, same is the case of TELCO selling trucks and Bajaj auto selling scooters.

Selling skills or salesmanship is needed in competitive environment when customer has a choice to buy either this or that. Salesmanship is also needed when a salesman is trying to sell a product to a customer who is already having it with him/her, e.g., shop salesman selling to a shopkeeper.

To understand salesmanship one must understand the definition of sale in modern context properly where a salesman is required to sell a product to same customer repeatedly. We have already discussed definition of sale in earlier Chapter no.2 in sales management section which is as follows:

1.4 Modern Definition of Sale

"Sale is exchange of goods, services or knowledge for money where the seller gets profit and both buyer and seller get long-term satisfaction"

With this definition of sale, following factors got focused and are important to sale

1. There should be exchange
2. Money has to be paid. If money is not paid sale remains incomplete
3. Seller should get satisfied with the profit he earns.
4. Buyer should be satisfied with the purchase and there should be no feeling of being cheated.

5. The satisfaction of buyer and seller should be long-term so that they are willing to do business again and again.

We will discuss selling skills required in different situations in details in chapters dedicated for them next.

1.5 Exercise

1. Observe the selling skills of the roadside vendors and understand the use of AIDAS formula by them; check various method used by roadside vendors to attract the attention of the consumers.
2. Visit exhibition stalls and critically observe the display of materials; what changes would you have made if you were handling the stalls. Prepare the plan, draw diagrams for the same.
3. Visit exhibition stalls and observe the stalls with maximum visitors; critically discuss the reasons for attracting the maximum consumers and find which factors of the following helped them get the maximum consumers
    - Innovative product
    - Demonstration of the product utility
    - Affordable pricing
    - Better consumer promotions (offers)
    - Attractive display and decorations
    - Position of the stall
    - Size of the stall
    - Quality of sales persons
    - Aggressive behaviour of sales staff
4. Work as stall salesman for a day or two and find out the challenges faced by them; prepare report for the same.
5. Visit a shopping mall and critically observe the behaviour of the various shop salesman; find which behaviour is most effective and why.
6. Observe the behaviour of the salesman that visits your home.

CHAPTER 2 SELLING PROCESS INDUSTRIAL/ INSTITUTIONAL SALE

Learning Objectives:

- Selling process in Industrial/Institutional products and skills for effective salesmanship
- Sales leads
- Prospecting
- Negotiation process

2.1 Advanced Sales Training in Industrial Sales

Industrial sale needs emphasis on different aspects as against normal sales pattern. A consumer purchases a product, and gives importance to the brand. This is not so in case of industry, it is said that industry does not purchase a product or a brand but is interested in purchasing a need satisfier of good quality at lowest possible price. So the emphasis is not on WHAT YOUR PRODUCT HAS but HOW YOUR PRODUCT SATISFIES THE NEED AT LOW COST. So the formula for industrial sale is different from consumer product sale. Industrial product sale can be denoted as follows:

S - Survey of potential customers

P - Prospecting the customers

A - Approach the customer

N - Need development/negotiations

C - Close of sale

O - Order processing

Let us look at the formula in detail.

2.1.1 Survey

Not all industries but all the products. So visiting all the industries to sell your product will be futile. It will also be time consuming and will be wastage of money also. So it is better to survey the industries first to find the possible buyers.

As similar industries buy similar products, the vendor company should find the different uses/need satisfying qualities of the product, and decide as to what all type of industries will need the product. Once the industries that will utilize the product are identified then it becomes easy to locate them. Following methods are used to locate different industries:

1. Yellow Pages

Most of the industries are registered in Yellow Pages under the industry type. It becomes easy to find the names, telephones and address of the industries easily.

2. Industry Directories

Regional industrial directories are available with the local industrial bodies like Chamber of Commerce and Industry. Once can pick up the details of all the companies in area. The only problem here is the directories are not UP TO DATE, so the information needs verification.

In United States of America industry registration is done under various classifications, the industry registration number shows its classification and so it becomes very easy to identify which industry will buy your products.

3. Administrative offices of industrial areas

The Industrial areas are managed by Industrial Development Corporations (IDCs). These IDCs have all the details of the industries in their record.

4. SSI registration centers

All the Small Scale Industries (SSI) are registered with SSI registration centers to avail government subsidies. This SSI registration centers can give details of information.

5. Manual survey

One can employ surveyors who can do manual survey of entire industrial areas at cost.

2.1.2 Prospecting

Once the survey to identify the potential/probable industries is over, one is required to PROSPECT them. Prospecting involves following:

1. Quantum of expected purchase

It is important to know what the quantity the industry is likely to purchase. What will be the frequency of this purchase? What will be total business that can be generated from this industry? The quantum of business will decide as to how much importance and what priority should be accorded to developing the business with the company.

All industries that buy the product, the seller is selling may not be potential buyers; if the seller is having lower capacity of production he may not be interested in selling to bigger industry and the bigger industry may not be interested in buying from small lot supplier as the cost of placing orders increases, in the same way a bigger industry may not be interested in supplying to smaller industry who will buy smaller lots as it increases, the cost of servicing the client.

2. Competition present

While prospecting the customer it is important to know who is currently supplying the products and at what rate with what quality of product and service. The seller must ask question to self, Is it possible for him to give better quality of product and better quality of service at SAME PRICE?, or Is it possible for him to give same quality of product and same quality of service at LOWER PRICE? If the answer to both questions is positive then only the seller should go ahead and try to become supplier to the industry being prospected.

3. Procedure of purchase

All the industries follow different methods/procedures in purchasing their requirements. They may follow the following procedures:

(a) Purchase by floating tenders.

(b) Purchase by rate contracts for particular period.

(c) Purchase from more than one vendor simultaneously on quota system.

(d) Purchase through new vendors/same vendor depending on the price quoted as and when the requirement is felt.

(e) Exclusive purchases from same vendor (generally a subsidiary).

(f) Purchase through purchasing agent.

(g) Purchase decisions are made by technical staff and executed by purchase department.

The marketer should find out the purchase procedure and plan strategy accordingly.

4. Reputation of the customer

(a) There are many industries that do not specify the requirements and then find faults in supplies and reject the materials. The material is then purchased at further discounted rate. This is a policy of such companies to get price advantage.

(b) There are many industries who keep ambiguous clauses in their purchase orders. These clauses are then used to deduct penalty from payments, e.g., delivery reached the company gate after office hours increasing the cost of inspection and accepting delivery. The penalty charged may be more than the waiting charges claimed by the transporter, if this clause is known the supplier may ensure that the deliver reaches in time or ask the transporter to wait outside the industry gate and make the delivery next day.

(c) There are many companies who give oral/telephonic orders which are contravening to their normal set principles. As such orders are EMERGENCY/IMMEDIATE ORDERS the vendor supplies them as a special service and relation building measure without getting WRITTEN ORDERS. The payment is then delayed and reduced under one context or other by the purchaser; it is found to be that companies NORMAL PROCEDURE to reduce cost of purchase.

(d) There are many companies who keep collecting rate quotations from different vendors and use it for squeezing the existing vendor to further price cuts.

(e) There are many companies who do not care for quality. Their purchase managers are interested in their individual benefits rather than companies, benefit and purchase products from the vendor who parts with commission for purchase managers.

(f) There are many companies who are very much concerned about the quality of supply and service and still demand lowest price. So the vendor who gives best quality of product and service of product and service of lowest rate gets the orders.

The marketer must check the reputation of the buyer and plan the selling strategy depending on the reputation to safeguard their interests.

2.1.3 Approach

Once the customer is prospected properly the sales person knows as to how much importance should be given (Relative importance as all customers are important for a sales person) to the customer. One also knows as to whom he must approach and how to get proper hearing. He can also prepare himself with the USPs (Unique Selling Propositions) of his products and the advantages he has over his competitors.

Approach should always be with appointment with the concerned person. The sales person should always reach the place at least 10-15 minutes before appointed hour. He should always be prepared with his sales/brand talk and should emphasize on the aspects which are attractive to the customer. He should try and do demonstrations of his products utility and leave literature with the customers for reference in his absence.

2.1.3.1 Planning of Sales Call

It will be a good idea if you plan your sales call well in advance. You already know who all are going to be present for your sales call (knowledge of DMU- decision making unit from your prospecting), you also know their need (Prospecting), you also know the features of competition, so you can plan your sales call properly emphasizing on the unique features of your product , similarities of your product with competition and the advantages you purpose over competition.

Your planning can include utilization of sales aids like, OHP, LCD projectors, computerized presentation on power point which discards actual samples of products and demonstrations.

You may plan visit of the DMU to an industry which is using your specialized products successfully. This is possible only when the industry using the specialized products is not in direct competition with the new buyer.

You must use this opportunity to build customer relationship by way of offering technological advancement offers which will separate you from the clutter of suppliers and help get the order successfully.

Some industrial products need safety certification from various organizations like fire department, industrial safety department etc. if you start selling these products without getting these certifications you may get an order which you cannot execute (see Box 2.1)

2.1.4. Participants in buying decision

One must understand the participants in the buying decision before planning the sales call as all the participants may have different view point about the purchase decision. Every participant will have company's welfare in their mind but their objectives may be at cross purpose to each other, e.g., the manufacturing department will look for best quality of materials at any cost but the purchase department may be looking for lower price and acceptable quality. Let us look for participants in the buying decision:

- **Initiators:** The process of buying starts at the stores where the store keeper observes that the inventory level is falling below re-order level; at this point he informs the buyers that the material needs to be purchased. The initiators can also be the new product department who are looking for components to be fitted in the new product they are developing.
- **Buyers:** These are the persons from the purchase department who will send purchase order directly to the supplier when it is straight re-buy; in case it is modified re-buy, these people will call the suppliers that were shortlisted before for new task and ask them to send their fresh quotes for fresh negotiations for the supply. When the purchase is for new task the purchase department will start the process of identifying various suppliers who may be able to and willing to supply the required quantity of materials in required quality specifications and ask them to submit their quotations.
- **Gatekeepers:** Gatekeepers are the people who handle the flow of information from suppliers to buyers and from buyers to the decision makers. They maintain the confidentiality of the information. The sales person should be aware of these gatekeepers as they may be interested in favoring a particular supplier and may withhold critical information about suppliers and selectively pass it on to decision makers to get favorable decisions for certain suppliers.
- **Users:** Users are the persons from manufacturing department who use the materials in production process and give favorable or unfavorable opinion about the materials. If the materials is not of required quality specification these people will reject the materials.
- **Influencers:** Influencers may be from within or outside the organization that is closer to the decision makers and the decision makers have high regards for their opinions. Influencers may or may not have stake in buying decisions and their casual remarks about the supplier or a particular instrument/material may be taken seriously by the decision makers.
- **Deciders:** For all high volume frequently purchased items and all high value products a decision making unit (DMU) is constituted by most of the organizations. The responsibility of this DMU is to ensure that the inventory of the products under considerations is maintained properly and there is no wastage or over stocking and the price and quality negotiations are properly done and all possible suppliers have been considered. This is done to ensure that quality of the products purchased is best, the supplier selection is right and inventory control is maintained.

Box 2.1 Preparation of Sales Call

This writer Suresh Abhyankar's first job in marketing was in a Mumbai-based company where the product was photosensitive electric switches. At that time in early 1070s, it was a new idea but was very useful one for many industries who consume lots of electricity to light their areas.

Mr. Suresh Abhyankar started his job with zero training as the owners of the company -a trading agency - importing these switches were new in business. With no formal training Mr. Suresh Abhyankar used to visit various small-scale industries to no result. He spent first one month visiting small and medium-scale companies and then in second month started visiting bigger companies. He was successful in the first company he visited-Colorchem-where one Mr. Borkar who was an Industrial engineer from MIT (USA) and had joined as works manager recently. Mr. Abhyankar happy with the development visited NOCIL and was successful there also. But NOCIL people said that their industry has all flammable chemicals and they will require seeing the fire and safety certification before they could process the order. When enquired with COLORCHEM they also insisted the certification and the process of getting the order was postponed to next year as getting the certification from the bureaucracy is time consuming and expensive work.

2.1.5 Need developments/negotiations

We will look at both these aspects separately as both of them are very important aspects of sale.

Need development:

(a) Many a times, it is possible that the product you want to sell is not needed by the customer as it is, but the sales person may propose its use in place of (AS REPLACEMENT) some other product/assembly of products to customer's advantage (cost saving/time saving/ease in operation/reduction in labor element etc.). This will require consistent persuasion/demonstration of the technical staff to prove the utility and saving, e.g., use of plastic panels in place of steel panels in automobiles, use of aluminum casting of engines in place of cast iron in automobiles etc.

(b) It is possible that you are trying to sell new technology in place of old with considerable initial investment. Here also considerable persuasion is required to prove that in the long run the new technology is going to be beneficial.

(c) It is possible that you are selling new technology that may increase the cost of manufacturing a little but can also allow the buyer to increase the selling price of their products substantially to offset the cost and generate more profits.

Negotiations

Negotiations are of different types they are:

(a) Price negotiations (b) Service negotiations

(c) Quality negotiations (d) Feature negotiations

A customer is interested in buying required quantity of product with required features at required time at required price with required service (supply on time, with after sales service). A sales person must try to find out what is needed by the customer and while accepting to give something should also try to compensate it which something else (extra quantity, liberal delivery time, immediate/advance payments etc.)

The negotiations will always depend on the negotiating power of buyer and seller and the negotiations can proceed only in the ZONE OF NEGOTIATIONS (See Figure 2.1). If sellers offer is not acceptable to buyer he will refuse to buy and if buyers demand is not acceptable to seller he will refuse to sell. The buyer will compromise on his demands and the seller will compromise on his offer depending on the POSITION OF STRENGTH they are holding.

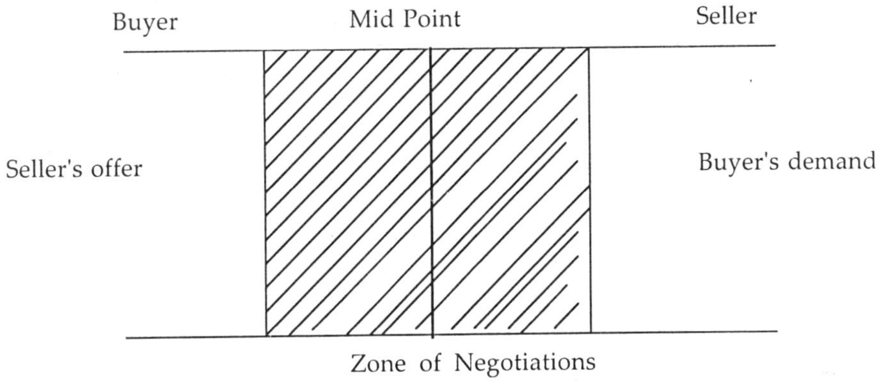

Fig. 2.1: Zone of Negotiations

Position of strength:

(a) **Buyer:** If the number of vendors is more than one and all are in position to meet the requirement of the buyer, the buyer is said to be in position of strength and can negotiate the deal favorable to him.

(b) **Seller:** If the seller is holding monopoly of sorts (No other vendors are able to meet the buyers demand) he is said to be in position of strength and can negotiate the deal favorable to himself.

The skill of negotiation lies in hiding the weaknesses and pretending to be in position of strength. The person who can prove himself to be in position of strength wins the negotiation. Care should be taken by the seller to show that the situation is a WIN-WIN (WIN for both buyer and seller) situation, as he cannot humiliate the buyer (as it may prove to his disadvantage in future) and force him develop new vendors in your competition.

2.1.6 Close of sale

After negotiating the deal it is time for close of sale. In Industrial sale the close of sale has lot of importance as:

(a) The order is taken/negotiated by sales person but is supplied by dispatch department. So the dispatch department needs to be properly instructed about negotiations.

(b) The order is given by purchase department and is received by receiving stores. It is important that the receiving department knows what to expect in what quantity, at what quality levels and at what time (delivery schedule).

(c) It is important for the accounts department to know what is being purchased by whom at what price and under what payment conditions.

To clarify the situation for all parties involved, in industrial sale an instrument called PURCHASE ORDER (PO) is utilized. The PO will have complete details of the negotiated deal. The copies of PO are circulated to each party involved to ensure the terms are followed strictly.

2.1.7 Order processing

After collecting the order it is important that it is given for processing with proper instructions. The order must be processed as per the PO for getting repeat orders.

A good sales person will ensure that the PO is explained properly to the production managers for making required changes in product specifications as required by the buyer and ensure that the supply schedule is properly understood by the production planning people. All these precautions will avoid unnecessary delays in supplies and rejections.

Important areas in order processing

Following areas are very important in order processing

- Explain the specifications of the product to the manufacturing department
- Explain the schedule of supply to the manufacturing department
- Explain the quality specifications to the manufacturing department
- Explain the terms of supply to the dispatch department
- Explain the terms of payment to the accounts department
- Explain the terms of service and installation to the service department.

If proper importance is given to each of these areas of supply the customer will get satisfied and will become a long-term relation for supplier.

2.2 Exercise

1. Visit Industrial area of your town and meet various small and medium-scale manufacturing unit operators; discuss with them their selling process and pricing strategies.
2. Visit distributor of any large-scale industrial organization and find out how they manage their sales on regular basis.
3. Visit any institution like school, college, hospital and find out how they buy their requirements.

Case Study 2.1 Adhesive Selling

Kishor Singh was working with industrial adhesives manufacturer with Satpur Industrial area and Nasik surrounding as his area of operations. Industrial adhesives market is fairly competitive market and the margins are low on most of the products except some specialty products and patented products. Kishor Singh was working on the order from Mahindra and Mahindra which was going to be fairly large in size and was going to be a continuous order. Kishor had approached the works manager Mr. Apte of Mahindra and Mahindra through a friend of Mr. Apte.

After the negotiations about the rate and service were over Mr. Apte asked Kishor Singh to get holding strength report of his adhesive from an independent laboratory on or before 15th June and then collect the purchase order. Kishor Singh asked his technical department head to get the required report and forward it to Mr. Apte and Kishor Singh went on a week long holiday. When he came back on 15th June he found the laboratory report was not ready and it takes at least three days to get it. He called Mr. Apte and explained the delay and requested him to give him another four days, Mr. Apte told him he will try and see what he can do but the chances are that the order will go to the other party.

Kishor Singh lost the promising order. Can you find the reasons for the loss of order?

Case Study 2.2 Laptops

Mr. Khanna of Wipro computers was trying to break in to Synergy Institute of Management's suppliers. Synergy Institute of Management purchase 120 laptops every year which they gave to their new batch students every year, last two years the order was being bagged by HCL. Company's sales officer who was student of the Director in some other institute. Khanna met the director several times and convinced him of unique features of his laptop, but the director said since his institute is giving the laptops free he would like to purchase the laptops at the lowest possible rate with the minimum required configuration.

Khanna had discussions with senior managers and convinced them that if they bag the order of Synergy they will also bag orders of another two institutes and was able to get rates which were ₹ 1000/- less than the HCL and lower than the other bidders (this time Dell was also in the fray). Synergy agreed to purchase the laptops from Wipro and made purchase order. Khanna insisted on 50% advance along with the PO which Synergy refused. Synergy said we do not give advance to anyone; we are willing to pay 50% on delivery and rest after 30 days. Khanna refused and the order went to Dell who accepted the payment terms and also reduced rate by another ₹ 500/- which was higher than Wipro by ₹ 250/-

The delivery period was 45 days from the date of PO; in your opinion is Khanna right? Should he have accepted the payment terms of Synergy? What went wrong from his side?

Case Study 2.3 Electronics Sale

Mr. Sahastrabudhe was working with an electronic industry and had become expert in electronic control panels. As he wanted to start his own business he resigned from his job and with money he got from provident fund he managed to get a shed for himself and loan from a nationalized bank for the machinery. Mr. Shastrabudhe caught hold of some raw materials suppliers who were willing to give him credit up to thirty days. With the little money he had, he could only manage to pay salaries of one skilled and one unskilled worker for duration of two or three months. In such situation Mr. Sahastrabudhe found that he cannot directly approach big factories that paid only after 90 days. Banks were willing to give him loan as working capital after looking in to his performance over two year period and the suppliers were willing to give him higher credit period after they look in to at least one year performance. Mr. Sahastrbudhe was not in a position to supply large quantities to any big unit and wait for 90 days to get the payment.

While discussing the matter with a purchase manager of a large organization he had a chance meeting with Mr. Shah who was also supplying the same control panels at much higher rate to the same factory. Mr. Shah later contacted Mr. Sahastrabudhe and gave him a proposal to become supplier to him and promised payments within a month.

What should Mr. Sahstrabudhe do? Should he try to contact more companies and try and convince them about the better quality better price but need for immediate payment or should he accept Mr. Shah's offer?

Case Study 2.4 Scab Insulations

Sunny, the sales and service Manager of SCAB Insulations was worried about the higher after sales costs incurred in the supply of insulations to Industrial Solvents and Chemicals Ltd. (ISCL). The cost escalation was due to frequent visits required to ISCL and the labour cost involved. The similar situation was expected to be happening in Polyolefin India Ltd. (PIL). Both these contracts were negotiated by Sunny and there was a fear of wiping out the profits in the contract. Next week he has to face the review meeting with Mr. Menon when he will also be giving his proposals for new customers which he was soliciting.

Background and History of Company

SCAB Insulations was a company established by Mr. Menon way back in 1976. Earlier Mr. Menon was working with Lloyds' Insulations a multinational company involved in insulation works in shipping industry. Now SCAB insulations were a principal contractor to Mazgaon Docks Ltd. and Shipping Corporation of India. Along with shipping industry SCAB insulations were also having long-term contracts with chemical companies like NOCIL, BAYER, and HP Refineries etc.

SCAB Insulations were having a team of six sales and service executives and Sunny was promoted to sales and service manager position on the basis of his good performance as executive. Earlier the executives will bring in the leads and then Mr. Menon will do the price negotiations before signing the contracts. After Sunny was promoted he was allowed to do the price negotiations for the new customers he will develop and was offered profit percentage from the sales generated.

Pricing strategy

Insulation work is done on all the boilers, vessels and pipelines carrying liquids in chilled or heated conditions. Boilers require double insulations-

1. From inside with refractory materials
2. From outside insulation materials

Vessels and pipelines require insulations from outside only. The pricing involves following components

1. Glass wool
2. Thermocol
3. Wire mesh
4. Binding wire
5. Plaster of Paris
6. Galvanized iron sheets (GI sheets)
7. Screws
8. Cost of labour (skilled and unskilled)
9. Repairs and maintenance work with or without material cost
10. Cost of supervision
11. Overheads like material handling, conveyance etc.
12. Profit margins

While giving the quotations higher quotations are required to be given for an old plant and machinery as it leads to frequent visits for repairs and maintenance. Industrial Solvents and Chemicals Pvt. Ltd. and Polyolefin India Ltd., was both running their plants for many years and the plants had served their purpose. Because they were old plants frequent leakages in the pipelines was a common occurrence which was leading to cost escalation and so drop in profits and loss of total commission to Sunny.

If the contract is terminated the loss could be stopped but there is one chance of recovery of these losses if both these companies go in for refitting leading to fresh requirement of insulation which can lead to higher profits in the long run. Sunny does not understand what he should do and what reply should he give to Mr. Menon in the next meeting.

Case Study 2.5 Civil Contracting

Sandip Patil completed his engineering degree in civil stream and wanted to start a construction company, he had financial backing from his father and so he started going through newspapers for tender notices requiring civil works. He started filling tenders at "NO Profit NO loss" basis thinking that he should establish his company first and then start thinking of earning profits. He was rejected by most of the times not knowing what is going wrong, when enquired most of the times the answer was standard your tender was not found to be suitable on technical grounds.

Through his father's contact he approached an established contractor and asked him what must be the reason for rejection on technical grounds? The father's friend said your rejection is on the grounds that your firm has not handled any projects earlier, you must get experience first for getting eligible to bid for tenders. The father's friend offered him subcontract in his ongoing project which can become his certificate of experience. Sandip Patil accepted the subcontract and did some more subcontracts with other established construction companies and now he is taking independent contracts.

What was the mistake of Sandip Patil at the beginning?

Case Study 2.6 Automobile Components

Dilip Kulkarni was working in an automobile company and observed that major cost component in automobile industry are imported equipment and parts. One of the parts was the telescopic folding door joints for the boot compartment and large emergency windows of the buses. He tried to develop manufacturing of the same and was successful in doing so.

Since the cost of locally manufactured product was much lower than the imported product and the quality was equally good he could establish the business very fast. In a short while he was supplying to major automobile industries and also the bus body builders. He appointed a team of sales people who covered the clients on a regular basis and maintained the flow of orders satisfactorily.

One day while going through the tour program of one of his sales executives (Mahesh Mishra) he found that he had planned a visit to Surat to contact a workshop converting normal cars in to luxury sedans. He called Mahesh and enquired the reason for the visit, Mahesh said that the workshop owner is very famous and has converted cars for many celebrities; Mahesh wanted to see if there is any scope for sale of their products.

Dilip Kulkarni asked Mahesh as to how many cars in his workshop were converting every year? The answer was 4 to 5 Dilip asked Mahesh to cancel his trip to Surat and said send an information brochure by post and ask for the order. Mahesh was disappointed and felt that a sure shot opportunity of sale was lost.

Is Dilip Kulkarni's action right? If you agree or disagree give reasons for the same.

CHAPTER 3 SELLING PROCESS – CONSUMER GOODS

Learning Objectives:

- Selling process in consumer goods
- Professional selling for fast moving consumer goods in competitive environment
- Types of calls
- Effective selling techniques
- Role of relationship

Selling process in Consumer Products: In consumer products selling process can be very simple and also very complex depending on the selling situations and the product being sold. As said earlier when the consumer wants to buy a product, selling does not required much of selling skills, a salesman with basic selling skills can effectively achieve his objective of selling the products. Let us looks at the basic selling skills in detail.

3.1 Basic Selling Skills

In the basic selling skills the formula AIDAS is very popular. This formula is useful in following selling situations:

1. Roadside vendors
2. Exhibitions and stalls
3. Retail shops
4. Door to door sales
5. Selling to retail shop owners
6. Ethical sales (to doctors)

The full form of AIDAS formula is as follows:

A = **Attention** – attract the attention of the customer, the roadside vendor may make various types of sounds or noises to attract the attention of the customer. The retail counter/door to door/seller to retail shops or the medical sales officer may attract the attention of the customer by wishing him. It is also possible to attract the customer by putting up a huge display of the product.

I = **Interest** – generating interest in the product to be sold, generally this done by actually allowing the customer to hold the product in their hands and handle it. While doing this the sales person talks about the product and explains how the product is useful and beneficial to the customer.

D = **Desire** – generating desire is also done by telling the customer how the product is better than the other products in the same category and why it is important that the customer buys it then and there for his/her advantage.

A = **Action** – it is the actual sale by taking the cash and handing over the product to the customer.

S = **Satisfaction** – here the sales person gives assurance to the customer that he/she has done the right thing by purchasing the product and it is a right decision.

The AIDAS formula is very useful in pharmaceutical sale also, it can be used as follows

A - Attention of the doctor

I - Creating interest in doctor's mind by talking about the diseases currently spreading, and the available medicines from your company that can chec the spread effectively. Then talk about the medicine promoted by the company for curing the disease,

D - When the doctor is sufficiently interested in the product to try the product on his patients.

A - Give samples for trial purpose (Action)

S - Satisfy his queries about the availability of the product/medicine at all chemist's shops and why it is better than competition.

3.2 Advanced Selling Skills (Professional Selling in Competitive Environment)

Many companies have their products already established in the market and selling the product is not a problem but selling the product in required quantity is a problem due to competitive atmosphere. The required (targeted sales) can be generated only by professional skills and not by applying basic selling skills. In the competitive atmosphere the professional sales person is able to corner a bigger chunk of available market (market share) with his/her professional selling skills. The advanced selling skill has seven steps to success which are as follows:

3.2.1. Planning and preparation

In this step the sales person does planning and preparation for his sales. This involves following steps:

- **Planning for the customers (route) to be visited:** A sales person must plan for the customers to be visited because he/she should not visit a customer too early or too late (gap between two visits should be fixed as per the PJP discussed earlier in Chapter 2). The customer should be aware of your frequency and he should expect you on that day at that time. This way the customer is also prepared to purchase the products you are selling.
- **Planning for the day's target (quantity to be sold):** In this step the sales person decides the day's target based on the monthly target and the market potential, a good professional sales person will keep track of his/her daily achievement and rework the target in such a way that he/she achieves (individual sales person may plan for higher than given target by his/her sales manager) the planned target at the end of the month.
- **Planning for customer target for the day:** In FMCG a sales person visits many customers in a day which forms his/her route/market for the day, sales done to all these customer totals to the day's target. Professional sales person plans his/her achievement through individual customers and leaves nothing to chance, this way he can control his/her day's achievement customer call to customer call. For this he/she uses the previous visits call data showing stock holding and purchases of that day and estimates how much stock of the product the shopkeeper/retailer may be holding based on his average off-take (sale to customer) and how much he is expected to purchase/how much sales person should sell on that day. E.g., if a particular retailer was holding say 10 units of the product and purchased another 20 from the sales person and his expected off take is 20 the sales person can again plan to sell another 20 units to the retailer (10 + 20 = 30 – 20 = 10). The total of these retailer/customer wise estimates must be always more than that of the target for the day.

Planning of customer targets reduces the selling efforts to a large extent as the pressure sale is required to be done on a less number of customers and that to it will be with a pre decided sales/brand talk making it much easier than done without any preparations. This is well illustrated in Fig. 3.1 below

Table. 3.1: Customer Wise Day Target Plan

S. No.	*Name of retailer*	*Cat.*	*Stock*	*Sold*	*Expected stocks*	*Target planned*	*Gap coverage plan*
1	Prakash stores	C	1	3	1	3	
2	Chandan stores	A	10	24	8	24	
3	New Maharashtra stores	A	8	24	10	24	
4	Mahalaxmi department store	C	2	3	2	3	
5	Regal bakery	C	2	3	1	3	3 extra
6	Kohinoor coop consumer society	B	5	6	2	12	
7	Deepak kirana	B	4	6	3	6	
9	Daily needs	A	9	12	5	12	

10	Shree Sai Variety stores	B	5	6	3	6	3 extra
11	Kamal kangan stores	B	4	6	3	6	
12	Health chemists	A	15	48	12	48	12 extra
13	Kanak Medical stores	A	14	48	10	48	12 extra
14	Adi Ganesh stores	A	20	48	14	48	
15	Mahesh stores	B	5	6	3	6	3 extra
16	Baking Aroma	C	1	3	2	3	
17	Vijai bakery	B	3	3	3	3	
18	Regal Restaurant and stores	C	3	0	1	3	3 extra
19	Daga Dry fruits	A	12	24	8	24	12 extra
20	Shanti kirana stores	B	6	6	4	6	
Total			129	299	95	288	48 extra
Target for the day 320. Gap between target planned per customer and actual target is 32 needs to be covered. 48 extra planned with 8 customers where pressure sale is required till the gap is filled.							

- **Preparation:** The sales person must prepare himself for the visit for this he/she must ensure that the required stock to achieve target is available with the distributor/ warehouse. The sales person should ensure that any promises made to the customers in previous visits are fulfilled, if the promises were not fulfilled the reasons for not doing so should be known to the sales person. The sales person should check the current price list and should have it with him. The sales person should carry all his selling tools (bag, samples, price list, Point of sale [POS] material, advertising schedules daily report, order book/bill book etc.) and if the sales person is using delivery van for spot sale the van, driver and helpers are ready in time to reach the market as per schedule.

3.2.2. Approach

The sales person should approach the customer in proper manner and greet him. Following care must be taken while approaching the customer.

- **Grooming:** The sales person should be properly groomed and be in formal dress, if the sales person approaches the customer shabbily dressed and ill groomed the customer will have bad impression about the sales person and will not pay proper attention to what he/she is talking.

- **Greet the customer in a proper way:** though the conditions today are changing and greeting in western style by "Hi", "Hello" or "Good Morning/Afternoon" is an accepted practice greeting in traditional style always has better effect and creates closeness instantly. So following traditional or regional greeting may be used.

1. Marathi – RamRam, Namaskar,
2. Gujarati – Jai Sri Krishna, Kem chho,

3. Parsi — Sahebji
4. Muslims — Salam Alekum
5. Hindi belt — Jai Sia Ram, Namaste,
6. Bengali — Nomoskar
7. South — Namaskara swami
8. Sikhs — Sat Sri Akal

- **Do not carry you cigarette in the shop:** entering a retail shop with burning cigarette or mouth full of tobacco/gutkha is treated to be disrespectful and should be avoided totally.
- **Remember the key person by name:** since the sales person visits every customer periodically the sales person should ensure that he/she knows the key person (the person who is in charge of giving the order/purchasing the product in that retail shop) addresses the customer by the name. This has good impact and a friendly atmosphere is created which is useful for achieving the targeted sale. For this the sales person should carry a diary in which he/she can write the name of key person with contact details. Next visit the sales person should refer to the diary before entering the retail shop and use the detail. Over a period of time sales person can start remembering them.

Box 3.1 Ganesh Ghurye is not Getting Sale

Ganesh Ghurye is not getting sale

Ganesh Ghurye who worked for SKACO Company was trained in Mumbai initially and then posted to Nashik. Ghurye's family had a cutlery shop in Girgam in south Mumbai, since he was getting in bad company his parents put him in this job through a known person in SKACO. The Nasik area that was covered by the sales officer posted in Pune earlier was separated so that the increased coverage could result in higher turnover. Industrial area set up in Nasik MIDC and Satpur MIDC was expected to give that higher purchasing power to Nashik residents.

After being put up in Nashik he was required to travel up to Dhule and cover the area on a given itinerary. The ASM SN Bose found that the area was not showing any growth in sale after Ghurye was posted their. SN Bose discussed the matter with the distributor Shah Traders over phone who said Ghurye works the market daily but is unable to get any business and Bose should personally come and check the reasons.

SN Bose reached Nashik by Varanasi express and he knew that Ghurye was working Nashik road market that day. When SN Bose contacted Ghurye he was surprised to see Ghurye and his attire. Ghurye had not taken bath, had not shaved, was wearing crumpled clothes and was wearing Hawai chappels; Ghurye was not carrying sales bag and was carrying only a diary. The shopkeepers looked at him and just waved him off saying they do not need anything currently.

SN Bose asked Ghurye to go back to his lodge and get dressed and groomed properly and come to the market with his sales bag. When Ghurye returned they worked the same route again and this time Ghurye was able to get good amount of orders. SN Bose then had a quiet talk about the importance of proper dressing and grooming.

3.2.3 Stock check

This the third and most important step in professional sales calls. In this step the sales person finds out what is the current stockholding of the retailer, if the stockholding is as per his/her estimate he is sure of achieving the targeted sales, if the quantity is less the sales person can plan to sell that much extra quantity but if it is more than the estimated stock he was expected to have, the sales person will encounter resistance to the quantity he/she has planned to sell and he/she should plan the next step of brand talk in such a way that the retailer agrees to buy targeted quantity. One more thing that can happen and is very important in Indian context is that of stock rotation and FIFO (first in first out) arrangement. In India the stock with expiry dates needs to be replaced (in western world once the product is purchased by the retailer it is his responsibility to sell and if the retailer is unable to sell it before expiry date it is a loss to the retailer and not the manufacturer.) So the sales person should ensure that the FIFO is followed strictly and no stock is nearing expiry date. While doing the stock check the sales person can also arrange the display of the product to improve off takes.

Advantages of stock check: advantages of stock check can be listed as follows

(a) Correct stock position is found.

(b) Correct sale during visits is established.

(c) Condition of stock is checked leading to timely replacements.

(d) FIFO is maintained.

(e) Display can be arranged while checking the stock.

(f) Stock of competition also can be checked.

(g) The position of stock and the planned sale leads to decision of how the brand talk is done.

3.2.4 Brand talk

In this step the sales person talks about his product why and how his/her product is good for the customers and is superior to the competition and how much quantity the retailer should purchase/order. For doing brand talk the sales person is required to have proper and in detail product knowledge. It is important for the sales person to do the FAB (feature advantages and benefit) analysis of the product he/she is selling in advance and use it at the time of doing brand talk. Brand talk is an optional step for established products in the market as everyone is aware the product's features benefits and advantages. In case of established products the sales person only tells the retailer how much quantity he plans to sell on the basis of the stock check during this step.

Brand talk helps to do following

(a) Brand talk in new product introduction to explain the need of product placement in retail shops.

(b) Brand talk for growing product to explain the need for extra quantity of product to be purchased.

(c) Brand talk for maturity product to explain advantages over competition.

(d) Brand talk for declining product to explain continued utility of product.

(e) Brand talk to remove misconceptions about the product.

(f) Brand talk leading to sell required quantity.

(g) Brand talk to increase stock pressure.

(h) Brand talk for explaining promotions and enlisting in promotions.

(i) Brand talk to retain goodwill etc.

Table. 3.2: FAB (Feature, Advantages and Benefit) Analysis

Product	*feature*	*Benefit*	*Advantage*
Horlicks	Increases the nourishment value of milk	Extra nourishment	Cheaper than competitor
	Can be taken in water	No expense of milk for getting nourishment	
	Respected for over 150 years	Proven value	
Lifebuoy soap	Antiseptic soap	Kills germs completely	More hygienic
	Available in many fragrances	Choice for every customer	Choice for every customer
ENO's Fruit salt	Easily dissolves in water	Quick result	Faster relief
	Reacts with acidity	Longer relief	Permanent relief
	Available in many flavors	Choice to customer	Choice to customer

For an established product being sold for many years one is not required to give brand talk in a classical manner as most of the time the retailers are aware of all the features and benefits and the advantages over the competition, but as said earlier in planning process that you may be required to push extra units of the product to achieve the targeted sale of the day and in such situations you may be required to give the features benefits in a dramatized way to create an atmosphere where the retailer thinks that buying extra quantity is a necessity at that point. A good sales person puts the facts in such way that the customer thinks that he must buy the quantity suggested by the sales person.

3.2.5 Objection handling

While doing the previous step of brand talk the sales person tells the retailer how much quantity he should purchase (A professional sales person never begs for an order he decides how much he wants to sell) the retailer may or may not agree with the sales persons decision and he objects to the quantity planned by the sales person. When the retailer objects to the quantity being sold, the sales person should handle it in a proper way. The planning done during first step comes handy at this time. He can give various reasons that he has planned in case there is an objection to the quantity being sold. E.g., he may say "the advertisements planned during this period are much higher than the previous period because of which there is higher off take expected for the product".

The retailer may raise objection not for the quantity but service conditions being offered by the sales person/distributor. In such case the sales person should listen to the objection carefully and promise to resolve the matter before the next visit. The sales person should not promise anything that he/she cannot fulfill, in such cases it better to tell the retailer that he will forward the matter to the higher authorities and get the matter resolved. E.g., for credit issue with the distributor he can say "I will ask the distributor to accept 2-3 days post dated cheque this time". If the retailer is asking for increased frequency of visit the sales person may say "you start buying higher quantity regularly and I will put you in higher grade where you will get more frequent visits" But if the retailer is asking for say change in pricing which is not in the sales persons authority he/she should say "I will forward your request to higher authorities and try to get favorable decision, but it may take some time". Remember honesty always pays in long run.

Most of the unprofessional people call this step as problem solving. But, use of the term, Problem Solving leads to misconception that you are trying to solve problems of retailers related to your product. Basically, there may not be any problems related to your product leading to skipping this stage. If the term objection handling is used you can think of the following objections.

(a) Objection to quality of product.

(b) Objection to features of product.

(c) Objection to packaging of product.

(d) Objection to advertisements of product.

(e) Objection to promotional efforts of product.

(f) Objection to service of product.

(g) Objection to profit margin of product.

(h) Objection to distributor's behavior.

(i) Objection to payment conditions of product.

(j) Objection to availability of POP of product

(k) Objection to quantity being sold to retailer etc.

Once you think everything as objection you can be well prepared to handle the objection leading to increase in your quality of call and efficiency of your presentation.

Objections raised by a customers or the questions asked by the customers to more about the products are treated as "Buying signals" by all the experienced sales people as customers who are interested in buying a products will only raise objections or ask relevant questions to understand the features of the products well before they buy the product.

Methods of Objection handling

Following methods are useful in handling objections:

- **Listen and do not interrupt:** While customer is making complaint, listen carefully to understand what he wants to say. The customer may get pleased to find someone listening to him. Answer only when customer has finished. Answer completely and rationally which will please the customer.

- **Agree and counter:** Agree to what the customer is saying which will calm the customer. Many times, customers are emotionally charged they will not listen to reason, if you calm them and counter to prove them wrong they will accept it.
- **Question the Objection:** Question the objection raised by customer, say "Do you mean to say that ......" and restate the objection in such a way that it answers the query. e.g. If a customer says "the packet of snack food is too small "you can restate it as - "Do you mean to say that it will be finished in one sitting and you will not be required to store it loose, yes it is correct, the small packet will ensure that every time you eat, it is going to be factory fresh."
- **Trial Close:** This is also called as "suppose test". It is found that many a times the customer raises false objection if you want to know whether the objection is true or false, you can use suppose test. You should ask the customer "suppose I clarify this point will you buy......" If the objection is true the customer will say yes and if it is false he will not buy. In that case you ignore him.
- **Hidden Objections:** Sometimes, the customer may not come out with objection clearly, in such case the salesman should probe and ask "Do you have any doubt about .... Then be assured that it is not true. E.g. If the customer has doubt about waterproof jacket and he is not clearly saying it you can say" do you have doubt about its waterproof quality, then be assured it is definitely water resistant. You can check it here if you want to".
- **Forestall the objection:** If you feel that customer may raise objection for a particular feature of your product. You can raise it yourself in your brand talk to avoid, e.g. If you are selling bright curtain cloth and you know that customer's raise objection about the color fading early you can tell the customer in your brand talk that "the color is fast and it will not fade easily."
- **Straight denial:** This is not advisable, but in many cases if the customer is not listening to reason and adamant, you will be required to deny objection clearly, e.g. If the customer is insisting on low quantity purchase and benefit of quantity purchase and benefit of quantity discount scheme and also extra credit you should firmly say "sorry it is not possible, it is against company rules".

3.2.6. Close of call

In this step the sales person takes the order confirmation from the retailer. Effective brand talk/presentation will lead to reduction or elimination of objections. And if whatever objections are raised are handled properly close of call becomes easy. Close of all means achieving your goal/ objective in making the call e.g. getting the order or affecting the sell.

Methods of closing call

- **Ask for the order:** You can explain the stock position and the off-take to the key man and tell him (if you are seasoned/professional) that you are sending so much quantity/ ask him how much quantity you should send, e.g., if the retailer had 4 units in your last visit and you had given 10 and today he has again 4 units you can safely tell him/ask him for order of 10 units.

- **Summarize and ask:** Summarize the discussion and ask for order, e.g., after explaining the promotions/advertising schedule you can say "in view of the promotions/advertising company is doing shall I send .... Quantity".
- **The alternate close:** In this the salesman uses sentences like "shall I send you ten units or five or "shall I send delivery in the morning or evening"
- **Action agreement:** In this method, the salesman says sentences like:
  (a) "OK! I will get these expiry goods replaced and send quantity".
  (b) "OK! I will ask the distributor to accept 10 days post dated check and send you 10 boxes".
- **The Objection close:** In this the sales person shows disagreement with the customer and accepts the order e.g.:
  (a) "I am not satisfied with the quantity you are ordering. I am sure you will ring me up to ask for extra quantity after 2-3 days."
  (b) "We do not give discount on small quantity like this but as you are a special customer I am accepting it".
- **Concession close:** The sales person accepts to offer extra concessions to finalize the order, e.g. He says "so I will finalize the order with extra concession that you asked".

3.2.7. Detail work

Professional sales person will not run away after getting the order of effecting the sale. He will do detail work like –

(a) Arranging display.

(b) Merchandising.

(c) Putting up POP (Point of purchase materials like stickers/danglers, posters etc.)

(d) Do general talks and thank the retailer.

All these things are done to create goodwill and developing good relations leading to favorable response on his next visit and generation of CONSUMER OFFTAKE to ensure good order in next visit.

3.3 Recognizing the Behavioral Type of Retailer

Every retailer will have his behavioral type and needs to be tackled in that way to get the results. A sales manager should train the sales officer in recognizing these behavioral types and deal with them in proper style. Some of the behavioral types are given below

a. No man: He says No to everything, his characteristics and methods to handle are given in Table 3.3 below

Table. 3.3: "No man" characteristics and methods to handle

Characteristics – "No man"	*How to Handle him*
Dull	Stay positive
Traditional	He lives in the past, so refer to past successes of your products and ideas
Keeps referring to past times	Develop as much evidence as possible for your ideas.
Not tempted by new products and ideas	Prepare in advance for all his likely objections in detail.
Views change as threat little	When you launch a new product go to him late with success stories at other places.
Strict follower of rules	
Does not take any risks	
Has lot of reasons for not buying the products	
Negative attitude	

b. Know it all: This type of customer thinks that he knows everything, this customer tries to show that the sales person who is supposed to be up-to-date on current knowledge is not so and so he should listen to the customer. Know it all customer shows characteristics and so he should be handled in way shown in table 3.4.

Table. 3.4: "Know it all" characteristics and method of handling him

Characteristics — "Know it all"	*How to Handle him*
Dominant	His weakness is that he thinks he knows it all - so appeal to his knowledge and flatter him
Sarcastic	Don't get angry, stay calm, do not retaliate
Considers himself superior	Persist with your presentation, accept his comments, support your ideas with facts
Tries to tell salesman his job	He will always think that he is the best, so let him feel happy about it
Threatens	
Shows-off	
Drops names	
Puts salesman down	
Does not trust the salesman	

c. Friendly customer: He is friendly with everyone, may be overfriendly Table 3.5 shows his characteristics and methods to handle him.

Table. 3.5: "Friendly customer" characteristics and methods to handle

Characteristic – "Friendly customer"	*How to Handle him*
Warm - hearted, Talkative	He will get you in all sorts of irrelevant discussions, do not get side tracked come to the business at hand
Trusts the salesman	Tell him, lets complete the business first and then talk peacefully
Undisciplined	Avoid open questions and frame your questions in such a way that he answers in "yes" or "no"
Welcomes salesman	Do not become very cold and unresponsive that will hurt him.
Cracks a lot of jokes	
Avoids business talk	
Likes to be popular	
No value for time	
Generally has 1-2 friends chatting in his shop	

d. Frustrated fighter: He works very hard but unsuccessful in achieving his goals (may be unrealistic) and so is very frustrated.

Table. 3.6: "Frustrated fighter" characteristics and how to handle

Characteristics – "Frustrated fighter"	*How to handle him*
Easily upset and angry	He will shout while talking to you, be calm and listen to him (do not smile while he is shouting), this will reduce his anger
Impulsive	He will become personal which is his style, be calm and do not take it personally (as it is he is abusing the company salesman and not you personally); be pleasant to him.
Gets insulted easily	His basis for anger will be emotions, so offer him logic and stick to your facts
Generally tense	Despite his anger there will be areas of agreement, look for them and capitalize on them.
Always complaining	
Loves to reject salesman	
Makes personal attacks	
Shouts at salesman	
Complains to supervisors	
Puts down products	
Believes all salesmen are wasting his time	

e. **Indecisive:** He is afraid of taking any decision, his characteristics and method of handling is shown in Table 3.7.

Table. 3.7: "Indecisive customer" characteristics and methods to handle

Characteristic – "Indecisive"	*How to handle him*
Shy	Reduce his indecision by giving advantages of buying now
Hesitant	Explain disadvantages of delaying the decisions
Doubts salesman	Be patient, give him lots of information, do help him decide and give him confidence
Keeps on asking for more information	Answer all his objection which are raised to postpone the decision, so answer all his objections very firmly and confidently
Has no confidence	
Is easily threatened	
Says he will buy next time	
Needs to be reassured	

f. **Tough customer**: He is very strong and tough minded and is difficult to convince, his characteristics and methods of handling are given in Table. 3.8.

Table. 3.8: "Tough customer" characteristics and methods to handle

Characteristics – " Tough customer"	**How to handle him**
Determined	He is well aware and knowledgeable, so you cannot bluff him. Be prepared with complete knowledge about your products and competition.
Forceful	He will constantly interrupt you, be calm and be factual in answering all his objections.
Drives a hard bargain	While he is talking, listen to him carefully, you may benefit by some point he raises.
Always wants discounts	He is trying to impress you, so use some flattery by appealing to his knowledge.
Refers to advantages of competitive products	
Impresses you with his importance to your business	
Thinks highly about himself	
Untrusting	
Interrupts your presentation	
Aware and knowledgeable	

g. Positive thinker: His basic attitude to business is positive and wants to do good business profitable to one and all.

Table. 3.9 "Positive thinker" characteristics and methods to handle.

Characteristics - "Positive thinker"	*How to handle him*
Constructive	Remember he is mature person, be mature with him.
Reasonable	Be well prepared with all facts to answer his all queries.
Intelligent	Faithfully follow steps of call, he will cooperate.
Asks relevant questions take	He is intelligent so be careful and don't him for granted.
Listens to your answers	Be completely honest and fair with all dealings with him.
Takes quick sensible decisions	
Enthusiastic	
Focus is on the future	
Raises reasonable objections	
Interested in his and your business	
Clever fair negotiator	

h. Low reactor: This type of customer shows no reactions to persons or situations, his characteristics and methods to handle are given in Table 3.10 below

Table 3.10 "Low reactor" characteristics and methods to handle

Characteristics- "Low reactor"	*How to handle him*
Does not talk	Ask him open questions and probe to make him talk.
Not sociable at all by	Try to build friendship with him gradually friendly gestures.
Does not commit himself	Do not remain silent even if he is not responding
Good listener	Try to be more enthusiastic and friendly.
Avoids answering questions	
Does not raise any objections	
Appears to have no trust in you	
Does not get excited by anything you say or show	
Shows no emotions	

3.4 Selling Techniques for Counter Salesman

Counter salesman in any shop is much luckier than the shop to shop sales person; for counter salesman the customer has come with intentions to buy and the salesman has to ensure that he gives proper attention to the customer and sell products of various types totaling to higher amount to the customer, the shop to shop sales person has to create the need and then try and sell the products he wants to sell.

In spite of this advantage many counter salesmen are unable to sell products to the customer and the customer walks out and goes to another shop. The counter salesman should understand that when the salesman sell anything to a customer he is not obliging the customer but the customer is obliging you by buying the products at your shop when he has choice of not doing so.

3.4.1 Selling skills required by counter salesman

Counter salesman should understand that he is there to give proper customer service and be prepared for the same so he should follow the selling steps as follows

Planning and preparation: The basic objective is to ensure that every customer that comes to the shop must purchase something and every customer buying should buy more products in more quantity. To achieve this objective the counter salesman should plan his sale and prepare for the same. Following things need to be done for the same

- Arrange the products properly maintaining FIFO (first in first out) in the shelves in proper display to ensure that all the products are visible to the customer when he/she comes. Display of products can lead to impulse buying.
- Arrange the products you want sell (for stock clearance or for high profit margins) in higher quantity in bigger display, customer always feels that the bigger display is due to high customer demand and wants to try the product if not tried and keep buying if already purchased.
- Ensure that the place is clean and dust free, customers do not like unclean and dusty places.
- Always be properly dressed and remain well groomed, customer do not like unkempt salesman and avoid buying from them.
- Know by heart prices of all the products or put price tags on all the products to avoid confusion, if you quote different prices the customer will feel that you are trying to cheat.
- Ensure proper lighting of the counter, one can switch on extra lights when customer comes, customers feel good by such gestures, and they think that it is a special treatment for them.
- If customer is not buying products being sold at your counter, try to escort them to the counter that sells the products they require.
- Keep smiling and don't be rude to any customer

Attract customers to your counter: Counter salesman should try and attract customers to his/her counter by doing the following:

- Ask the customers passing by whether they would like to see any products from your counter

- Inform the customers about new varieties that are on display now
- Tell customers that they can see the products and not buy the products if they do not want to

Actions when customer visits your counter: when the customer comes to your counter you should ensure that he leaves only after buying something. Following things should be done

- Ask what they want to buy and show the best variety in that product
- If the customer finds it above the budgeted price ask them what range the customer is interested in and show products at upper limit of the range quoted by the customer.
- Show maximum varieties till the customer is happy and keep all the products liked by customer aside and make the customer feel that you expect the customer to buy more than one.
- Keep smiling face and do not show any disapproval about the customer being choosy.
- Do not talk about the price unless customer asks for it, let the customer choose the best and if the customer finds the products unaffordable he will buy other at lower price.
- Show the latest arrivals only after customer has selected what he/she has come to buy, this can lead to additional purchase immediately or in next visit.
- When the purchase is over ask how the customer wants it packed, in one packet or separate packets or gift wrapped.
- Say thank you and come again to every customer.

3.5 Sales Calls for Direct Selling

Direct selling is becoming popular in many products especially the financial instruments, the selling technique required for it is a combination of institutional sale and then the simple AIDAS formula which we have already discussed. This sale is done in two steps as follows

A. Lead generation: Lead generation is the most important part of direct selling, if the lead generated is proper sale becomes much easier for the sales person. Many companies use many different methods for lead generation. Some of the methods are as follows

Collecting information from secondary sources: if the customer you are looking for is required to be higher income group one can collect the data from the automobile dealers (owners of cars/two wheelers), electronic shops (buyers of high end models of TV, fridges etc.), from shopping malls (buyers of products in excess of say ₹2000/-), from banks giving credit/debit cards (monthly expenditure in excess of -xxxx amount per month) etc. this information is supposed to be confidential but most of these establishments or their employees sell the information for some consideration.

Collecting information through primary survey: Many organizations employ demonstrators and ask them to put up a stall/table in any mall/multiplex or at the entrance of some exhibition, these demonstrators ask various customers to enter a simple game of fun after entering their personal details of a form and as the game is simple give small gifts to every customer who fills the form. This information is then scrutinized to get the leads.

Telecalling: Telecallers are employed to systematically contact customers from particular high income localities and find out if they are interested in buying the products being sold by the organization.

The leads so generated are then passed on to the sales team for further action.

B. Sales calls: Sales person needs to know the actual buyer and then attempt the actual sale he is required to do two types of calls as follows

Cold calling: Cold call is the visit to the prospective buyer to find out

Whether the lead generated is good

Who is the actual buyer?

Details of the buyer's financial condition

What product can be easily sold and

What needs to be done to convince the buyer about the need to buy the same?

This information is collected from the family members and friends of the prospective buyers. Many organizations use junior/trainee sales persons for doing cold calls and then the senior persons go for actual sales call.

Hot call/Actual call: Once the prospect becomes hot (definitely capable of buying the product) the hot call/actual call is made. Since all the information is available about the prospective customer the selling becomes easy (seller is prepared to answer all the expected queries in a positive way)

3.6 Effective Selling Techniques

One cannot give any universally effective selling technique, what one can always talk about what one should not do to offend the customer. If the customer is not offended the chances of effecting sale increases, following tips can be useful to become effective or result-oriented sales person.

- **Try to find out the customer's intentions:** Customer may not always be interested in buying the products being sold; many customers try and get maximum information about various products compare analyze the features and take decision for purchase in future. In such cases do not show displeasure but try and show as many varieties as you can and give maximum information it is always possible that the customer may change the intentions and by on impulse. In any case if you are helpful the customer will definitely come to you next time and buy.
- **Customer is always right:** Do not cross the customer and try to prove him/her wrong, if you try to prove him wrong the customer will go on defensive and retaliate aggressively to prove he/she is right. This will spoil the situation unnecessarily, instead if you say yes you are right and I would like to show you some additional information and give information contrary to what the customer is saying with details the customer will understand that he/she is wrong. At this point do not confront the customer and embarrass him/her.
- **Find out customer needs:** If the sales person tries to find why the customer want to buy a product the sales person can change his sales pitch/brand talk to suit the customer need and be effective.
- **Be supportive to customer:** Many customers are afraid to take buying decision and are unsure about their decision, if the sales person finds that the customer is in the dilemma

of whether to buy or not to buy, sales person can be supportive and assure the customer that the decision to buy is the right one and the customer should go ahead and do it.

- **Presentation techniques:** Presentation techniques helps generate sales and increase the quantity per sale. Use of presentation folder is common practice in personal selling when it is done one to one basis; use of slide projectors or LCD projectors is very effective when the presentation is done to a large number of people at a time following precautions are very useful in doing the presentation.
- **Using presentation folder:** Hold the presentation folder in such a way that the viewer is able to see it properly. Do not read from the folder but keep talking about the page open in front and give more information than it is present on the paper attracting the attention of the customer towards what you are saying rather than what is written on the paper, paper is only a support point for you. Try and get eye contact with the customer and talk confidently.
- **Using slide/LCD projector:** Prepare the slide with 3-4 bullet points per slide of what you want to talk. Use bright colours on the slide, wherever possible use attractive illustrations, use font size that will help all the listeners to read to contents properly. Talk confidently with maintaining eye contact with maximum people.

3.7 Role of Relation Building

Relation building is very important in all types of selling situations. Relation building makes it easier to approach the customer, the atmosphere is friendlier and the customer trust on the seller is much higher. The customer also tries to build relationship with the seller as the customer thinks that if the relations are better he/she can expect better service and priority treatment.

Sales person should take care that the relationship does not become disadvantageous to the company interests and the customer is benefiting and the cost of company interest. The relationship should benefit the company more as the relationship is being built with the intentions of getting better business.

3.8 Exercise

1. Categorize various daily use products that are being used by your family in to various companies; find out which company products are most used by your family. Talk to nearest retailer and ask him how he procures these products and who comes and sells these products to the retailer.
2. List all the retailers you visit and critically analyze why you frequent some of the retailers and why you do not visit again. Prepare a report on the relation building activity done by the retailer you visit with high frequency.
3. Have you received a product a product that has not satisfied you even when the claim made by the company in their promotional suggested so? Have you made complaint about it to the retailer? If yes what was the reaction of the retailer to your complaint? If you have not complaint make a formal complaint and analyze the reaction of the retailer.

4. Make a visit to the distributor of any company and find out how he arranges to sell the products in his area of operation and find out what is the qualification level of his sales representatives and the amount of training they receive.
5. Try and analyze behaviour of your friends to the types of customers given in the chapter; try to handle them in the way given as per type and see if you get success in your arguments or no.
6. Prepare FAB analysis of five known products to you.
7. Try selling any common product to your friends, ask them to be critical and ask lot of questions to you. Check as to how many times you succeed in selling.

3.9 Questions for Practise

1. In what types of selling situation can one use AIDAS formula effectively?
2. Why is it necessary to use advanced selling method for FMCG products to retailers?
3. What is missionary sale? Why is it called as missionary sale?
4. What is the difference between cold call and normal call? When is cold call used and for what purpose?
5. List effective selling techniques and their importance.

Case Study 3.1 Panasonic

Mr. Acharekar wanted to purchase a cordless telephone for his house; his earlier experience suggested that the life of the cordless instrument is about 3-4 years so he wanted to purchase an instrument which is not very expensive. He went to Panasonic show room and enquired about the cordless telephone, the sales took him to the cordless counter and showing him a display of various models said these are the various models available and the rates are tagged to them you can choose any one of them. Mr. Acharekar asked him some questions about a model costing ₹2000/- the salesman said you will get a booklet along with the phone which gives all details. Mr. Acharekar said he is an illiterate person can the salesman explains? The salesman said that Mr. Acharekar does not look like illiterate person, at that moment Mr. Acharekar started going towards the door and said he is not interested in purchasing anything there.

The shop supervisor saw Mr. Acharekar moving towards the door without purchasing anything and he intercepted Mr. Acharekar who explained his problem. The shop supervisor not only explained all the features of the instrument but also demonstrated them. Mr. Acharekar bought the cordless and went happily.

What was the mistake of the shop salesman?

Case Study 3.2 Batra

Batra the newly appointed sales officer for a cosmetics company was working on his route for launching a new product. The shopkeeper listened patiently the brand talk and looked at the picture of the product in the sales organizer, finally shopkeeper asked to show the product sample. Batra started going through his bag and then remembered that he has removed the sample from his bag previous evening to show it to his girl friend and did not take a fresh sample in the bag. The shopkeeper refused to place any order, the same thing happened in next few shops and then Batra decided to go back and fetch the new product sample from his distribution point. By the time he returned it was lunch time and no key persons were available in any shops. Batra could not achieve his day target and his productivity for that day was only 10%.

What was the mistake of Batra?

Case study 3.3 Sunil Balgu

Sunil Balgu the sales officer went to his distributor M/s Harishchandra's office on Monday morning and enquired about the quantity of promotional stocks of Boost refill where a PUSH promotion of one free on every one dozen Boost refill purchased was on. The distributor gave him the stock register which was updated only up to Thursday and the deliveries of Friday Saturday and Monday were not deducted. Sunil Balgu took the Thursday figure and went to the market, he booked good amount of orders that day and told the distributor to stop booking orders in scheme any more as he had sold the stock out already.

When Sunil Balgu went to office next Monday after finishing his tour the ASM Mr. Arora called him in his cabin and started firing, Balgu did not understand why the ASM was angry even after doing a good amount of sales during the tour. The ASM showed him the letter he had received from M/s Harishchandra which said - promotional stocks available on Monday 20 dozens orders booked by Mr. Sunil Balgu 60 dozens (copies of orders booked by Balgu attached). Please send 40 units Boost refill free along with next dispatch or send a credit note for the same.

What was the mistake of Sunil Balgu?

Case Study 3.4 Importance of Key Man

Mr.Vijay Parmar sales officer in SKACO company was working a particular Ghatkopar MG Road route for last three months and sales were dropping drastically, this route was supposed to be important route in his area and he was not getting proper orders. He could see the stock pressure dropping continuously in the route and many stock outs. The shopkeepers used to give him one reply "Is bar chalega". He talked to the previous sales officer and asked him what must be reason? The previous sales officer said the dealers were good and should give orders.

They decided to work together one day and the previous sales officer who travelled by train asked Vijay at Ghatkopar station and they worked together. That day the orders were very good, at the end of the day the previous sales officer said "all these shopkeepers are complaining about you, they do not know you and they said you do not visit their shops". Vijay was surprised he said "they do not know me is right because I have not met them earlier, but I do come every time to these shops and I always meet someone else" The previous sales officer asked "what time do you reach these main shops?" Vijay said around 1330 hrs because I start from Amar Mahal side as I come by bus.

What is going wrong in Vijay's case? Can you give him suggestions?

Case Study 3.5 Attentiveness

Mr. Niranjan the sales executive of an electronic company found that his sales in a particular showroom is dropping drastically after he appointed the new demonstrator; Akshay the new demonstrator was the best one selected during the interviews with fluency in Hindi, English and mother tongue Marathi, he was good looking and smart. Niranjan expected that the sales in the most important showroom for his products will go up but instead it had gone down and was sliding continuously.

Niranjan visited the showroom two or three times and made Akshay do mock calls and found that he was very convincing. When Niranjan discussed the matter with his ASM Mr. Bapat the ASM suggested you send mystery customers to the showroom to check on Akshay. The report of the mystery customers was shocking, Akshay was either smoking outside the showroom or chatting with his friends (in person or on mobile) and was not attentive to the customers; the other demonstrators who were attentive then showed their company products to all the customers and were able to convince them to purchase those brands.

Suggest action against Akshay to Mr. Niranjan.

CHAPTER 4

SELLING OF SERVICES

Learning Objectives:

- Selling of services marketing in personal selling
- Tools for personal selling
- Value added selling

Selling of services is a different ball game altogether, it is easy without any efforts where the service is an urgent need of customer and is very difficult when the customer is unaware of the service and its need. Let us look at the classification of services before we learn the selling skills for the same.

4.1 Classification of Services

Services are classified by the industry they serve as follows

Table. 4.1: Classifications of services

S.No.	*Industry*	*Services*
1	Business services	a) Secretarial b) Security c) Catering d) Event management e) Training f) Software providing and utilization g) BPO (Business Process Outsourcing)

2.	Entertainment	a) Movie, television program production and broadcasting
		b) Amusement parks
3	Hospitality	a) Hotels & lodgings b) Restaurants and cafes c) Catering services
4	Trading	a) Wholesale trade b) Retail trade c) Online trade
5	Finance and Insurance	a) Insurance advising b) Loans and advances c) Investment, brokerage and advice d) Real estate buying and selling advice
6	Education	a) Schools and colleges etc. b) Training and consultancy c) Coaching classes
7	Transportation	a) Air, sea, road, train travel service b) Car hire, charter or leasing services c) Goods transport by air, sea, road, train d) Liquid, gas transport through pipelines e) Postal and courier service
8	Public utilities	a) Electricity supply b) Water supply c) Drainage and sewerage services d) Garbage collection and disposal
9	Government	a) Defense of country b) Protection of people and property (POLICE) c) Health and education providing d) Good relations with other countries
10	Health	a) Hospitals and clinics b) Gymnasiums, sports complexes and spas c) Weight gain/reduction programs d) De-addiction programs e) Mental asylums
11	Telecommunications	a) Broadband, e-mail b) Telephone, fax, c) Satellite data transfer d) Video conferencing

If we look at the services the services which are run by Government undertakings like public utilities and Government departments does not need any marketing efforts and selling skills as they are monopolies and are needed by everyone. The marketing and selling skills are essential where the services are run by private organizations and are open to competition.

The gap between marketing of services and selling of services is very thin, there is very little that a seller of services can do when the customer is not aware of the service, so the sales person is doing both marketing activity (creating awareness and need for the service) and selling activity that is of actually selling the service to the customer. To understand the marketing and selling activity one must understand the marketing mix of services and its importance to the sales person of the services.

4.2 Marketing Mix of Services

Unlike marketing mix of goods where the marketing mix consists of 4 "P"s (product, price, place and promotions) the services marketing mix has three more elements and has 7 "P"s each one of it is very important for marketing services and is as follows

- **Product:** In services if your product is differentiated from other service providers selling of that product becomes comparatively easier. E.g., if all the food stalls are selling traditional Indian snack foods a food stall selling Chinese food has easier job as there is no competition.
- **Price:** If your price is much below the competition with promise of better service you have an advantage in selling the service.
- **Place:** If the place of service being provided is closure to the customer or has some unique qualities selling of service becomes easy. E.g. the barber/kirana shop nearest to your house is always most preferred service provider. If your location of a restaurant/hotel is at exclusive location you get better business.
- **Promotions:** if you can afford to promote your service better than competition you get better response. E.g., Kingfisher/Jet Airlines
- **Process:** If your process is unique or different then the chances of your selling improves tremendously,.
- **People/service providers:** if the service providers are better than others selling of the service becomes easy, e.g., tuition/coaching classes having renowned teachers (coaching service providers) getting customers becomes easy, if your hotel has renowned chef, customers come to you easily.
- **Physical evidence:** If the physical evidence of the service provided is better than others getting customers becomes easy, e.g., ambience of multiplexes and malls which is part of physical evidence attracts more customer.

4.3 Selling Skills for Services

If the sales person of the services avoids offending the customers he is better placed to sale the service easily. Following tips are very use full in selling services.

a. **Grooming:** Sales person of the services needs to more properly groom himself than consumer products sales person as the expectations from a service providers are higher by the customers; and better groomed person can assure better service than others.

b. **Keep smiling:** If the sales person of services has smiling face the customer gets assured that the services marketer is doing good business. Good business in services is only possible when lots of people are buying the services provided by the marketer.

c. **Do not show fatigue:** If the service provider looks tired the customer is unsure of the quality of service that may be provided and avoids buying it from tired looking service provider.

d. **Customize service:** Try to assure the customer that the special requests by him/ her will be accommodated may be at extra cost.

e. **Never say no:** Even if the customer's demands are not in your normal procedures, never say no directly, always say "you will look in to the request and see what can be done". You may refuse the request latter but at least the customer has a satisfaction that you tried and the customer carries good impression about you which helps promote your business.

f. **Try and build relations:** Relation building is most important in services as customer feels more secure at the hands of known service provider.

4.4 Selling Process Services

Selling process in services is a mix of industrial/institutional and consumer sale. Industrial/ institutional because the clients for services are mostly organizational buyers for their employees and like consumer sale because the service specifications are not rigid and appreciation of service is subjective and depends on individuals that are using the service, e.g., if you are running a travel agency the contract is negotiated and finalized by the HR department for various employees that are going to use the service, but every individual employee may have his/her own specific demands to be fulfilled like - the driver of the vehicle should be able to speak English/Hindi/ regional language, should not have any habits of tobacco, etc., and should be well dressed and young/middle aged -(within the given framework) to avoid any complaints against service providers.

So to get clients the formula of industrial sale SKACO needs to be used and while negotiating the contract the brand talk (with FAB analysis) and objection handling steps need to used.

When the customer approaches the service providers following care needs to be taken

- The customers must feel at home and relaxed when he comes to service providers, so there should be a reception desk that will be manned be highly trained person that will make the customer feel that he/she has come to the right place. Many times it is found that the employees of service providers become arrogant and do not behave properly with the customers that have approached on their own. The arrogance of employees can start the downfall of the service agency. (Many hospitals, restaurants, hotels and travel agencies etc. have lost their business only because the employees become arrogant and misbehave with customers)

- The customer should not be made to wait (most of the time the employees are talking over the phone to some other customers and keep doing the same making the customer that have come in person feel that he/she should have called over phone rather than coming in person) and be given proper attention. The customer prefers to come personally because he/she needs to get all doubts cleared before the purchase of service, it is a clear buying signal and if the customer is properly attended for the sale is 100% sure.

- Service provider should have all his selling tools (brochures, posters, hand books, albums, price lists, different plans to choose from etc.) ready for sale and should use them as and when required to do the brand talk.

- The sales person should be aware of the competition and their schemes so that proper comparison can be given between the products (FAB analysis) e.g., though our prices of the tour are the same we provide four star accommodation while our competitors settle for three star accommodation etc.

- Customer when being served should be given the promised service, as the quality of service is subjective in nature, customer's will differ in their opinion about it, but if the promised service is not provided which is objective in nature people will always carry strong negative opinion about its and will have adverse impact on future sales, e.g., air port pickup and drop facility for all customers individually is one of the promised service by the hotels if the hotel does not provide it or settles for one car for four customers sharing basis or orders a auto rickshaw instead of a car the service provider has gone back on the promise and this is not acceptable to many customers.

- The physical evidence of the service must be as expected by the customer e.g. if a customer buys your service for travelling from one place to another in a Volvo and you end up giving a Volvo type body of an ordinary bus which is not comfortable enough the customer will never come back and may try to cancel the trip and look for another service provider. The customer will give you enough bad mouth publicity to affect your service.

4.5 Upgradation of Service Time to Time

Customers availing a particular service expect to get better and better service every time, if the service does not show improvements they do not expect to be charged higher for the same service, since the service provider needs to increase the charges periodically they start losing the regular customers if they do not improve the service quality, e.g., customers of travel service will expect following upgradation of service

Step-1 Customer buying ticket from the service provider by visiting the service provider's office, and boarding the bus at the service provider's office

Step-2 Customer buying the ticket from a booking agent nearer to his residence and boarding the bus on a pick up point nearer to residence

Step-3 Customer buying ticket online and service provider sends a vehicle for pick up at the residence

Customers are happy to pay little extra charge for the upgraded service and in fact are happy to get better service at little extra charge.

4.6 Loyalty Bonus to Regular Customers:

Customers using service on a regular basis from a service provider expects to get extra attention or better service or a discount for the loyalty they show towards the service providers;

the service provider must recognize the regular customers and give special service or a discount for the loyalty of the customer, e.g., if you are a regular customer of a hotel he should not charge you higher rates during peak season and should accommodate you even when you have forgotten to book the room well in advance.

- Many service providers operate loyalty schemes as follows
- Frequent flier programs in airlines
- No charge for spouse during week end stay for executives in star hotels
- Discount in room rates and all the other services for people who assure a minimum number of stay in all star hotels in a year.
- Discount in food bills for regular customers of a restaurant
- Discount in rate for regular customers by tourist taxi operators
- Discount in rates for housing societies by maintenance service providers on contract.

Box 4.1 Gupte gets a room

Gupte gets a room

SKACO company ASM Patankar got a message that the sales director is visiting Goa market along with Southeast Asia director next week .Actually the southeast Asia director wanted to see the carnival festival in Goa, but when in Goa he wanted to see the Goa market also. The regular sales officer working in Goa was on leave as he had got married a week earlier. To ensure that the market is in good shape. Patankar decided to send Gupte a sales officer working in Mumbai to cover it before the visit and ensure that everything was in order.

Gupte reached Panaji in the evening and found that all the lodges were full due to the tourist season and was unable to get any place. He tried all the places but in vain, he was worried as to where he should spend the night; because it was Sunday and evening he could not even contact the distributor and make some arrangement through him. The regular sales officer had some relative in some village near Panaji and he used to stay with them. Gupte called Patankar and asked him what he should do, he was in no position to pay high rents in expensive hotels.

Patankar used to work Goa market as a sales officer before he was elevated to ASM position and he used to stay in Panaji in Santosh lodge on 18th June road; since he used to stay there for two weeks at a stretch every two months he and the manager of the Santosh lodge Mr. Angle had become good friends. Many times when the lodge was full Mr. Angle would give his own bed to Patankar and go home for sleeping.

Patankar asked Gupte to go to Santosh lodge and talk to Mr. Angle giving Patankar's reference; when Apte did that he was surprised that Mr. Angle offered him his own bed in the office and said "I will give you a room tomorrow morning. Gupte was given a room next morning and was not charged for Sunday night.

4.7 Tools for Personal Selling

Selling tools are all those materials that help the sales person achieve the positive sales results. The selling tools are of following types

- **Product sample:** Most useful selling tool, when a sales person shows the actual product to prospective buyer the impact on the customer is three fold; one– customer can view the product, two–customer can touch the product, and three –customer can listen about the qualities of the product.

- **Price list:** The sales person must have updated price list of the product being sold so that he/she does not make any mistake in quoting the price and negotiating the price.
- **Presentation folder:** it is important for a sales person to carry a presentation folder which shows the product varieties if any, the product advertisement details, product promotional details etc. The presentation folder gives authenticity to the sales talk made by the sales person and also helps him convince the customer better.
- **Catalogues:** Catalogues are the printed folders that show information about the company, its product range, list of current and valued customers, major projects handled etc.
- **Product brochures:** In engineering organizations the products are larger in size and complex in nature; so they cannot be carried as samples, in such case cases one can carry product brochure that can show product photographs, product design layouts, product uses etc., this helps the customer to get fair idea about the product and helps the sales person achieve sales.
- **Daily sales report:** In consumer sales daily sales report is the most useful tool that helps to plan the customer wise sales and record stock availability and sale made for future reference. Daily sales report also helps the sales person classify the customer according to the customer's buying capacity and frequency of purchases and this helps in planning sales promotions better.
- **Stock report for available stocks:** Sales person must have the current stock position at the supply point with him without which the sales can be lost, e.g., if a sales person takes order for a particular product for particular quantity in a particular variant and the stocks are not available at stock point the order cannot be supplied and the customer goes for the alternative product from the competitor. Next time when the sales person approaches the same customer he is unwilling to give order to the sales person fearing repeat of the previous occasion.
- **Stapler:** A sales person may be required to staple merchandising materials at a customer point; if the sales person is not carrying the stapler he/she misses the opportunity to do the merchandising which helps enhance the offtake.
- **Tixo tape:** A Tixo tape helps the sales person put the posters and point of sale materials in the retail shops.
- **Sales bag:** A sales person must carry a sales bag along with all his selling tools; sales bag ensures that all the selling tools are carried regularly and also makes the sales person look smart.
- **Measuring tape:** Measuring tape is a useful selling tool for shop salesman in textile shop. The sales person can measure the required length of the cloth and give to him.
- **Scissors:** Scissors helps the textile shop salesman cut the required cloth length.
- **Display units:** In an exhibition stall or a retail shop display units help display the products properly and attractively which helps the sales person to sell the products effectively.

- **LCD /slide projector:** If the sales person is required to do presentation about the product its uses, feature and benefits in front of a gathering of customers it is better the sales person uses a LCD/slide projector and a screen to project images and information in creative manner so that the presentation becomes effective.

4.8 Value Added Selling

When a reseller adds value to the product he has purchased before selling it further to the next customer it is called as value added sale. Value added sale is a common practice observed by all the customers regularly. Common examples of value added selling are as follows

- **Pan shop:** A panwala sells pan with its ingredients after mixing them in a proportion, this is value addition sale and he charges extra for proportionately mixing the ingredients.
- **Vegetable vendors:** Vegetable vendors clean the vegetables and remove the soil from it, spray water on them to keep them fresh before selling, the cleaning is value addition.
- **Firewood seller:** The firewood seller cuts the wood is smaller sizes so that it can be easily used in the kitchen, this is value addition.
- **Kirana shop:** Kirana shop owners supply grains after cleaning sometimes after milling them and supplying fresh atta to the customers is value added selling.
- **Vegetable suppliers with home delivery:** In many cities now vegetables are supplied after cleaning and chopping them ready for the house wives to fry and make any dish or mix a salad, these suppliers also supply enough of flavoring agents like coriander, green chilies etc., just enough for use in that dish. This is value added selling

One can make a long list of such value added selling, the essence of value added selling is selling goods and service together to enhance the profitability out of the selling the goods and attracting maximum number of customers towards the seller.

4.9 Exercise

1. List all the services you buy on a regular basis and find out how these service providers approach you for getting the business.
2. What are the services being used by you that can be classified as essential services? Are you being served properly by essential service providers? If the answer is yes or no; find why they are able or unable to satisfy your service needs.
3. Think of the services that are needed but are not available; prepare a business plan for the same and check whether these services are commercially viable or no.
4. Explain the marketing mix for services
5 Explain the special selling skills required for selling services
6. Explain in detail the process of selling service
7. Explain the importance of up grading of services regularly.

Case Study 4.1 Travel Agent

Mr. Ramchandran contacted his travel agent to book his tickets for his tour from Pune to Delhi on 15th June and then evening flight to Lucknow and returns to Pune on 16th June and asked the travel agent to book hotel accommodation in Lucknow. Mr. Ramachandran expected a morning flight to Delhi, evening flight to Lucknow on 15th and return flight from Lucknow in the afternoon so that he can be back in Pune 16th evening and went to Bengaluru. The travel agent booked him as follows

From	Date	ETD	To	ETA
Pune	15th June	1630 hrs	Delhi	1800 hrs
Delhi	15th June	1700 hrs	Lucknow	1800 hrs
Lucknow	16th June	1030 hrs	Delhi	1130 hrs
Delhi	16th June	1300 hrs	Pune	1430 hrs

Mr. Ramchandran was shocked to see the tickets on his return from Banguluru on 14th evening, he fired the travel agent and refused to accept the tickets and booked his tickets directly (he was forced to by executive class, 30% more fare) and decided to change his travel agent.

What was the mistake of the travel agent?

Case Study 4.2 Selling Formula

Sagar Bankhele joined Good housekeeping Ltd., as sales executive, the company based in Mumbai was involved in housekeeping contracts of various software companies. Some of their clients opened their offices in Pune so the company opened their branch also in Pune. Sagar was appointed basically to develop business in Pune.

After getting trained in Mumbai, Sagar started working in Pune and started contacting various organizations for getting the business but even after working for 45 days he was unable to develop any business lead and was frustrated. He then went to his institute and contacted his professor who taught them sales management; after listening to Sagar's plight the professor gave him only one suggestion and that is use SPANCO formula.

Next month Sagar met the professor and said "the formula worked I have two leads in negotiation stage". What part of SPANCO formula must have worked for Sagar?

Case Study 4.3 Selling Startegy

Mr. Varma the sales manager for Good hospitality Pvt. Ltd. which was running Hotel Amantran in central part of city was worried about his banquet sales. He started thinking about the matter and decided to list all the facts about the Hotel.

Background: Hotel Amantran was started by Mr. Purohit some twenty years ago and was very famous for its veg. thali meals and other veg. dishes. Mr. Purohit went on purchasing the shops adjacent to Amantaran and slowly acquired the entire building. Initially he thought of starting a lodging house but looking at the size of the plot and developing commercial establishments in the vicinity decided to go for a three start hotel with banquet and conference halls for small and big functions.

The business so far: Since the hotel started the business so far for the hotel was limited to birthday parties for school going children and some felicitations with high tea. Commercial establishments were not using the banquet or facility even when the rates offered were competitive in fact much lower than other hotels.

Current situation: Mr. Purohit appointed Mr. Verma who had successfully worked in Hotel Three Diamonds as sales manager in charge of banquets. Mr. Varma found that most of the commercial establishments were interested in giving business to Amantran, in fact many executives would prefer to come even for lunch regularly because it was the nearest hotel and restaurant to their offices. The major objection was they served only vegetarian food and did not serve any liquor.

Varma's suggestions to Mr. Purohit: Mr. Verma suggested following to Mr. Purohit

1. Start a separate non-vegetarian restaurant on the roof top with a liquor bar attached to it.
2. Serve veg. and non-veg. food in banquets
3. Offer banquet hall for evening parties and allow customers to bring liquor and charge corkage to them.
4. Offer Conference hall to commercial organization for their meetings and offer beer and liquor along with food.

Mr. Purohit a teetotaler and pure vegetarian was not ready to accept the idea as yet, meanwhile another hotel owner was showing interest in opening another three star hotel with all these facilities in the same area.

Do you agree with Mr. Verma's suggestions to Mr. Purohit? Give reasons for your answer.

Case Study 4.4 Punctuality

Prashant was highly charged by the services marketing project he had done, the project was need for housekeeping services in urban India and the results were very positive showing that the customers are willing to pay higher housekeeping charges if the maids are efficient and do the work as expected by them. Prashant's cousin had said that in USA one can call housekeeping agency and ask them to send housekeeper for required work, the housekeepers come and do the job and go, the satisfied customers clears the bill to the company.

Formation of Service Company: Prashant started the company that can supply housekeepers on demand and wanted to recruit housekeepers willing to go through the training process, so he gave an advertisement in local news paper which was popular among lower income group. He also contacted Government run employment exchange and they put up a notice on their notice board. Prashant contacted employment agencies specialized in unskilled and semiskilled employees and registered his company with them after paying registration fees. The response was very poor and those who came wanted guaranteed income service and were not interested in unsteady income.

Since Prashant had started advertising his service in newspapers and internet he started getting requests and so he recruited the candidates that came by and had a training program to train them in handling washing machines, vacuum cleaners, dishwashers etc., and started sending them to the clients.

Though he was paying his employees auto fare to travel and was willing to help them procure their own two wheelers; invariably these employees travelled by city bus service to earn that much extra (difference between auto and bus fare) which must be most expensive and worst in frequency and punctuality in entire India. From the nearest bus stop these employees walked to the destination and were late by at least 45 minutes to one hour sometimes longer than this. The employees were in a hurry to get back home and so finished the work fast and the work was not done satisfactorily.

Soon Prashant's company was labeled for unsatisfactory work and not punctual and he stopped getting work.

Where did Prashant go wrong?